OF MIKES AND MEN

OF MIKES AND MEN

From Ray Scott to Curt Gowdy:
Broadcast Tales from the Pro Football Booth

By CURT SMITH

Diamond Communications, Inc.
South Bend, Indiana
1998

Of Mikes and Men

Copyright © 1998 by Curt Smith

10 9 8 7 6 5 4 3 2 1

Manufactured in the United States of America

Diamond Communications, Inc.
Post Office Box 88
South Bend, Indiana 46624-0088
Editorial: (219) 299-9278
Orders Only: 1-800-480-3717
Fax: (219) 299-9296

Library of Congress Cataloging-in-Publication Data

Smith, Curt.
    Of mikes and men : from Ray Scott to Curt Gowdy :
broadcast tales from the pro football booth / by Curt Smith.
        p.   cm.
    Includes bibliographical references and index.
    ISBN 1-888698-11-X (alk. paper)
    1. Sportscasters--United States--Biography. 2. Football--
United States--Anecdotes. I. Title.
GV742.4.S65 1998
070.4'49796332'092273--dc21   97-35177
                                                     CIP

CONTENTS

Other books by Curt Smith

America's Dizzy Dean
Long Time Gone
Voices of The Game
A Fine Sense of the Ridiculous
The Storytellers
Windows on the White House

For My Family

ACKNOWLEDGMENTS

"This is how pro football ought to be," John Madden will observe as snow shrouds Lambeau Field. "Cold. Freezing. The fans into it. Guys hitting each other." In *Of Mikes and Men*, radio/TV announcers tell how pro football ought to be — and was, or is.

Many people helped write this book. They were generous with their time — and I cannot help but be generous in my gratitude.

First, the Voices. For details, see "The Announcers" chapter. I also wish to thank the Pro Football Hall of Fame in Canton, Ohio, for its *nonpareil* aid — especially John Bankert, Pete Elliott, Joe Horrigan, Don Smith, Tricia Trilli, and, above all, Pete Fierle.

Miming John Steinbeck, Doug Gamble suggested *Of Mikes and Men*'s title. Kerri Donaleski compiled the index and transcribed hundreds of hours of tape. Jill and Jim Langford of Diamond Communications and staff Shari Hill and Jaime Noce took the project from manuscript to finished book with insight and care. Juanita Dix crafted the design from text to jacket. My wife, Sarah, now terms herself a football savant. Thanks, too, to my literary agent, Bobbe Siegel, CBS Radio producer Howard Deneroff, and network publicists Dan Bell (Fox), Helene Blieberg (CBS), Andy Dallos (ABC), Greg Hughes (TNT), Ed Markey (NBC), and Dan Quinn (ESPN).

Any fumbles are mine alone. Completed passes involve the names above. Finally, let me thank the reader — for your interest, and concern.

PREFACE

The poet Walt Whitman asked, "Where is what I started for so long ago? And why is it yet unfound?" The National Football League started more than 75 years ago. In time, broadcasters helped find its niche — the dead-end kid turned weekend ministry.

Today, the NFL says grace at the head of America's sports table. Return to its, and radio's, 1920 debut. Football sprang from towns like Canton and Decatur — born of proximity, exuding blood and guts, and colored black and blue. The NFL was long akin to wrestling — except that wrestling had a niche.

Tools were primitive in radio and early television. A telephone, as microphone. Box seats, as press box. Broadcast booths sat *inside* a scoreboard. Compare their Conestoga to the '90s Porsche of skycams, downlinking, and computer generation. You can't. To paraphrase Ring Lardner, interest was once a side dish the NFL forgot to order.

Television changed pro football, and helped pro football change us all. In 1946, fewer than 17,000 TV sets dotted America: visiting Aunt Martha on Sunday, families trekked Monday night to the P.T.A. Today, nearly 80 percent of homes flaunt two receivers — and 70 percent have three. Aunt Martha channel-surfs — and teachers study the red-dog blitz.

Time, said historian Arnold Toynbee, "is on the side of the barbarians." However personal and arbitrary opinion may be, it is clear that TV sides with the NFL. For decades, the rectangular tube has ferried plot and theme into living rooms, general stores, and gentle small towns. Stop-action, slow-motion, and instant replay affirm pro football as quick, compact, and chockablock with verve.

"The sport that is most popular on TV," says former Cowboys' president Tex Schramm, "is by definition *America's* most popular sport." Unlike basketball, huddles spur anticipation. Unlike baseball, both teams move at once. Unlike hockey, a football hails visibility. Voices top its chart. Jack

Whitaker — football's e.e. cummings. Dick Enberg — Oh, My! Curt Gowdy — cowboy legend in his time. Each mines an alchemy of look, sound, and feel.

"Always," notes Verne Lundquist, "the game is the thing." Yet broadcasters spur TV's ideal sport. Merle Harmon used drama like Edgar Bergen did a mannequin. Charlie Jones denotes homework and authority. Ray Scott's voice crossed John Huston and James Earl Jones. When he intoned, "Starr. Dowler. Touchdown. Green Bay," ten million spines would quiver. Different behind the mike, they cleaved off it, too. You will not mistake, say, Pat Summerall for John Madden.

Consider an announcer's life, style, and view of his profession. Each may be solemn, theatric, or satirical. In these pages, football's best Voices link you with events on and off the field — the NFL as talking history. You will grasp why a Gallup Poll says that 43 percent of America's most avid fans are hooked by age *eight*.

Relive Ken Coleman re. Jimmy Brown, Chuck Thompson on high-topped John Unitas, and Jack Buck wounded in the same place and in the same World War II battle as Lindsey Nelson — and not knowing it for 25 years. Also, Chris Schenkel vamped by Julie London, Marty Glickman on Pearl Harbor Day, the world on Howard Cosell, and Frank Gifford and Tom Brookshier, in a prop plane, mixing scotch and courage as their pilot tried/prayed to land.

Think of the 1950s and '60s Giants — the *first* America's Team — midwived by TV and football growing up. Next, images that grace autumn memory — Doomsday and Steel Curtain, Landry and Lombardi, Hail Mary, the Immaculate Reception, and Green Bay — football's Mayberry. *Of Mikes and Men* recalls their mix of Mount Olympus, the Pyramid at Giza, and the Czar's Winter Palace. A fan would no more miss them than trade his Y.A. Tittle card.

With the possible exception of the Equator, it is said that everything begins somewhere. This book etches the NFL's rise from hardscrabble sprig to parish sport. Its tales flow from print articles and talks by phone, tape, TV, journal, or in person over the last decade. Many were told specifically for this book, and to benefit the Pro Football Hall of Fame, which will receive a portion of the proceeds.

"Fumbles, penalties, and interceptions," says Art Donovan, the Colts' 1953-61 tackle. "Try telling me pro football isn't a generous game!" I wish to thank the Voices for *their* generosity — and retelling what pro football was, and is.

CHAPTER

THE ANNOUNCERS

More than 600 National Football League players served in World War II. Sixty-six were decorated. Twenty-one never returned at all. First and ten? Down and out? Half-a-century ago, the real touchdown was to be alive.

Most stories in *Of Mikes and Men* concern the last fifty years of America's, and pro football's, life. They stem from announcers who span the era from Red Grange through Sam Huff via Cookie Gilchrist to Steve Young. I am especially grateful to Lindsey Nelson and Mel Allen, who related tales before their deaths, respectively, in 1995 and '96.

Years after the fact, Voices stir the tender ear of memory. We know where we were, say, when the Eagles beat Green Bay, 17-13, for the 1960 title (at a relative's home, enjoying the day after Christmas). We remember the broadcaster, and what he sounded like (Ray Scott and Jack Whitaker). Play-by-play was a small boy's link to a wider world.

On the following pages are the names, and faces, of each announcer. Enjoy. Relive. Let the Voices of pro football evoke memories and sounds and sights that recall the past.

KENNY ALBERT. Saint Francis of Assisi said, "Give me a child until he is seven, and you may have him afterward." Before seven, Albert belonged to broadcasting. He inhaled sport from father Marv, did cable play-by-play at 15, and aired NYU basketball as a student. After graduating, he worked for Home Team Sports, WTOP-Washington, the NHL Radio Network, baseball Yankees, and hockey Capitals, Islanders, and Rangers. In 1994-95, the New York native called one game or more in each of sport's Big Four. Then, he moved to Fox and began its El Dorado of good cheer — the NFL (also, NHL) on TV's newest stage.

MARV ALBERT evoked the mot "Been there, done that" — Peacock baseball, boxing, hockey, pro and college hoops, World Championship of Basketball, and 1988-92-96 Summer Olympics. He also buoyed NBC's professional football coverage as a lead announcer. Passion: "I'm living a dream come true." Ubiquity: Try turning the knob without hearing Marv's trademark "Yesss!" Show-biz: In "Late Night With David Letterman"'s 11 years at NBC, Albert appeared a record 74 times. His third book was titled, *I'd Love to But I Have a Game — 27 Years Without a Life*. In 1997, fired by NBC, that life took a stunning turn.

MEL ALLEN. As 1940-64 Voice of the New York Yankees, he became an institution — and made "How about that!" a household term. Few recall that he shone at football, too. Mel aired 1950s Giants' and early-'60s Redskins' radio, and evolved into TV's top college Voice. He did the yearly East-West Game (a then-post-season poobah), 14 Rose Bowls (the then-Granddaddy of college/pro ball), and Movietone NFL newsreels. *Variety* termed him "among the world's 25 most recognizable voices." Round or oval ball — no matter. Allen was peanuts, beer, and the United States Marine Band — a palatine behind the mike.

CHRIS BERMAN. In the early 1950s, Milton Berle was dubbed "Mr. Television." Berman is "Mr. ESPN." In October 1979, the new network (age, one month) hired Berman (24). The two bloomed in league — Chris, as studio host, anchor, and commentator, making ESPN sport's grandstand and "SportsCenter," its parade. The Connecticut native's first love is football. It shows on Sunday's "NFL Countdown" and "NFL PrimeTime." Berman has won six Emmys, 11 Cable Aces, and five National Sportscaster of the Year awards. In 1996, he began hosting "Monday Night Football"'s halftime. For sport's Uncle Miltie, there is rarely a time out.

TERRY BRADSHAW. Pittsburgh's 1971-84 quarterback faced linemen topping 300 pounds. Today, he is Fox Television's 800-pound gorilla. Watch its pre-game show: Terry dominates — a mix of Willie Nelson, Uncle Remus, and Tennessee Ernie Ford. Catch The World According to Bradshaw via gospel and country and western albums, a syndicated radio talk show, prime-time Fox cameos, and visibility to wow Madonna. You almost forget what came before: 1978 Player of the Year, four-time All-Pro, four Super Bowl victories, 1983-93 CBS analyst (in '94, joining Fox), and Hall of Fame '89. Always, he is rustic, unorthodox, and utterly himself.

THOM BRENNAMAN was to the broadcast, not manor, bred. The son of Marty Brennaman was born in Hoopsland — Chapel Hill, N.C. — graduated from Ohio University, and took his first job at WLW-Cincinnati. He did Reds' radio, covered the Bengals' loss in Super Bowl XXIII, then walked to WGN-Radio in 1990. In 1994, Brennaman, analysts Anthony Muñoz and later Ron Pitts, and Fox TV commenced the NFL together. In 1996, Thom-Ron proved adept at calling afterthoughts, not just glamour boys, on Fox's World Football League coverage. Brennaman also covers the Arizona Diamondbacks and baseball's "Game of the Week."

JACK BRICKHOUSE's calling card was "Hey-Hey!" He made the Monsters of the Midway seem even larger. Even as a young man, Brickhouse played in Peoria — his home town. Then, in 1942, Bob Elson entered the Navy, and Brickhouse inherited his niche as Voice of the Cubs and White Sox. In 1948, Jack moved to WGN, and for 24 years sold cigars, sacked pomp, and floated down a river of hand-clapping as WGN's Voice of the Bears. He pricked analyst Irv Kupcinet, who jabbed back — football's Hope and Crosby. On December 29, 1963, his act turned national over NBC-TV. "Hey-Hey!" The Bears beat the Giants for the NFL title.

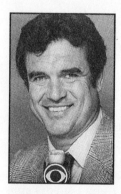

TOM BROOKSHIER heaped new meaning on the term "break a leg." Colorado '53, Tom became a gifted Eagles' defensive back. In 1961, he suffered a broken leg in a game. Convalescing, Brookshier received a call from a Philadelphia radio station, offering work. A year later, he retired, did Eagles' radio, and joined CBS-TV in 1963. Tom called Ray Nitschke "the madman of the Packers" in 1967, and fluffed a Super Bowl VI post-game interview with Dallas' Duane Thomas. By contrast, he and Pat Summerall forged TV football's pre-eminent '70s team. "TV's like playing," he laughs. "You see good and bad along the way."

JAMES BROWN is TV's host with the most — anchoring Fox's "NFL Sunday" pre-game show, its studio hockey and boxing, and PBS specials. Ironically, Brown's real love is hoops. The Harvard All-Ivy was drafted by the NBA Hawks; instead, did Washington radio/TV (e.g. Bullets' play-by-play/analysis); and in 1984, joined CBS. For 11 years, Brown co-hosted the NCAA hoops championship. He also hosted the 1992 Winter Olympics and Heisman Trophy Award show, and did NFL play-by-play and college hoops analysis. In 1994, J.B. joined Fox's infant coverage — bringing order to the proceedings and panache to his role.

JACK BUCK is cause and mirror of the NFL's appeal. Wounded in World War II, Jack spent V-E Day in a Paris hospital. Returning home, he went to Ohio State and audited Woody Hayes' course on football theory. In 1954, he trekked to St. Louis, joined the spiring KMOX, then vaulted to network football. The American Football League's first Voice also called the 1960s and '70s NFL on CBS-TV — usually, the Bears or Cowboys — airing the Ice Bowl and Super Bowl IV. Then, in 1978, he began the first of 17 years as CBS Radio's "Monday Night Football" anchor — his sidekick, Hank Stram. Mixing bite and lite, Buck never scents of bland. (Pete Rozelle Radio-Television Award, 1996.)

JOE BUCK proves that life/love isn't wasted on the young. Raised in St. Louis, Buck aired Triple-A baseball at 20, graduated from Indiana University, and joined dad Jack at Busch Stadium in 1991. Three years later, joining Fox at 25, Joe became the youngest-ever Voice to call the NFL on weekly network television. In 1996, Buck began Fox's baseball "Game of the Week" and aired the World Series: only Vin Scully, at 25, had done it at a younger age. Each fall, Buck leaves the summer game for Sports Everest USA. Joe's NFL ties come naturally. His maternal grandfather, Joe Lintzenich, flanked Red Grange in the Bears' 1930-31 backfield.

ERIC CLEMONS. Carl Sandburg hailed Chicago's "big shoulders." Born in the Windy City, Clemons used his to attend Columbia College, break into broadcasting in Chicago and Mobile, and join ESPN's "SportsCenter" in 1987. For five years, he lit sport's nightly window on the land, then moved to Boston's WHDH as anchor/reporter. In 1994, Eric became a reporter for Fox and added play-by-play to his '96 *vitae*. Sandburg called Chicago "the hog butcher of the world." Clemons calls the NFL from the Pack via the West Coast offense to D.C.'s hogs. "As a panorama," he says, "there's nothing like it in the world."

KEN COLEMAN seats luck at his table. Born in suburban Boston, he applied in 1952 for Browns' play-by-play. "They didn't want a native," he explains, "but a fresh face from outside Ohio." Fourteen years later, Ken left Cleveland for return to Boston. More luck: The Red Sox had not won a pennant in two decades, but made the World Series in Coleman's second year. In between, he etched the Browns on their 125-station radio network and CBS-TV's coast-to-coast coverage — seven championships, six network title games, and a marriage of team and time. Jack Buck termed him the best NFL Voice of *all* time.

CRIS COLLINSWORTH scents of the insouicant boy next door. The Florida graduate buoyed the 1981-88 Bengals: Rookie of the Year, two Super Bowls, three Pro Bowls, four 1,000-yard seasons, and 417 catches. In 1989, he ran a down and out to HBO documentaries, Wimbledon tennis, and "Inside the NFL." In '92, Collinsworth added NBC's Notre Dame and, later, NFL coverage. Cris has been an analyst, pre-game studio commentator, and Olympic track and field reporter. He also hosts WLW-Cincinnati's "Sports Talk" radio show and has a law degree from the University of Cincinnati. Just call him counselor.

BOB COSTAS grew up on Long Island, attended Syracuse University, and called his first pro football telecast, at 24, in 1976. His big-time brace links anchor, host, and play-by-play: the Super Bowl, Summer Olympiad, World Series, baseball "Game of the Week," and weekly NFL and NBA. From the top, Costas merged humor, depth, and passion. He hosted NBC's "Later .... with Bob Costas," dots its prime-time "Dateline," and has virtually retired two awards — the Emmy "Outstanding Sports Broadcaster" and "National Sportscaster of the Year." "What more can he do?" Al Michaels marvels. "Knowing Bob, he'll think of something."

RANDY CROSS, like pro football, spans the Mason-Dixon Line. Born in Brooklyn, the UCLA two-time All-American now lives in Alpharetta, Georgia. Blue *and* gray hail his NFL high deeds and holidays. The 1976-88 guard and center played in three Pro Bowls, was a four-time All-Pro, and helped the 49ers win Super Bowls XVI, XIX, and XXIII. In 1989, Cross traded downs for dialogue, joining the 49ers' network, CBS. When, in 1994, Columbia lost the NFC to Fox, Randy crossed the street to NBC. He does Peacocks' AFC analysis and some Notre Dame and other college games — to wit, the 1995 Fiesta Bowl.

HOWARD DAVID is CBS Radio's Ubiquitous Man. David does "Monday Night Football," the NFL on Sunday night, NCAA "Game of the Week," and Super and Fiesta Bowls. His resumé also blares Olympic speedskating, Masters golf, U.S. Open tennis, Saturday baseball, and "Sports Central USA." Formerly of Mizlou Television, a sports syndicator, the NBA New Jersey Nets, and hoops show, "Above the Rim," the Maryland graduate now does Princeton football and basketball's Milwaukee Bucks. Born in Brooklyn, Howard doesn't have to "Wait Till Next Year!" On-air events are as closeby as tomorrow.

DAN DIERDORF was born in football's cradle — Canton, Ohio. "Guess my path," he laughs, "was preordained from the start." It led to the University of Michigan (as All-Big Ten tackle) and St. Louis Cardinals (1971-83 offensive lineman and member of the 1970s NFL Team of the Decade) and, after retiring as a player, radio/TV. In the mid-80s, Dierdorf did KMOX Radio analysis, CBS Radio/TV play-by-play, and hosted a talk show, "Sports Open Line." By 1987, he talked his way to sport's Golconda — "Monday Night Football" — where, lucidly and exuberantly, Fortune's Son is talking still.

JOHN DOCKERY is a thinking man's announcer. The fourth of seven children, he worked in his dad's tavern, was class president at Brooklyn Prep with honors in Greek, and still played four sports. Dockery then graduated from Harvard, played baseball in the Red Sox' organization, was cut by the Dolphins, and in 1967 signed as a free agent with the Jets. Retiring at 32, he became a self-styled "three-headed monster" — analyst/reporter/entertainer — ex-jock turned sideline pioneer on CBS and, later, NBC. Dockery defines the "scholar-athlete" — airing '92 Olympic wrestling and weightlifting and attending Columbia Graduate School of Design.

JIMMY DUDLEY. You recall him now — "So long and good luck, ya' heah!" — punctuating each Sunday in the Big Ballpark by Lake Erie. Dudley etched Graham and Motley, became Jim Brown's Boswell, and warmed Municipal Stadium's 1950s snowclad taiga. How antipodal: the Virginian's lyric tone softened football's pell-mell. As Voice of the Browns, Dudley told stories with restraint and charm. He covered three NFL championship teams, broadcast the '48 baseball Indians' first world title since 1920, and made the huge lakefront bowl Cleveland's Main Street of the mind.

DICK ENBERG worked his way through Central Michigan University, earned graduate degrees at Indiana, and entered broadcasting with Bob Kelley on 1960s Rams' radio. In 1971, he went big-time as host of the TV series, "Sports Challenge." Joining NBC in 1975, Enberg corkscrewed into a latter-day Curt Gowdy. Its Renaissance Man has called — "Oh, My!" — the Super Bowl, Olympics, Rose Bowl, Wimbledon, Ryder Cup, World Series, and NCAA basketball. NBC's top NFLer since 1980 renders poetry, respectability, and good manners — treating emotion with respect, not contempt. No one moistens a handkerchief like Dr. Dick.

ROY FIRESTONE. Art Buchwald said, "My priority is to find the serious in the irreverent and then treat the irreverent more seriously." Glib and reflective, Firestone excels. In 1981, his "SportsLook" series debuted on ESPN. For 14 years, Roy interviewed hundreds of personalities — restless and inquisitive, exploring fields from betting to the law. By contrast, irreverence drapes his persona as master of ceremonies and stand-up comic. In 1987, Firestone did analysis for the first year of the NFL on ESPN. Today, Roy does documentaries and other features for the network that he helped to build.

JOE GIBBS conveys a word at ease with his on-air image — *gentleman*. Gibbs became the Redskins' coach in 1981, and a year later won the Super Bowl. By 1992, he had a 124-60 regular-season record, four NFC titles, and two more Lombardi trophies. Like Sarah Bernhardt, Gibbs then quit at the top of his game. "I want more time for my family," he said — also, for Joe's public speaking, religious work, and ownership of a NASCAR racing team. Today, the unself-conscious Gibbs elevates NBC's sixty-minute "NFL Live" pre-game show — bringing intellect to a medium which celebrates the shallow and clichéd.

FRANK GIFFORD. The 1952-63 halfback/flanker linked USC roots, movie star looks, and sundry skills to take Manhattan: 1956 MVP, seven-time Pro Bowl selection, and El Cordobes of the Giants' offense. Giff then moved to television: "Wide World of Sports" host, Emmy's 1977 Outstanding Sports Personality, and 1971-core of "Monday Night Football." Dry and whimsical, Gifford helped "MNF" become longer-running than Lucille Ball, "Bonanza," or even "Gunsmoke" — gracing prime time more than 400 times. "That fact says something about TV," he jokes — and perhaps about football's Dorian Gray. (Rozelle Award, 1995.)

JERRY GLANVILLE doesn't believe in 24-hour time periods. The former Houston and Atlanta coach does Fox analysis, aids HBO's weekly "Inside the NFL," and drives in the NASCAR Super Truck Series. Versatile and anti-mellowspeak, he is even a member of the Atlanta Country Music Hall of Fame. In 1974, the North Michigan University graduate cracked the NFL as Lions' assistant coach. From 1977-82, he built the Falcons' defense — a.k.a. "Grits Blitz." Glanville then went from Buffalo via Houston back to Georgia. Each Sunday, he sings "On the Road Again" — joining Kevin Harlan on the NFC on Fox.

MARTY GLICKMAN entered broadcasting the year that Franklin Roosevelt began a second term (1937). He retired in 1992 — outlasting nine presidents, four American wars, and the Baltimore Colts. Glickman called the Jets and Knicks for 16 and 21 years, respectively. The Giants, however, were his stairway to The Big Apple's heaven. Glickman began in 1948, and did their play-by-play for 23 years — helping make New York, New York a football, football town. A stutterer, Glickman took speech lessons as a child. The Syracuse University football and track-and-field star has proceeded to give them for the last half-century.

BOB GOLIC. On and off the field, the '78 Notre Damer shakes down the echoes. Golic was a football and wrestling All-American and Lombardi Trophy finalist. Drafted by New England, he played 13 years for the Patriots, Browns, and Rams. Bob's Everest was Municipal Stadium as an All-Pro and 1985-87 Pro Bowl star. Retiring in '92, he went Hollywood in film and television. On NBC's series, "Saved By The Bell: The College Years," Golic played Michael Rogers, a rugged resident advisor. Ironic: He was no Mr. Rogers to offensive linemen. In 1994, Bob became a Peacocks' analyst. Today, on CNN's "NFL Preview," he continues to advise.

CURT GOWDY. *Webster's* defines *eclectic* as "selecting from various systems ... or sources." Another definition might be *Gowdy* — "selecting from various sports to become TV's paradigm for a generation." Gowdy was ABC's — then, NBC's — 1962-79 pro football *duce*. His starbrights include the first AFL-NFL championship, Joe Namath's Super Bowl, Xmas 1971 double overtime, and Immaculate Reception. Curt called seven Super Bowls, seven Olympics, 12 World Series, and two decades of "The American Sportsman." In 1970, he became the first sportscaster to win the Peabody Award for broadcast excellence. (Rozelle Award, 1993.)

JIM GRAY. NBC's roving reporter has navigated a map of vivid stops. Prior to 1988, the University of Colorado alumnus did the America's Cup, NBA, and Top Rank Boxing as ESPN's West Coast Bureau Chief. As an NBCer, he then buoyed the pre-game "NFL Live" and the "Profiles" section of the '88 Seoul Olympics. Shifting to CBS, Gray covered the Super Bowl, World Series, NCAA hoops, Masters golf, Winter Games, and "NFL Today" pre-game show. In 1994, he returned to NBC and today reports for "NFL Live" and "NBA Showtime," adds post-game football analysis, and hopes to reprise his 1996 Olympics coverage.

TIM GREEN. Every vocation needs a scholar and a gentleman. At Syracuse, the All-America lineman and Lombardi Trophy finalist was an Academic All-American, Phi Beta Kappa, 1986 co-valedictorian, and major in English literature. Green played with Atlanta and New England, retiring in 1993, then vaulted to Fox as an analyst. Spare time links National Public Radio commentary, the syndicated magazine show, "Extra," and a potpourri of prose. Tim has written four novels, including *Ruffians* and *Outlaws*, and the non-fiction *The Darkside of the Game* — ironic, since he lights the oral and written word.

GREG GUMBEL was selling hospital supplies in 1973 when brother Bryant, a star at WNBC-Television in Los Angeles, told him about a sports job at Chicago's WMAQ-TV. Gumbel had no training, but got the post. Too, others at ESPN (1981, as "SportsCenter" host), Madison Square Garden Network (Knicks' and Rangers' Voice), and CBS (the NFL, NBA, Olympics, baseball, and pro/college hoops). Greg hosted the 1990-93 "NFL Today," then moved to NBC when CBS lost football. He hosts "NFL Live"'s half-time and pre/post-game shows — "then go home, curl up in the leather chair, and put headphones on and block out the world."

PAT HADEN. In 1992, Ross Perot conceded that "Bill Clinton is a Rhodes scholar. So am I. R-O-A-D-S." Haden is the Real McCoy. Pat came out of USC to become a Rose Bowl hero, get his law degree from Loyola University, and quarterback the Los Angeles Rams. In 1978, the Touchdown Club named him its NFC Player of the Year. Retiring in 1981, he traveled to CBS Radio and, ultimately, TNT — with Verne Lundquist, forging a bright and literate team. "If there's a reason for my style," he says, "it's the two years [1975-76] I spent at Oxford. The reflective part of me had a chance to grow." R-O-A-D-S, indeed.

TOM HAMMOND gives new connotation to the term *thoroughbred*. Born in Lexington, the University of Kentucky equine genetics major lent his pre-NBC pedigree to events like the Keeneland Summer Select Yearling Sales, the world's leading thoroughbred auction. In 1984, he called the Peacocks' first '84 Breeders' Cup and soon mated NBC full-time. Hammond now does its pro and Notre Dame football, the NBA, and track and field, and has hosted the U.S. Gymnastics championship, World Professional Figure Skating title, and 1992-96 Summer Olympics. Horse racing remains in his bluegrass blood: Hammond calls all of NBC's equestrian events.

KEVIN HARLAN's father is Packers' head Bob Harlan. Raised in Green Bay, the son found sports all-consuming. Harlan took to broadcasting in high school, worked for KCMO-Kansas City in college, and graduated from the University of Kansas '82. Soon, he was doing Kansas and Missouri football/hoops, radio's nationally syndicated "Sports Sunday," and the 1985-93 NFL Chiefs. In 1991, Kevin joined NBC, becoming Fox's three years later. Today, Harlan calls its NFL and boxing, TNT pro basketball, the NBA Timberwolves, and sports on Mutual and NBC Radio — somehow finding time to talk football with his dad.

MERLE HARMON cloaks football with a warmth and insight that eclipses the bare and statistical. Raised in Illinois, Harmon graduated from the University of Denver, did college football for ABC, and began his fidelity to pro ball in the early 1960s. He did the AFL on ABC, called the Steelers and Jets on local radio, and anchored TV's mid-'70s World Football League. Said the *Los Angeles Times*: "He smacks of those golden days of Red Barber, Mel Allen, and Ted Husing." *TV Guide* called him "maybe the best radio play-by-play football man ever." Always his voice, meticulous and clear, beamed through the window of Mid-America.

DAN HICKS rode out of the Old West via the Deep South to Manhattan. The Arizona graduate began his TV career at NBC in Dan's home town of Tucson. In 1989, Hicks moseyed to Atlanta's CNN, hosting "Sports Tonight" and "College Football Preview." In '92, his roundup led to NBC, New York — its outposts, men and women's golf, the NBA, French Open, and American Cup Gymnastics. Hicks anchored Peacock diving/swimming at the 1996 Atlanta Olympics, first-ever pay-per-view coverage of the Summer Olympics, and NBC's "Prudential Update." Plus, the NFL, calling games light-years distant from Tombstone and OK Corral.

JIM HUNTER ascribes tangible causes to CBS Radio's appeal. The Seton Hall graduate gives Columbia one-stop shopping. Football: co-host, pre-game and halftime Sunday and "Monday Night Football" and "NFL Preview." Baseball: "Game of the Week," All-Star Game, and playoff play-by-play and the weekly call-in "Inside Pitch." Hoops: NCAA host. Olympics: 1992-94 Winter Games in Albertville, France, and Lillehammer, Norway. The long-time anchor of CBS' "Sports Central USA" also brings his extempore material to Camden Yards as Voice of the Orioles. Listening, you feel free to sample Hunter's full course of knowledge and aside.

KEITH JACKSON. "I never was very good at interoffice politics and cocktail parties," Jackson says of his removal after one year as "Monday Night Football"'s Voice. Instead, he is among football's finest mikemen — his Georgia yamp as fresh as a day behind the rain. The ex-Marine launched "MNF" in September 1970. The next year, ABC staged a spree of musical chairs. Frank Gifford replaced Keith — who, in turn, succeeded Chris Schenkel on the NCAA "Game of the Week." His new homes became South Bend and Happy Valley, not Yankee Stadium or Lambeau Field — the perfect backdrop for the five-time Sportscaster of the Year.

TOM JACKSON's autobiography — *Blitz* — describes a path from Cleveland (his boyhood hero, Jimmy Brown) via the University of Louisville (two-time Missouri Valley Conference Player of the Year) through the 1973-86 Denver Broncos (two Super Bowls, three Pro Bowls, and team marks for most seasons and games played) to 1987- ESPN suzerzainty. Jackson is its studio analyst for "NFL Countdown" and "NFL PrimeTime" — ESPN's pre-game and wrapup Sunday shows — and the 1996 Cable Ace award recipient as "Best Sports Analyst." A writer said: "Tom played in the Mile High City, which is fitting. At ESPN, his talent is a mile wide."

RON JAWORSKI *would* rather be in Philadelphia. From 1977-86, the "Polish Rifle" passed the Eagles to career yardage (27,000) and touchdown (175) records and into their only Super Bowl. UPI named him its 1980 Player of the Year. Retiring in 1989, the ex-Ram, Dolphin, and Chief traded the T-formation for a microphone on the Quaker City's WIP and WYSP Radio. In 1990, Jaworski was hired as an analyst by ESPN on its weekly "Edge NFL Matchup" and "NFL Prime Monday." The Youngstown State graduate also thrives at business — managing golf courses, a restaurant, and several fitness centers. Dub him pro football's W.C. Fields.

ERNIE JOHNSON, JR. From 1990-94, he hosted Turner Network Television's studio coverage. Johnson's act then moved to game sites — apt, since he grew up in stadia across the land. Ernie's father was a Braves' pitcher and, later, pioneer on cable television's WTBS. His son graduated from the University of Georgia, joined WSB, Atlanta, in the mid-1980s, and in '90 emigrated to TNT. Among satellites in his orb: Turner's Goodwill Games, the Pan American Games, and '92-94 Winter Olympics. Above all is TNT's Sunday night coverage: Like the NFL, Ernie rides cable's wave that his dad helped begin.

CHARLIE JONES is among sport's most recognized/recognizable Voices — for 38 years airing NFL football, the last 33 on NBC-TV. Other travels with Charlie: golf, boxing, soccer, Wimbledon tennis, track and field, the Summer Olympics, and nine different college bowl games. The ex-USCer's historic firsts include the first Super Bowl, AFL title game, NBC "SportsWorld," World Cup gymnastics, Senior "Skins" golf, a multination athletic event in China, and the Colorado Rockies' opening game. All aired the voice as unique as any in broadcasting — whiskied and deep-voweled — akin to sandpaper searing glass. (Rozelle Award, 1997.)

HARRY KALAS. For years, John Facenda's voice-over buoyed NFL Films. "He could make a laundry list sound dramatic," muses its Steve Sabol. "I called it his 'retreat from Dunkirk' voice." When Facenda died in 1994, Kalas assumed much of the narration. His face mimes the Vienna Boys Choir — and voice, a wrecker demolishing cars. For the past quarter-century, the Illinois native, University of Iowa graduate, and Voice of the Philadelphia Phillies has also done Notre Dame football and Big Ten hoops. Harry's home-run call is "It's out'a here!" It is a phrase unlikely to be applied to *him* by grateful NFL fans.

ANDREA KREMER has spanned both coasts, following and enhancing pro football. Born in Philadelphia, she graduated from the University of Pennsylvania, was sports editor of a weekly paper, and joined NFL Films in 1984. Through '89, she produced, directed, and reported for its nationally syndicated "This is the NFL." Kremer won a 1986 Emmy for her special, "Autumn Ritual," before going to ESPN. Today, its Los Angeles-based correspondent specks the sports network's "NFL Countdown" and "NFL Prime Monday" and does interviews — e.g. Joe Montana, Don Shula, and Steve Young — for its "Outside the Line" series.

JIM LAMPLEY calls his career "idiosyncratic." It is also of a piece. In 1974, Lampley started at ABC as a sideline announcer on college football after being chosen by a nationwide talent search. His breakthrough year came a decade later: Jim hosted "Monday Night Football"'s halftime — succeeding, which is not to say replacing, Howard Cosell — and co-anchored 1984 Winter and Summer Olympics' late-night coverage. Postlogue links NBC and CBS play-by-play; a 1993 role as "NFL Live" host, succeeding Bob Costas; and as Cosell would say, a "plethora" of non-network jewels. Brightest is Lampley's niche as Voice of HBO Boxing.

VERNE LUNDQUIST. Born in Duluth, he grew up in Texas — inhaling its sense of impatience with limits of any kind. First, Verne became the 1970s Voice of America's Team — succeeding Texas' Broadcaster, the late Frank Glieber. In 1983, he joined CBS to call figure skating, college and pro hoops, The Masters golf, and NFL with Dan Fouts or John Madden. Enter TNT in '94 — and the NBA, more golf and ice skating, and Sunday night football. Recall John Connally re. Lyndon Johnson: "His were child's dreams [that] could be as wide as the sky and the future as green as winter oats because this, after all, was America."

JOHN MADDEN. In grade school, the Sister Superior told Madden's parents that he talked too much. "Boom! Blast! Wow!" He still does, yet brings a bawdy irresistibility to his work. "One knee equals two feet," he says. Who knows what it means — or cares? Madden is Gleason, and a Nation reacts with glee. Madden evolved from Raiders' head coach at 32 to Lite Beer spokesman to CBS analyst. Always, he blared a pastiche of charm, bravado, and evident love of football — sport's Big Daddy patch of raw personality. In 1994, he followed the NFC from CBS to Fox. Gesticulate, or Telestrate: Madden is the best at what he does.

PAUL MAGUIRE. America sees a Good Time Charlie straight out of "Grumpy Old Men." The AFL evokes Maguire's 1960-70 career as Chargers' and Bills' punter and linebacker. Historians recall that as a wide receiver — *mirabile dictu* — Paul led the country in receiving yardage in 1959. Welcome to a most unusual man. Maguire has been an NBC analyst since 1971 — jabbing, riposting, laughing. Even a 1991 heart attack left the Western New York resident uninhibited and unchanged. "The only difference is that I couldn't have salt, but I never liked salt, anyway," he says. "I was the kind of guy who gave up rutabagas for Lent."

MARK MALONE. The Arizona graduate was Pittsburgh's first-round draft choice in 1980. He apprenticed to Terry Bradshaw — later, became the Steelers' quarterback, throwing five touchdowns *v.* Indianapolis in 1985 — and ended his career with the Chargers and the Jets. Malone then turned to broadcasting — his base, WPXI-TV, Pittsburgh — before trading the Steel City for Bristol, Connecticut. At ESPN, he hosts "Edge NFL Matchup," covers football for "SportsCenter," and is a sideline reporter on "Sunday Night NFL." Aiding Pittsburgh charities, Mark's touch with kids today is as sure as his passing for Steelers USA.

SEAN MCDONOUGH inherited his father's genes. "He'd take me to games in Foxboro," Sean says of *Boston Globe* columnist Will McDonough, "and I'd hang around the players. I enjoyed that more than the Patriots enjoyed most games." McDonough's son was raised in Boston, graduated from Syracuse, did minor-league baseball, and became a *wunderkind* — Red Sox' TV at 26; CBS baseball, 30; and Winter Olympics, 32. At Columbia, Sean has also done golf, college hoops, and pro and college football. "I hope to be here," he says, "when the NFL returns to the network which nurtured it." NBC's Will McDonough might sing a different tune.

DON MEREDITH. As 1960-68 quarterback, the ex-SMUer helped make the Cowboys America's (Emerging) Team. Moving to TV, Meredith — a.k.a. Dandy Don, or Danderoo — became a prodigious jolt of Americana, "Monday Night Football"'s bodacious, homespun star. He gilded 1970-73's "MNF," moved to NBC, then returned to Cosell and Co. from 1977-83. The tableaus linger: "Turn Out the Lights, the Party's Over"; "Howard!" uttered between amusement and disdain; musing, "He says we're number one," of an obscene, finger-wagging fan. "I didn't even know that much about football," Dandy Don often said. His genius was that America didn't know, or care.

AL MICHAELS. A man stuck in the mud with his car was asked by a wayfarer whether he was stuck. "You *could* say I was stuck," he said, "if I was going anywhere." Michaels has gone places since his boyhood a block from Ebbets Field. Hired by ABC in 1976, Al co-hosted its first Super Bowl and was named "Monday Night Football"'s play-by-play Voice in 1985. Are you ready for some football? Today, the three-time Sportscaster of the Year weaves with Frank Gifford and Dan Dierdorf a seamless quilt of football on the air. His defining line — "Do you believe in miracles? Yes!" at the 1980 Winter Olympics — is remembered to this day.

MATT MILLEN is often called "Little Madden" — in truth, fusing his own blend of analysis and showmanship. For 12 years (1980-91), the Penn State All-American lifted the Raiders, 49ers, and Redskins. Everywhere he went, sunshine followed — the only player to win four Super Bowls with three different teams. Millen then joined CBS, tumbling to Fox in 1994. Today, he and Dick Stockton forge its No. 2 broadcast tandem. At CBS Radio, Matt and Howard David are *primus inter pares* — calling "Monday Night" and the Super Bowl. Said one writer: "Millen's so good that even Notre Dame fans forget he went to Happy Valley."

VAN MILLER. On October 17, 1959, the *Buffalo Evening News* bannered, "Buffalo To Have Team in New Football League Next Fall." Always, Miller has been its prosopopeia — carrying the Bills to Upstate New York's cities, farms, and postcard towns. The Dunkirk, NY, native also broadcast the NBA Braves and is sports director of Buffalo's CBS affiliate, WIVB. "Why shouldn't I keep going?" he says. "I was a bus boy at the Last Supper. My Social Security number is 4." In Buffalo, "Pro football isn't merely a diversion," said former Bills' guard Conrad Dobler. "It's a religion." Welcome to Upstate's parish priest.

TED MOORE. The '60s Packers meant Ray Scott, dulcet and sonorous. Their radio Voice also flushed with providence. In 1960, Moore joined the Pack: They won their first championship since 1944. By turns, he called titles in 1961-62, Lombardi's 1965-66-67 trifecta, the Ice Bowl, and first two Super Bowls. In '65, Moore broadcast Don Chandler's phantom overtime field goal that beat Baltimore, 13-10, in the Western Conference playoff. Five years later, he traded Lambeau Field for Memorial Stadium! No problem. Even as the Colts' new play-by-playman, Ted's heart remained in football's Smallville, USA.

ANTHONY MUÑOZ graced the '90s film "The Right Stuff" — having brought that to football as an 11-time All-Pro. In 1980, Muñoz was the Bengals' first-round draft choice. Soon, he justified their fealty. He became three-time NFL Offensive Lineman of the Year, unanimous member of the NFL Team of the '80s, 1991 NFL Man of the Year, and played in two Super Bowls. Muñoz is perhaps pro ball's best-ever offensive lineman. Retiring in 1992, the two-time All-American worked at TNT, CBS, and 1994-95 Fox. Says former partner Thom Brennaman of the born-again Christian: "If everyone were like Anthony, this would be a far better world."

BRENT MUSBURGER. From the start, this son of Oregon liked having the final say: As a minor league umpire, he once threw out 26 players and managers in a single year. Later, the Northwestern graduate got it as a Chicago columnist and Los Angeles news anchor, breaking in at CBS in 1975. Then 35, Brent became its sports quintessence: Masters golf, U.S. Open tennis, the NBA, college hoops and football, and host and anchor of "NFL Today." At Northwestern, he was suspended for a year for having a car on campus. The dean said he should enter the Marines. Instead, Musburger shaped sports broadcasting's 1970s and '80s profile.

LINDSEY NELSON. "I'm glad I did it," Nelson said of his frantic schedule. "I'd just hate to have to do it again." Over four decades, the Tennessean called events from the Cotton Bowl to the World Series to the NBA "Game of the Week." He also brought his voice, crusading and exact, to 19 years of NFL-TV. From 1974-77, Lindsey added Mutual Radio's "Monday Night Football." Always, his rhythmic country gabble and glaring sports coats — in time, he owned nearly 350 — made him a presence. Before his death in 1995, Nelson was a professional and professor of broadcasting — teaching America the definition of class. (Rozelle Award, 1990.)

MERLIN OLSEN. If a football broadcaster is possessed of an easy familiarity, he evolves into an extended member of the family. Merlin leapt from Utah State (nuclear physics major) via the Rams (Hall of Fame defensive lineman) to become a father figure to America's kinetic cult. At NBC, he and Dick Enberg formed a superb 1978-88 tandem. Olsen never made it to a Super Bowl. Announcing, he did five. Merlin also starred in two Peacock series — the gentle "Father Murphy" and "Aaron's Way." How unique was No. 74? What other football player could make FTD florist delivery ads a series of National Good Feeling?

RON PITTS calls football a family affair. His father, Elijah, keyed the five-time champion 1961-69 and '71 Packers. The junior Pitts played with Buffalo (1985-87) and the Pack (1988-91) before trading miked helmets for lavalier mikes. The Academic All-PAC Ten UCLA graduate became an ABC analyst and Black Entertainment Television (BET) correspondent — also, covering the NFL for cable's Los Angeles-based Prime Ticket. In 1994, Pitts joined fledgling Fox as a color man — calling NFC and, later, World League Football telecasts on cable FX. "Football is in the genes," says Ron — less Pit(ts) Stop than Marathon.

MEL PROCTOR. Talk about life imitating art. Growing up in Colorado, Proctor watched sports and "The Fugitive." In 1995, he wrote the definitive book on the TV series. His other avocation became Mel's job. The Colorado College graduate has done football (Mutual, Turner, and NBC-TV/Radio), baseball (Orioles and Padres), and hoops (the NCAA on CBS and Washington Wiz [nee Bullets]). He also plays the recurring character Grant Bessor on NBC's "Homicide: Life on the Streets." Wry and fluent, the three-time Maryland Sportscaster of the Year — unlike the NFL — has never wandered from the points of his past.

JAY RANDOLPH is the son of a politician — U.S. Senator William Jennings Randolph — who trooped to America's other favorite game. Jay began sportscasting in Clarksburg, West Virginia, in 1958. Fast-forward to Dallas Cowboys and SMU radio, St. Louis Cardinals' TV, and NBC's pro and college football, men and women's golf, NCAA hoops, and three Olympics Games. Not spiky, like Paul Maguire, or theatric, like Lindsey Nelson, Randolph is breezy and relaxed — also, a three-time local Emmy recipient. "Ah, football and politics," he muses. "Both are competitive, fought in the trenches, you rarely have ties, and you're exhausted when you're done."

BEASLEY REECE entered North Texas State University's music school on an early-'70s scholarship. As a walk-on, he proceeded to make football rhythms of his own. Reece was drafted in 1976 by Dallas, and played nine years with the Cowboys, Giants, and Buccaneers. In 1988, he signed with Hartford's NBC-TV affiliate, WVIT, and is still its sports director and anchor. In '91, the network made him an NFL analyst — also, reporter and boxing interviewer on the 1992-96 Summer Games. Eddie Gomez, playing bass with pianist Billy Evans, called the jazzman's goal "to make music that balanced passion and intellect." Reece scores.

RAY SCOTT. "CBS' National Football League coverage didn't make a move to any big game without him in the late '50s and early '60s," *TV Guide* wrote of the NFL's best-ever mikeman. From 1956-74, Scott exteriorized pro football as Voice of the Green Bay Packers. He called four Super Bowls and nine title games, spurned happy talk for spartan discourse, and used his Cadillac of a voice to sell more fans on the NFL than any broadcaster who ever lived. Football's TV Caruso was also its Godfather. In 1952, Scott conceived, sold, and later broadcast the NFL's first network series — DuMont's Saturday "Game of the Week."

LON SIMMONS crashed into America's Passion via its National Pastime. He pitched in the baseball Phillies' organization, hurt his back, became a carpenter, and decided that to make the major leagues he needed a different kind of tool. Lon began radio at Fresno, California, leapt in 1957 to San Francisco's KSFO, and soon aired the transplanted Giants. Football meant the 49ers of Tittle and Brodie and McElhenny and the Alley-Oop and shotgun formation and Kezar Stadium. "San Francisco was packing the NFL," he recalls, "when the rest of the country thought it kind of an odd eccentricity." Again, California leads the way.

PHIL SIMMS shows that blondes *can* have more fun. The Morehead State alumnus and No. 1 draft choice was the Giants' 1979-93 quarterback. Peaks: 1985 Pro Bowl Most Valuable Player, '86 All-Pro, two-time Super Bowl champion, and Super Bowl XXI MVP. Simms holds team marks for career TD passes and most passes attempted and completed for a game, year, and career. In 1994, Phil threw a pass to ESPN as a studio analyst — a year later, joining NBC. He now flanks Dick Enberg and Paul Maguire on the Peacock's top announcing team — gracing other events like "Quarterback Challenge," "Run to Daylight," and even the NBA.

BOB STARR mixed precision, a Sooner lilt, and *bass* voice into five decades of play-by-play. Bob has sampled baseball, college basketball, and the 1966-70 Patriots, '71 49ers, 1972-79 Cardinals, and '80-89 and '93-94 Rams. "The NFL's so different," he says by comparison. "You have fewer games, so each means more. The intensity — when I'm done at the end of a three-hour telecast, you have to decompress." The sweat reflects Starr's work ethic, which has triumphed by necessity: His teams never won a conference title. How apt that this Prince has struggled Valiant(ly) with a parade of comic clubs. His wife's name is Brenda Starr.

DICK STOCKTON was born in Philadelphia, grew up in New York, graduated from Syracuse, and took his grace and homework to a roundup of network stops. The NFL: 1976-77 NBC, '78-94 CBS, and '94- Fox. Baseball: '75 World Series — calling Carlton Fisk's Falstaffian home run — and CBS in 1990-92. Dick has done pro and college hoops, the Pan American Games, and Winter Olympics. His Agincourt was '94 in Lillehammer: Bonnie Blair and Dan Jansen stir reminiscence, even now. Stockton and Matt Millen form Fox's No. 2 NFL team. As a kid, Dick cheered the Giants. He now airs their Giant-killers — the once-Lombardi Pack.

HANK STRAM. Football's dapper analyst/ex-coach is perhaps its most innovative. The Purdue alumnus graduated in 1960 to the new AFL. For 15 years, he coached the Kansas City Chiefs (nee Dallas Texans) — making Super Bowl I, winning the 1962 six-quarter AFL title game and Super Bowl IV, and four times being named AFL, AFC, or NFL "Coach of the Year." Stram joined CBS-TV in 1975-76, coached the Saints in '77-78, and then returned to Columbia. Through 1995, he and Jack Buck made radio's "Monday Night Football" a fetching and inspired hit. Today, Stram co-hosts "NFL Preview" — still wedding Beau Brummel and Computer USA.

PAT SUMMERALL. As a football Voice, he vaulted higher, more enduringly, than any former athlete. Pat grew up in Florida, went to the University of Arkansas, and as a 1952-61 Cardinal and Giant taught off-season school. He then chose the 4-3 over 4+3. Summerall joined CBS Radio, moved to TV in '67, and ultimately set a blue-chip consortium for play-by-play. The *New York Times* parodied Pat calling Hemingway's *The Old Man and the Sea*: "Old Cuban. Sea. Marlin. Harpoon. Sharks' feast. Brave old guy. Broken knife. What a struggle. John?" — as in Madden, who joined Summerall in 1994 when Fox lured the NFL. (Rozelle Award, 1994.)

JOE THEISMANN, as in Heisman, cleaves America into two broadcast camps. Many prefer hearing him to being at the game. Others pray that laryngitis will silence him forever. At Notre Dame, Joe was an All-American and Heisman Trophy runner-up. He joined the Canadian Football League in 1971, became an NFLer three years later, was its 1983 MVP, and played at Washington through '85. Retiring with a broken leg, Joe moved to CBS and, then, ESPN in 1988 — obliging the latter's "Sunday Night NFL," "NFL Countdown," and "NFL Prime Monday." On any show, the New Jersey son and Cable ACE award recipient's voice seems forever in bloom.

CHUCK THOMPSON. In the late 1950s, the Colts were sport's most compelling franchise. From Virginia to Little Italy, they seduced a region — and their Voice, its heart. Born in Massachusetts, Chuck moved to Maryland in 1949. Fans prized his fairness and schoolboy voice — shared a love of Unitas, Berry, Lipscomb, and Moore — and reveled in Thompson's war cries: "Ain't the Beer Cold!" and "Go to War, Miss Agnes!" He called three Colts' titles — including '58's sudden-death — and moored CBS' 1960s and '70s coverage. When the Colts left in 1984, he remained with the baseball Orioles — not from, but forever of, Bijou by the Bay.

MIKE TIRICO. Term the Syracuse '88 graduate precocious and/or fortunate. Call him busy, above all. Tirico broke into radio/television as a student and by 1989 was named Central New York's top local broadcaster. He was the first recipient of SU's Bob Costas Scholarship, given to an exceptional broadcast journalism student. In 1991, Tirico joined ESPN, hosting the NFL and NBC on radio and a blizzard of TV. "SportsCenter," "College Football Scoreboard," and "NFL Prime Monday" star the Whitestone, New York native. Also, college hoops' studio and play-by-play. On Sunday, he would rest — except that the NFL holds sway.

BOB TRUMPY reached NBC by way of the University of Utah (B.A. 1968). That year, he signed with the Bengals as a 12th-round draft choice. In 10 years, Trumpy eclipsed most No. 1's. Retiring in '77, the four-time All-Pro turned to radio — WLW-Cincinnati's "Sports Talk" — and TV. Bright and voluble, Bob has teamed with Bob Costas, Don Criqui, and Marv Albert on NFL and college telecasts. In 1993-94, he and Dick Enberg — then, NBC's top coupling — became the first TV pair to call successive Super Bowls. Name it, Trumpy does it: boxing, golf, weightlifting, or volleyball. Paid by the word, he would own NBC.

LESLEY VISSER. A proverb says, "The style makes the man" — and woman, too. For 14 years, Lesley's writing distinguished arguably America's best sports section, the *Boston Globe*'s. Then, in 1988, she was signed by CBS Sports — among any network's first women (and first journalists to cross the divide between print and electronic media). At the *Globe*, Visser won a slew of awards — at CBS and, now, ESPN viewers and reviews. "My big joke is that many of the skills are the same," she says, "but now my hair has to be better. At the core I'm still a writer, but I love TV." Also, Dick Stockton — colleague and husband.

PETE WEBER received B.A. and M.A. degrees from Notre Dame — using his majors (Modern Languages and Communications Arts) to style a wise and winning narrative. He has been a Bills' analyst, pre- and postgame anchor, and hosted series starring Marv Levy, Jim Kelly, Bill Polian, and Frank Reich. He also loves the shinny sport — calling the Sabres, Kings, and Fighting Irish. In basketball, Pete has done the Seattle SuperSonics — baseball, minor-league Buffalo and Rochester. Invariably, though, focus returns to the Bills. Says the Illinois native and current Empire Sports Network host: "They're the hub of Western New York."

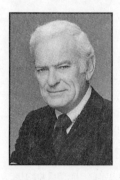

JACK WHITAKER has exalted broadcasting since before Dwight Eisenhower became President — spanning six decades of radio/TV from WCAU-Philadelphia to CBS in 1961 to ABC in '82. The St. Joseph's graduate has done CBS' Super Bowl I and Eagles' and Giants' play-by-play — hosted Columbia's anthology series, "Sports Spectacular," and covered sports for ABC's "World News Tonight" and "Nightline" — and buoyed baseball, tennis, track and field, the Olympics, racing's Triple Crown, and golf's four major titles. Here's to a superb writer, essayist, and two-time Emmy Award recipient — bard, archivist, and football balladeer.

BOB WOLFF has endured/enjoyed both sides now. In the early '50s, the son of New York City broadcasted the low deeds and high comedy of the sadsack Redskins. He gave the score, but didn't have to; listeners knew who was winning. Wolff also did the play-by-play of The Game That Made Pro Football — at Yankee Stadium, in the shivery twilight, on a December 1958 afternoon. Baltimore's overtime victory — "The Colts win!" cried Wolff. "[Alan] Ameche scores!" — catapulted the NFL to Big-Game America. For the *cum laude* Duke graduate: history, immortality, and solace from the Redskins' identity as hero of every dog that was under.

CHAPTER

2 BEGINNINGS

EARLY DAYS

Unlike Dumbo, pigskins weren't made for flying. Instead, they rivaled Atlantis in pro football's backlot youth. Forget glamour, kitsch, and the klieg lights of publicity. Players were barely household names in their own household.

Towering, 1920s and '30s baseball was wed to radio. By contrast, the NFL limped through most years one step ahead of the law. On September 26, 1920, Rock Island met St. Paul in the first game of pay-for-play football. Early announcers were paid little. Often, games weren't even broadcast. Most teams had to pay stations to put matches on the air.

In 1939, pro football's first telecast had two cameras, was broadcast by Allen Walz, and aired over RCA's experimental TV station: W2XBS. It sprang from Ebbets Field, starred the Brooklyn Dodgers and Philadelphia Eagles, and reached fewer than 400 sets. Few of the players even knew the game was being televised. "I certainly wasn't aware of it," recalled Brooklyn tackle Bruiser Kinard. "That sure is interesting."

For years, Bill Stern, Ted Husing, and Graham McNamee beat football's drum, but oblivion stilled its band. Below, their successors' entree to the NFL.

I WAS FOUR WHEN my parents moved our family to Columbia, Tennessee, 40 miles from Nashville. I spent a lot of time in front of the radio — but not to hear professional football. To us, it didn't exist. *My* time was Saturday afternoon. We would hear Graham McNamee and Ted Husing doing the big games from Yale and Harvard and Army. We heard a lot of the Columbia University games, and I didn't understand then that it was mostly because Columbia played its home games at Baker Field in New York City, and broadcasts from there did not require the network to go to the expense of traveling a crew. Some of those inflections inflicted by the announcers were as strange to me as my southern accent would have been to them. Speaking of a rules infraction, they would tell me that "Yale has been 'peen-a-lized.'" I didn't understand that long *e*. Still don't. But I listened. Still do.

— *Lindsey Nelson*

GROWING UP, I knew about Red Grange and [the University of] Illinois, and the Four Horsemen of Notre Dame. Pro ball was a secondary kind of sport. It wasn't until Grange came into the Polo Grounds as a professional [1925] and drew that enormous crowd for the first time [more than 70,000] that we began to be aware of it. I saw my first pro football game my sophomore year in high school at Ebbets Field between the Dodgers and Giants. It was exciting. The problem was that no one knew the league was alive.

— *Marty Glickman*

MY WIFE'S MAIDEN name is Lintzenich. In the early days of radio her father was the all-time punter of the Chicago Bears. He played with Red Grange and Bronko Nagurski. He was saying that's like being one of Elizabeth Taylor's husbands — nobody knows who the heck you are. But while playing for the Bears, he had a punt of 94 yards. I guess it's all in the timing.

— *Jack Buck*

I'VE OFTEN THOUGHT of that span of ten days, during which
Grange played five pro games. Ten days — and the NFL's niche
changed forever. Following his last collegiate game, he signed
a pro contract with the Bears, and agreed to go on a barnstorm-
ing tour. The deal would be 50 percent of the gross for the
Bears, who would pay expenses, and 50 percent for Grange. In
the first game, played in a snowstorm at Wrigley Field in Chicago, they drew 28,000. Then, that huge crowd at the Polo
Grounds. Think of his successors, and what they owe the Gal-
loping Ghost — Baugh, Walker, Hornung, Butkus, Harris, Montana, and the rest. Seeing his picture, they should salute.

— *Lindsey Nelson*

I WAS ONLY eight years old when Grange ran wild against Michigan in the dedication game at Memorial Stadium in Champaign
on October 18, 1924. So it was a real kick to sit on the dais with
him 50 years later and participate in a golden anniversary banquet in Champaign. A full house was on hand to commemorate
the most famous performance in football history.

My remarks that night included the Damon Runyon line
that "Red Grange was three or four men and a horse rolled into
one. He was Jack Dempsey and Babe Ruth and Al Jolson and
Paavo Nurmi and Man O'War." I recalled how Quin Ryan broadcast the Illinois-Michigan game on WGN Radio in 1924, the year
the station went on the air. A listener called WGN after Grange
scored four touchdowns in less than 12 minutes and suggested
the station get another sports announcer. "The one you have
obviously doesn't know a touchdown from a first down," the
caller said. "No man can score that many touchdowns in that
short a time!"

The Bears' George Halas was there to honor him. "Red
Grange had more impact on football than any man in this century," he said. "And even though there are 26 years left in this
century, my statement will still stand up when the hundred
years have passed." Then Grange spoke, mentioning a tele-

gram from President Ford, the ex-Wolverine football player. "When I assumed my present office," the wire read, "I never dreamed that I'd be congratulating someone who kicked the heck out of Michigan."

That day, they held a press conference to salute Red's return to campus. Grange remembered meeting Babe Ruth once in New York and getting some advice. "Kid," Babe said, "don't believe a damn thing they write about you, and don't pick up too many checks!" With typical modesty, Grange wouldn't take credit for making the NFL what it is today. "That," he laughed, "is like saying the Johnstown flood was caused by a leaky toilet in Altoona." Maybe, but to a defense Red looked like a tidal wave.

— Jack Brickhouse

AN EXTRAORDINARY day in pro football occurred at the Polo Grounds on December 7, 1941, Pearl Harbor Day. I was doing a pre-game show. Red Barber was doing the game, Connie Desmond color. And during the course of the game, they began to make public address announcements over the loudspeaker. Would Admiral So-and-so please call his office? Would General So-and-so please report to his headquarters? Would Colonel So-and-so please report to his base? The people in the stands did not know what was going on. *I* knew, on the other hand, that Pearl Harbor had been attacked. The news room in New York at 1540 Broadway would interrupt our broadcast of the game and make the announcements. Yet while we were aware of it, we didn't know the full extent of it. Remarkably, the first question asked when we heard about Pearl Harbor was, "Where is Pearl Harbor?!" No one knew. Of course, we found out soon enough. Eventually, the crowd knew that something was going on as these high-ranking officers were called out of the stands to report. Finally, the word spread throughout the crowd. The Brooklyn Dodgers won the game, and the Giant

fans went home very quiet, because it was the start of the day
of infamy — perhaps the most memorable of our lives.

— *Marty Glickman*

IN NOVEMBER 1941 I got a note from a former classmate, Jimmy
Coleman, who had played football at the University of Tennessee. He was writing about a proposed reunion in Washington
at an upcoming Redskins-Eagles' game. We had mutual friends
on both teams. The game would be played at Griffith Stadium
in Washington on a Sunday afternoon the first week in December. I have never managed to forget the exact date of that game.

On Saturday, wearing my army uniform, I took the train
from North Carolina to Washington. The next day, one of our
friends, the Eagles' Bob Suffridge, invited me to sit in on his
team's pre-game meeting and on the bench itself. "Be with
us," he said. "Take off your army hat and come on." He passed
me off as the Eagles' recruiting officer. Before this disguise I'd
had trouble getting credentials to the game. Now, I trotted
amid the players onto the field as thousands cheered. On the
rooftop, public address announcer Frank Blair, later NBC-TV's
newsman on the *Today Show*, looked over his notes. In the stands,
a young Naval officer named John F. Kennedy made himself
comfortable. On the Eagles' bench, I watched and waited. None
of us at Griffith Stadium or anywhere else would ever forget
that afternoon.

As the game progressed, we suspected that something unusual was happening, but we didn't know what. Frank Blair
kept calling for various members of the military establishment
to report to their stations. On the bench we asked each other
what was happening. No one knew. Harry Thayer, the Eagles'
general manager, was on that bench. At one point, coach Greasy
Neale said, "Harry, see if you can find out what's going on."
What was going on was that the Japanese had successfully completed their raid on Pearl Harbor and destroyed our Pacific Fleet.
The game itself was uninterrupted. Suffridge put on a great

performance, but the Redskins won, 20 to 14. As we went after the game through the crowds to a waiting taxi, we heard wild rumors. Some screaming fans said that enemy soldiers had landed in San Diego.

We went directly to the apartment of Ed Cifers, a Tennessee alumnus and Redskins' player. Then we went to a preplanned party the Eagles had at the Willard Hotel. Suffridge was still telling people that I was the Eagles' recruiting officer. But now I wasn't having trouble getting around. The mood had changed abruptly. My army uniform was my pass to anywhere. As I walked back through Union Station, a man rushed up, slapped me on the back, and said, "Give 'em hell, Lieutenant." I realized then that I had permanent employment. It wasn't the last steady job I had — but without doubt it was the most important.

— *Lindsey Nelson*

BROADCASTING AT Lambeau Field is one thing. Broadcasting in Canyon City, Colorado, is something else. Canyon City is a very small town near the Royal Gorge. I was there to do a high school football game one Sunday afternoon. We get there about two hours before the game and pull into this school, and we say, "Where's the field?" It was out behind one of the school buildings. We look around, and there's no press box. There are about two rows of bleachers. That, and a flatbed truck.

I went to the truck and asked the driver, "What you are here for?" He said, "I'm here for the game today." I said, "Can you tell us where they broadcast from?" He said, "Oh, you're the radio station doing the game." He told us to sit on the flatbed, and he'd back the truck up to the 50-yard line. Fine; we didn't have a choice. Then I look around, and say, "Where's the A.C.?" — the electrical outlet? He said, "I don't think we *have* one."

The closest A.C. was in a building fifty yards behind the end zone on the second floor. You couldn't even see the yard markers. I did the game from there looking through the window — and the guy with that truck had to run about 150 yards of line so we could reach the building and use the plug. I often remembered that day when I later did the Jets at Shea Stadium — by contrast, palatial. Talk about not starting at the top.

— *Merle Harmon*

I GREW UP LISTENING to Graham McNamee do boxing. Our radio was a rectangular box called an Arbiphone, the strangest-looking thing you've ever seen. To hear more than a jumble, you had to adjust three different dials. The speaker itself rested on top of the box, which looked like a big question mark. Worse, it *sounded* like one. But it made me aware of broadcasting.

Years later I went to the University of Tennessee. Our football games were aired from the second deck of a shack on top of the stands. And the only way to reach it was by climbing a wooden stepladder that swayed in the wind. Once there, you were stuck, because coming down was more terrifying than going up. In the '60s and '70s, I'd recall that ladder while doing pro football for CBS. No one will ever get me to knock technology.

One day in November 1939, I was spotting for Jack Harris, who did play-by-play of Tennessee games over WSM ["The Station of the Grand Ol' Opry"]. Remember that stepladder, and that there were no restrooms inside the broadcast shack. At halftime I climbed down to get the statistics from the Tennessee athletic department, which I'd then take back to the booth. I get there, and see Harris staring at me with a pained expression. "Here are the stats," I said. "*You* do 'em," he said.

Jack had drunk a second cup of coffee at brunch that morning, and I guess the extra cup was too much for him. So as he rushes off to find a restroom, I'm reading the stats. My broadcast career had begun! If Jack Harris had been content with a single cup of coffee, my life might have turned out differently. There but for the grace of Maxwell House go I.

— *Lindsey Nelson*

MY MOTHER LED me to NFL broadcasting. You may remember the radio show, "Information, Please." They had Franklin P. Adams, John Kiernan, the brains of America. The show was on literature and writing. They'd ask questions and award the "Encyclopedia Britannica" for people that got it right. Boy, my mother could pop in ahead of everybody. She made me check out a library card and waited outside till I got it. I had to read a book a week. She made me take typing in high school — the only boy in the class. The girls giggled when I came in. She made me take elocution lessons. I was outraged. I said, "Why?" She said, "Curtis, one day I want you to be able to stand on your own two feet and express yourself. You'll be in command when you do."

My senior year, we had the greatest high school team Wyoming ever had — 31 straight victories. Three of us became starters at the University of Wyoming. I went out for practice in December, just before the season started, and the coach, John Powell, called me over and said, "You're off the team." I said, "What do you mean? What'd I — do something wrong?" He says, "No, your mother was over here today and went in to see the principal. She doesn't like your English grade — thinks it's below what you should be doing. So she's ordered you not to be on the basketball team." I was never so mad in my life.

I told her, "How can you do this to me? You know basketball's my whole life. We've got such a great team this year — we've all grown up together." She said, "Get your English grade up." Talk about a pioneer woman! She meant everything she said. I got my grade up in 10 days. She taught me to get everything out of myself I could. When I did the NFL, my mother was the reason why.

— *Curt Gowdy*

AS A KID IN A tiny town in Indiana, the nearest football that you could see was in the county seat of Huntington — Dan Quayle's home town. I don't think I even got to a game until I was 16, because Bippus didn't have enough people to play football. I never thought too much about it — and nothing about the NFL or radio and TV. The only thing I thought about was Jim Thorpe. Growing up in Indian country, you asked, "Who's the greatest athlete?" The answer's always been, and still is, "Jim Thorpe." That's about as near as the NFL got.

— *Chris Schenkel*

IN THE PRIMITIVE days of pro football, the broadcast and broadcaster were not important. He was low man on the totem pole. I broadcast in the Polo Grounds for six or seven years out of the scoreboard in right field. There was no room anyplace else. The scoreboard was set up with boxes and rectangles where the inning, score, or team's name was inserted. We would peer through the apertures looking down on the field to see the play. Fortunately, the scoreboard was near midfield and I was close enough to the field to hear some of the comments on the sidelines. The problem was that when you came into the scoreboard to do the game, the first one in was the last one out. It was so narrow that all you had was a wooden bench and plank on which the broadcast equipment was set. No one could get by — no way to get out at halftime, or any time. So you'd remind yourself to go to the bathroom before the game.

Priorities.

— *Marty Glickman*

MY FIRST CONTACT with pro football came as a teenage broadcaster in Johnstown, Pennsylvania. Our baseball club was the Pittsburgh Pirates — and the football team, now the Steelers, was named after them. That's how dominant baseball was back then. The football club was coming to Johnstown to play a preseason game against the Erie Veterans. I asked a friend of mine with the Pirates if he could get me Johnny Blood — his real name was Johnny McNally, a great running back and their playing-coach — on my radio show. He arranged it, which was good enough. What I didn't expect was my bonus. The Pirates came to town on Friday. The game was Saturday. Art Rooney, long-time Steelers' owner, picked that time to sign the great Colorado football star (Byron) Whizzer White, later a Supreme Court Justice, to the unheard-of salary of $15,000. Was he criticized by the other owners! They said he had ruined football to pay anybody that outlandish kind of money! I didn't care. I got Johnny Blood and Whizzer White on my show. When you're young, priorities smack of *me*.

— *Ray Scott*

WHEN I GRADUATED from the University of Wyoming in '42, I was going to be a fighter pilot. I went into the Air Corps, and didn't know I had a ruptured disk in my back. I guess I'd hurt it playing college basketball. These were the early days of ruptured disks. They didn't know much about them. I had an operation in '43 — only seven years after the first disk operation ever performed — and got discharged from the Air Force after ten months in a hospital.

I still had a lot of back pain, and came back to Cheyenne. The neurosurgeon told me I couldn't work for six months. I was sitting around one day when the phone rang. It was the manager of the local radio station, Bill Grove. He says, "Curt, we've got a six-man football game we've sold tomorrow for $60. We don't have anybody to broadcast. Everybody's gone in the service." I said, "Bill, I've never broadcast in my life." He said, "Well, we used to cover you at the university when you played basketball there. And I know you're a sports fan. If you don't do it, it's either my wife or I, and we've never *seen* a football game."

I talked to my mother and she said, "Do it. It'll get your mind off feeling sorry for yourself." The next day she made me wear my long underwear to protect my back and drove me to the field — a vacant lot with a goal post on each end. I walked over and there were two soap boxes. True story. One soap box held an old-fashioned microphone. The other one was to sit on. There was a kid standing there named Dick Lane. He said, "I'm just here to do the commercials." I looked out on the field and said, "Wait a minute. Where are the yard lines? There's no side lines, no goal lines. How do you tell where the ball is?" Dick says, "Look, I'm just here to do the commercials. I don't know."

Just then a bus drove up, and let out both teams. They ran on the field, and my eyes popped. They had no numbers on their back. I said, "Do you have a roster? How do I tell the players?" He said, "I'm just here to do the commercials." They kicked off and I made up every name. The guys I met in the Air Force or played basketball against in college — BYU, Utah, Colorado. I guessed where the ball was. I didn't call a touchdown till the ref put his arms up. Somehow I got through it, went home, and soon the phone rang — Bill Grove again. He says, "Curt, that was great. You want to do our high school basketball games?" I turned to my mother, and she says, "Do it."

All this happened only three months after the neurosurgeon told me not to work for six. But it didn't seem like work. That's how I got started doing football.

— *Curt Gowdy*

WHEN I STARTED broadcasting, the goal of most sports announcers was to do baseball. The job was virtually year-round. You'd go south in March, and stay with the team until the end of the World Series. Football was a sometimes thing. It was just the weekend. It encompassed four months of the year, and that's all. The football season ended late in November, around turkey time. Now, of course, it ends late in January — and it starts a good deal earlier. The difference between baseball and football was evidenced in the men who made their reputations doing them. Bill Stern and Ted Husing were rapid-fire announcers with exciting voices. A fellow like Red Barber was a soft-spoken, laid-back broadcaster — like baseball. Baseball is a relaxed game to watch. You pay attention, lean forward with each pitch, and then sit back. A baseball game is a relaxed two and a hours in the sunshine. Football is a a clash between gladiators. Those who best broadcast the sport reflected football as war.

— *Marty Glickman*

CHAPTER

3

SEEMS LIKE YESTERDAY

TV TACKLES RADIO

Enter television in the late 1940s — and the NFL in scattered markets across the land. The picture was black and black; sight and sound, uneven; money, as small-timey as the pros. In 1951, the entire *league* got $50,000 in TV profit. (By dint of foil, a 30-second Fox-TV ad on the '97 Super Bowl cost $1.2 million.) Football meant those college guys, not the rag-tag NFL.

If lucky, a 1940s and early '50s announcer had a spotter (volunteer), a seat (often distant from the field), and wire to the production truck. Until 1953, he did not, however, have a network to inject health into pro football's weak TV pulse. Enter a curious tatter of the time — DuMont — adding Saturday night football to Gorgeous George, "Demolition Derby," "Colonel Humphrey Flack," and "Rocky King, Detective."

The post-war years were hardly America's glad tidings to the NFL. Still, it slowly stirred, like a still river shedding ice. In 1955, a major network — NBC — replaced DuMont on pro football's title game. A Chinese proverb suggested augury: "One generation plants the seed. Another gets the shade."

IN THE LATE '40S, I had been with a Pittsburgh radio station for a year when I convinced the Steelers' general manager to let us broadcast their four pre-season games. We stole them from their long-time flagship. We paid a ridiculously low amount of money and the general manager almost got fired for it. I'm glad there was no such thing then as tape — because those games were a disaster. Our first game was against the Chicago Cardinals at Comiskey Park. It's a miracle it wasn't our last. Football was so little thought of that we were put in the White Sox' baseball broadcast booth behind home plate. The booth was so far away it was almost impossible to make out the numbers or the players. It's hard to do a job when you can't see the job you're supposed to do. I wonder if guys today realize how far the NFL has come.

— *Ray Scott*

GROWING UP in the '40s, I couldn't have spelled the NFL. I'm trying to think if there *was* any NFL. There wasn't on the West Coast. I remember vaguely that the Los Angeles Dons had a game they played annually with the Rams for a *Los Angeles Times* charity. Then I went to USC and was told I'd be drafted number one by the Rams. I thought, "Hmm, that's nice. I'll play for the Rams." Still, I wasn't terribly concerned. I wasn't even sure I was going to play ball. It wasn't a big deal — more like wrestling than anything else that I knew in profesional sports.

It turned out that the Rams didn't take me as the top draft choice. Instead, I went to the Giants number one. I had to ask, "Who coaches the Giants? Where do they play?" Somebody said, "The Polo Grounds." I vaguely knew that it had something to do with baseball. I never saw [Giants' owner] Wellington Mara. Instead, he sent a letter, said it was really great to have drafted me and that I was their property, told me to report such and such a date, and that my contract was for all of $7,500. I had been offered $10,000 to play in Canada. I talked it over with my wife and said, "You know, let's go to New York. This will about pay for our trip. We'll see what the Big Apple's all about." I was a little curious, because I'd played at Yankee Stadium as a senior.

We beat Army, 28 to 6, and I had a good game in a blizzard. Wellington Mara scouted the game. That's why I was drafted number one. We stayed over on Sunday and went to see "Guys and Dolls." I'll never forget all those tall buildings, never dreaming that a year later I'd be back with the Giants. I'd figured I'd get out of USC and, like everyone else in my family, get a job and earn an honest living. Instead, I wound up doing what I'm doing now. Just kidding.

— *Frank Gifford*

IN 1952, I WAS at an ad agency in Pittsburgh when I was contacted by a Steelers' executive, Ed Kiley, and his Eagles' counterpart, Paul Lewis. Back then, each NFL home game was blacked out. That worried TV advertisers because they'd lose every city. Paul and Ed had an idea: Move one game to Saturday night and televise it nationally. That way, only one city would be blacked out. I approached my boss at the agency but we couldn't get a sponsor. The same two men came back to me in spring 1953. By now, *I'd* had an idea. I approached an executive friend of mine at Westinghouse whom I knew to be a football fan and asked him to meet me, Ed, and Paul. I was primed to tell him why pro football would be the coming thing — one game a week on Saturday night.

We talk. Finally, my friend says, "Ray, how much?" I said, "First, you have to decide how much to spend on commercials." Then I swallowed hard and said, "But for rights, time on TV and paying the announcers, three quarters of a million dollars." Small potatoes now, but then it was big. Amazingly, he liked it — so I go back to my boss and tell him the sponsors are interested. Next came getting a network. We went to CBS. They said, "Not on Saturday night — we've got Jackie Gleason." Here's some history. CBS then said, "If you can get Westinghouse to cancel 'Studio One' on Monday nights" — a very popular dramatic show — "we'll do it and have 'Monday Night Football'!"

Westinghouse wouldn't, so my boss went to NBC and they said, "Sorry. We have the 'Comedy Hour' with Sid Caesar and Imogene Coca." He went to ABC, and *they* had the "Saturday Night Fights." It looked like the idea was dead. Then, salvation. The station that I was a sports director at in Pittsburgh was owned by the DuMont Network — a distant Number Four behind CBS, NBC and ABC. They agreed to do it, and we went to Commissioner Bert Bell for approval. I'll never forget what he said: "Ray, don't you ever tell the owners, but we should probably pay you to do this."

As it turned out, 1953 was the first year the NFL went coast-to-coast on TV for an entire year. I did play-by-play. The late Herman Hickman, former coach at Yale, was the analyst — but wasn't with me at the game, but at a studio in New York! He'd analyze the first half and when the game was over he'd analyze the second. I was by myself for the announcing. Come 1955, and DuMont went out of business. That can't erase how this Little Engine That Could beat CBS, NBC, and ABC in the ratings — really, the moment that TV football began.

— *Ray Scott*

MY GREATEST MEMORY of DuMont came in Chicago. I went there to do a game and I'm riding down Michigan Avenue in a cab. I look up over a theatre and there's my name. Chuck Thompson. DuMont. The Bears' game was right underneath. It is possible that their priorities were a bit askew.

— *Chuck Thompson*

THE FIRST TIME I watched the NFL was at night on DuMont. I recall they used a white football, and Otto Graham throwing it around the field. Marion Motley plunging through the line. Chuck Thompson doing the games. It brought the Cleveland Browns to life for me. But it was for the most part radio football that I associate with those days. There wasn't that much television football and so I listened to the staccato radio tones of the much imitated Marty Glickman called out the plays for the Giants. I recall sitting and keeping score of football games. "Those of you scoring at home." I was a very sick young man at the time.

— *Marv Albert*

DOING GAMES IN Cleveland Stadium wasn't pleasant for DuMont or anyone else. Then I got smart, because it's difficult to try to speak while shivering. I started bringing an electric blanket. See, I discovered that engineers are bright people. They have plugs in their operation. I would plug it in, and I'd put on some slippers. Put my feet down on the blanket. My feet would be warm. That's an inside of broadcasting. Another was looking down from the roof of Cleveland Stadium. It was like looking at a chess board — a beautiful place to watch a game.

The field was far away, but you were over the top and doing television I saw the quarterback fade and immediately saw pass routes. People think of those great crowds at the Stadium. We didn't have them right away. The first 80,000 crowd was in '53. We played the 49ers and [quarterback] Frankie Albert. Otto Graham got nailed out of bounds by a fellow named Art Michalik. Had 16 stiches in his chin and came back in the second quarter. Then, came back out. George Ratterman took his place. Otto came back in the third quarter and hit the first nine passes he threw. And the Browns went on to win. It's funny what you recall.

Anyway, you couldn't beat Cleveland Stadium as the best place to broadcast. Even if my feet didn't think so.

— *Ken Coleman*

I ONCE DID A Steelers-Eagles' game in Philadelphia. It was a terrible, one-sided game. This TV executive from DuMont got me outside on the stadium roof at halftime. He said I didn't have the ability to make this bad game sound exciting. I told him, "Don't be stupid!" I said the people listening and watching at home could see what a lousy game it was. I refused to do it his way. Here's what hasn't changed from DuMont to now: TV people think the average viewer is an absolute idiot.

— *Ray Scott*

WHAT TERRIFIC COMPETITION there's been in the past half-century, and I'm not referring to the playing field or arena. I mean the bigger battle — selling each sport as the best buy for fans and sponsors. Growing up, baseball ruled the roost. When baseball was over, college football had its fling. College basketball aroused interest come championship time, but, oddly, I wasn't aware of pro football on radio in those early years. Sure, I knew about Sammy Baugh, Sid Luckman, Don Hutson, Bronko Nagurski — then, Otto Graham, Marion Motley and Buddy Young. Their *names* sounded like football players. But watching the pros in the early days was like taking an excursion to an off-Broadway play.

Then came TV, and the battle for sports dominance began. I was a telecaster for DuMont, and soon realized that Bert Bell, the commissioner, was monitoring the telecast to make sure that the sport was being sold to his complete satisfaction. One night after completing a Colts' game, I was awakened by Bell's gravel-voiced telephone critique. "Just checking you out," he rumbled. "Good call, good excitement, but a couple of flaws. You called tonight's game an exhibition game. We don't play exhibition games. We play hard-fought *pre-season* games. Get it? Once you said, 'The runner was tripped coming through the line.' Bob, this is a *tackling* game. These guys don't go around sticking out their legs to trip people. A final thing. In the last quarter, you wrestled a fullback to the ground. Bob, that's another sport. We're football. Otherwise, good job."

I thanked the commissioner for his observations, reset the alarm clock and went back to sleep.

— *Bob Wolff*

MY FIRST EXPOSURE to football was the NFL and the 49ers. John Robinson, who coaches at USC now, and I would go to Kezar Stadium, sneak into the games, and watch the 49ers. John always wanted to be a receiver, so he watched guys like Billy Wilson and Gordy Soltau. I wanted to be a lineman, so I watched guys like Leo Nomellini and Bob St. Clair. But it was a regional game — nowhere, you know, close to what it is today. We didn't have "Monday Night Football," ESPN Sunday night, double-headers. You'd read about them in the newspaper and go to a pre-season game and listen on the radio. Television wasn't the big thing in the early 1950s. Just being there was. I sort of miss the way pro football was when it and I were growing up.

— *John Madden*

WHEN I WAS growing up, I had no idea what the NFL was. The Cardinals drafted me in the [1953] second round. I was playing football at the University of Arkansas. And my dad was never really what you'd call a sports fan. But by then I knew what the NFL was, and I called him at my home in Florida and told him what I was being offered — $7,500 to play, and a $500 signing bonus.

He said, "Tell me that again." I did, and he said, "Son, if they'll pay you that money for playing anything, take it." Back then, nobody televised pre-season games. The Giants trained in Oregon. The Cardinals trained on the north side of Chicago. Most teams picked a distant location to train, because they didn't really want anybody to know what kind of team it was going to be. You'd go back to your home base and say, "Well, our pre-season record was 3 and 3," or 5 and 1, and nobody cared.

Didn't make any difference. Nobody knew who any of the rookies were. It was just keep it quiet. Let us sort of work things out on our own, until the time came when the regular season starts. Folks asked, "What have you been doing?" Little different now.

— *Pat Summerall*

CHAPTER

4

PIECE OF DREAMS

CBS-TV'S EYE

Mid-1950s America bought 10,000 TV sets daily. By 1956, their ubiquity helped pro football trade paper plates for Tiffany. That year the Columbia Broadcasting System began the first truly coast-to-coast coverage. Soon, its web linked Anaheim, Azusa, and Cucamonga — Jack Benny's famed litany — to the Lions' Bobby Layne, Chicago's Monsters of the Midway, and Cleveland's Jimmy Brown.

Finally, pro football had kicked apathy aside and crashed through into a kind of splendid network arcadia. CBS tied a deep and honest identity and surpassing ability to promote — tune in, each weekend, same time and channel! Recall the Sunday afternoon ghetto? Before 1956, Americans took a drive, visited relatives, or filled the beach — almost anything except watch television. CBS *literally* changed how we observe the Sabbath.

Ethel Merman was once asked if Broadway had been good to her. "Yes," she said, "but I've been good to Broadway." Post-1955, replace television for Broadway — and pro football for the Merm.

IN TV'S EARLY days at CBS, the voice mattered more than now.

It all stemmed from radio. If you had the pipes, you had a better chance of getting a job. That's how we got so many wonderful voices. Bob Neal, for instance, in Cleveland, as great a pipes as anyone's. Bob Fouts, Dan's dad, in San Francisco. Philadelphia, Byrum Saam. Had the nearest thing in voice quality and technique to Ted Husing I ever heard.

Jim Gibbons in Washington had the hardest job with his boss, George Preston Marshall. Gil Stratton and Bob Kelley were the Rams. Pittsburgh was Joe Tucker and Bob Prince. Detroit — Van Patrick. Van and I did many Thanksgiving Day Lion-Packer games. And Jack Brickhouse with the Bears and Cardinals. We did a couple of Giant-Bear title games, and saved me one time in Chicago. It was freezing, I had electric socks, and the batteries went dead. He was in the warm press box. So he sent his boots to me — the only way I got through the second half.

We had amazing camaraderie. Ray Scott in Green Bay, Ken Coleman with the Browns, Chuck Thompson of the Colts. Drank together, ate together. Now, they're so competitive. These pipes — I doubt that they'd help each other. Go ahead and die. Freeze your feet. But in our day, no way.

— *Chris Schenkel*

CHUCK, RAY, CHRIS with the Giants. We all had our own team, and were with them all the time. Now, guys come in, and you can tell that all week they've read out of the same press guide that other announcers read the week before. I liked it when teams had their own TV announcers. One year CBS decided to split the Voices up. Jack Drees was doing the Cardinals, and me the Browns. We worked together, each doing one half, and we went into both markets — Drees into Cleveland, and me St. Louis. When Ray heard about it, he said, "I'm not going to do that" — and he didn't work that year. What the format cost was inside material and color. Sometimes divide to conquer isn't the wisest course.

— *Ken Coleman*

THE REGIONALIZING was great for the announcers, because we became friends. We were a special fraternity — the Voices of the NFL teams — only 12 of us in the world. We didn't have as many pressures from people upstairs. You were the Giant announcer, period. You did the play-by-play, however you wanted to. I did have the Mara family check me out, at my request. One Monday after a game, [owner] T.J. Mara called me and said, "Chris, I'd better talk to you. You're our announcer, but you're rooting for the Giants." He wanted me to remember that there were two teams on the field. I couldn't believe it, because we were trying to sell football! But he was right. I listened to a recording — and I *was* shilling more than trying to tell the game. The why is that I was part of the family. I went to every Giant function. My wife, Fran, spent Thanksgivings with the other wives. Who to thank? My parents for conception at the right time so that my life began at the right time for the right league.

— *Chris Schenkel*

NOT ONLY DID each team have its own announcer, but the ballparks were different, too. One of the most difficult stadiums would have to be Cleveland's Municipal Stadium. You worked up on the roof, and in a shack. You climbed up a ladder to the roof, and then walked down to the booth. That can be a little difficult — depending on how much luggage you're carrying.

— *Chuck Thompson*

THE MOST TERRIFYING assignment that I ever had was crawling belly down over the snowy roof at Cleveland inch by inch, my heart pounding until I reached the door to the improvised TV booth. One slip and I'd be getting flight pay from CBS-TV — except that there was no runway below. Back then, TV accommodations were an afterthought. Broadcasters were shunted to distant positions most mortals feared to tread. I successfully made my rooftop adventure to that forsaken outpost along with my TV analyst, Curly Morrison, but I worried throughout the game about my return trip to the ladder which I had originally climbed to put me up into outer space. Today, TV accommodations are like luxury suites. The larger the sportcaster's audience the greater the pampering. Not that I'd have minded a little for myself.

— *Bob Wolff*

BREAKS ARE FUNNY. When CBS started doing the NFL, each team had its own regional network — and each network was sold to different advertisers. The logical guy to do the Packers was Earl Gillespie, broadcaster of the-then Milwaukee Braves. But Miller Brewing Company was his sponsor — and Ham Brewing Company helped sponsor the Packers. Ham said they didn't want anybody connected with Miller, so CBS asked if I'd like to do Green Bay. The kicker is that the Packers were a doormat at the time. CBS literally apologized for sticking me with them! They said, "Ray, if this works out we'll move you to a bigger team later on!" Can you imagine? If you find a bigger team than the Packers became, let me know.

— *Ray Scott*

CBS ANNOUNCERS were under the watchful eye of Commissioner Bert Bell. (See page 44.) He had this uncanny sense of how to popularize pro football. He had rules. Don't talk about fights or anything negative. We didn't have videotape at that time, just kinescopes. Somehow Bert'd get a kinescope, and critique us all. At the same time, Bert encouraged CBS to improvise.

In early TV, floor managers were vital — the guy with you in the booth in touch by headset with the producer and director. He'd get instructions, then tell you when to go to break. Not very direct. One day in '56 I got a call from Frank Chirkinian, the famous CBS director. He said, "What if I put a plug in your ear so I could talk to you directly, and we'd have better coordination? I could say, 'Let's focus on Player A,' and you'd be ready to talk about him when the camera did." We tried it the following Sunday, and it was fine when Frank wasn't telling me off-color stories. Try sharing *them* with your audience at home. The ear plug — or IFB, Intercepted Feedback — became part of CBS football, and now part of any live telecast you see, news or sports. Bad for floor managers — but great for you.

— *Chris Schenkel*

I GREW UP ON CBS' NFL coverage. It was a lot less depressing than the first pro football game I did. In the mid-'60s, I was just starting out and doing mostly radio in New York. The Continental Football League had just come into being. It had a Brooklyn Dodger franchise, and Andy Robustelli was their general manager. They played their games at Randall's Island, which meant poor lighting and other amateurish situations. I did the play-by-play — and had a disaster before the game between the Dodgers and the Hartford Charter Oaks, a truly fabled franchise.

Just before the game, they changed the numbers completely. Worse, you could hear the public address announcer booming over the crowd, which did not exactly elbow their way in. You'd hear the P.A. guy mention the ball carrier. You'd hear me mention the ball carrier. It was two different games that you heard at home. You couldn't see the yard line markers because of the lighting. The players were unknown, so I'd memorized their names. Big help. They went out and changed the numbers. I walked out of there thinking that I should really seek another career.

— *Marv Albert*

5

I'LL TAKE MANHATTAN

THE FIRST AMERICA'S TEAM

Forget the Dallas Cowboys, Atlanta Braves, or Chicago Bulls. The *first* America's Team came to define pro football as the NFL, suddenly and memorably, exploded on TV across the land.

The 1956-63 New York Giants won six titles, made household names of Huff, Gifford, Rote, and Robustelli, and sold pro football to the home of television, finance, and big-city ad men. Toots Shor's and 21 resounded with this new game — our team — right here — on top.

At the time, New York's glamour boys and afterthoughts linked CBS, the NFL, and Madison Avenue. Later, 10 of them found their way to Canton. "Making it in New York," said Giants' kicker Pat Summerall, "meant far more to the NFL than, say, succeeding in St. Louis or Detroit."

To millions — including Giant-haters — it also made watching pro football as natural as a smile.

IN 1952, MY first year as the Giants' announcer, football was still unknown, even in New York City, because the baseball Giants, Dodgers, and Yankees got all the space — TV, radio, or print. Marty Glickman and I did radio together. Harry Wismer

did the telecasts — and also Notre Dame games on Saturday TV.
Harry was bright. He came to me and said, "Chris, I'm worried
about not getting back because of weather from Notre Dame.
So if you'll prepare to do the game on TV, I'll give you $500. In
case I can't get back and you have to do it, I'll give you $1,000."
At the time I got $150 to do radio. So I went to the team owners,
the Mara family, and said, "This guy has made a deal with me."
They asked what it was. I told them, and they said, "Take it."
Harry then decided he didn't want to do the Giants any more.
So I moved in — me, and the Giants' 6,200 season ticket holders
at the Polo Grounds. It was lonely in that vast baseball park —
especially the day we were defeated, 63 to 7, by the Steelers and
used four quarterbacks because they kept getting hurt. How
bad were things? How's this? Two of the quarterbacks were
defensive backs — Frank Gifford and Tom Landry.

— *Chris Schenkel*

MY FIRST GIANTS' broadcast was 1948 when Charlie Conerly
joined the club, and I did games for 23 years. Between the mid-
'50s and mid-'60s, they were the toast of the town. A sense of
tradition began among Giants' fans in the 1930s. Even today at
the Meadowlands, people who watch are the same people, or
their progeny, who went to the Polo Grounds or later Yankee
Stadium. They saw personalities like Sam Huff, the colorful
middle linebacker, Jim Katcavage, Rosie Grier, Rosie Brown.
Gifford came in 1952. Later, he played only offense — but that
first year the All-American boy was All-Pro defensive halfback.
They stayed together for many years, weren't traded hither and
yon. When Huff was traded to the Redskins [1964], there was a
terrific hullabaloo about it in New York. One of the original great
Giants leaving? It seemed impossible. A far more innocent age.

— *Marty Glickman*

THE GIANTS' FIRST success came when Vince Lombardi came
in 1954. Then, in 1956, we moved to Yankee Stadium — and

that was the year pro football took off. Our title game at home wasn't even sold out [51,836]. The next year, Yankee Stadium was sold out for every game — 62,000-plus — and the Giants have sold out since. Suddenly the Giants were a success in New York, which was and is the media capital of the world. Television is not the smartest creature in the world, but they know a product. People began to say, "Hey, this isn't wrestling anymore." In '56, we and the Yankees won it all. We shared their stage and stadium with the Fords and Marises and Skowrons. Mickey Mantle and I shared the same locker — and were both MVPs of our leagues.

Today, most of the Giants live in the suburbs. We couldn't afford to even *go* to the suburbs. So we lived in town together — shared everything together. As far as the myth of my being a Marlboro man, I never was. Charlie Conerly and Cliff Livingston were. I didn't do that. But we did everything else.

— *Frank Gifford*

MY FIRST YEARS in the NFL were with the Cardinals. Their first thought was not winning. Their first thought was saving money. After the first five or six weeks of the season, it was clear that we weren't going to be in a playoff. So they started to cut the squad down — and if you were a kicker or an end, as I was, you had to do that and cover punts and run down on the kickoffs. I was traded in the spring of 1958 to the Giants, and immediately it got fun. The players took a pride in the organization. They dressed better. The equipment was better. The training facilities were better. The outlook on winning and losing, the coaches, were better. We got to New York that first year after training in Oregon and won a couple games. Seventeen of our families lived in the same hotel, which doesn't exist today, the Concourse Plaza, in the Bronx, about three blocks from Yankee Stadium. People say togetherness, and a sense of pride, are clichés. Tell that to the late-'50s Giants.

— *Pat Summerall*

WHEN I FIRST came to New York, Mel Allen told me, "Some day when the Giants are good, you're going to know what it's like to be the Yankee announcer like I've been all these years." He was right. You couldn't walk anywhere without being stopped, especially after a victory, in Manhattan. On Monday, I'd always go out to lunch to meet Giff or Kyle Rote. "There goes another one [Giant]!" they'd say. Boy, you felt ten feet tall. You were known when you entered a restaurant. You got the best table. You were part of New York — all because of winning. What iced it was this new phenomenon — television.

I learned about TV doing Harvard games as early as 1947 and '48. We may have had only 15,000 viewers on a four-station network, but they clamored for more. Stations were added. The ratings kept skyrocketing. You knew that TV was the perfect medium for football. Add the fact that our Giant teams probably had more character per person than any team ever assembled. In 1952, Frank Gifford and I were rookies. I kid him about what he wore then — patched-up dungarees. He says they were clean. I say, "Well, they were clean, but they were patched, Frank. You didn't have too many bucks at that time."

Giff became a star equivalent to anyone on Broadway. The team was exposed by the camera to America — and people embraced them, because they knew football players were pretty good guys. They came from college. At that time, they didn't come in the locker room with briefcases. They were making $22,000, not $2.2 million — and the announcers' salary paralleled them, as they do today. Today, they all make a lot of money. But money can't buy what we did — played a part in the making of the NFL.

— *Chris Schenkel*

IN 1958, I KICKED a field goal as time expired in the Giants' last regular-season game. ["The Miracle in the Snow" beat Cleveland, 13-10, and forced a playoff game that New York won for the Eastern Conference title.] I had already missed one from 34 yards, and I didn't know how long *this* was [49 yards]. All the line markers were covered by snow. When I got into the huddle, Conerly, the holder, told me, "What the hell are *you* doing here?" A real confidence builder. Back then, I just thought about winning for the Giants. I know now how lucky I was. We had coverage from all over the country. We had to win, or our year was over. The field goal gave me an identity.

I don't think it's been matched at any time, in any sport, how New York adopted the Giants. I was there from 1958 through 1961, and never at any restaurant did I pay for a check, drink, or anything. A rub down, a massage — everything was on the city. What made it click was the location and the time. All three networks were based in New York. Gifford and I had network radio shows. Five of our players worked for Philip Morris. Other teams were jealous because of the chances that came our way — broadcast and advertising. I assume they're over it by now.

— *Pat Summerall*

I STILL RECALL HOW Pat kicked that field goal. I couldn't even read the yard lines — that, and we didn't have the best seat in the house for broadcasting — the old Yankee Stadium bullpen. The Giants' great rival in those years was my Cleveland Browns. Their terrific games in the '50s and '60s produced one-way traffic. Bert Bell felt that if you broadcast locally, people wouldn't pay for something they could get for free. So TV stations were blacked out within 75 miles of any pro football stadium. People left New York for nearby cities in Long Island or Connecticut that telecast outside the blacked-out radius. If the Browns played in Cleveland and Municipal Stadium was sold out, people went to Erie, Pennsylvania, or down to Columbus to see the game on TV. Back to Pat. To this day no one knows how far his kick was. What we knew is there was no one the Browns would rather beat than the Giants — and the other way around.

— *Ken Coleman*

WITH THE BLACKOUT, fans in New York began putting super antennas on their roofs to get out-of-town stations. And
you could feel the surge — I gotta' go to Yankee Stadium to see
what it's like — an NFL game live. In New England, there
weren't any blackouts — so I got more letters from Boston and
Providence than New York, really. New Yorkers don't write
fan letters.

   When the Giants started selling out, the Maras gave me seats.
Then I bought some, because I knew I'd need them along the
line. Occasionally, I had tickets left — and I'd give them to Senator
[John] Kennedy or his father, and they became Giants' fans. You'd
look down and see Bobby and Teddy and the entire clan. Even
when Boston got a pro football team [in 1960, the AFL Patriots],
it still embraced our club. To this day, I go back there, and I'm
still the Giant announcer. When the Giants were in their last
championship game [1991], all sorts of New England sports-
writers called me for my reaction. You wouldn't know I hadn't
done a Giant game since 1964. Maybe they hadn't noticed.

— Chris Schenkel

THE GIANTS BECAME such an institution that today you can't
get a season ticket. They're left in wills, and there's a waiting
list of thousands. If that team played now, trust me: They would
be the real America's Team.

— Marv Albert

CHAPTER

6

SWEET SEASONS

GREAT DAYS/YEARS I

Marque teams and games spread like jam in their retelling. Vince Lombardi's Packers. Pittsburgh's 1970s four Super Bowls. The 49ers 1980s-'90s God Was in Their Heaven. By then, the NFL had a sustaining niche in network programming. A cause: overtime, in the urban twilight, with a stunning denouement.

If timing is all, December 28, 1958, had everything: football's best-ever quarterback, a lion's jaw of a Giants' defense, Yankee Stadium, national TV, and 50 million viewers. Pre-sudden death, pro football had never got more than $200,000 for its title game. The next pact brought more than three times that amount.

The Gallup Poll says that Americans would rather relive the 1950s than any decade of this century. Those who saw the Baltimore Colts' 23-17 dreamboat victory would agree. Before sudden death, football had courted viewers. This chapter performed the vows.

I'VE SEEN AS many losers as anybody in football and other sports. That's what made the rare wins sweet. The Cardinals haven't won a championship since 1947 in Chicago, where one year I broadcast them, or later in St. Louis or Arizona [moving there, respectively, in 1960 and '89]. Forty-seven was different. Owner Charlie Bidwell built what he called the dream backfield. Paul Christman at quarterback, Pat Harder at full, Charlie Trippi and Elmer Angsman at halves. They won the title, 28-21, over the Eagles. I'll never forget that game. It was played on a frozen field in Comiskey Park. Trippi went 50 yards [*sic*, 44] on one score, 75 yards on another, and Elmer had two TDs of 70 yards — the four Chicago touchdowns. One year; what a beaut. It's had to be to compensate for the last fifty years.

— Jack Brickhouse

ONCE IN A WHILE a team plays a perfect game — in the Giants' case, the title game in '56 against the Bears at Yankee Stadium. We came out on a frozen field, and had sneakers on. I tried both sneakers and cleats. I couldn't stand on either one of them. But the sneakers felt better, so I wore them.

It's funny what you remember. I recall a third and about nine or ten on our first drive. I was working against a good defensive back, J.C. Caroline, who was covering me man for man. I knew I could beat him on the outside. So I went down, made my little juke to the inside, and he bought it and fell right on his ass. Then I broke to the outside, and he still recovered and almost got there. The ball floated in the wind, and we got the first down. [Mel] Triplett went in from about the seven-yard line, and carried the referee and half the Bears with him. They had no traction whatever — and after that, no chance.

It might have been 35 to nothing at halftime [actually, 34-7]. Here's the nutty thing about the NFL. We won, 47 to 7. Earlier in the year we'd tied, 17-all.

— Frank Gifford

I COULDN'T BELIEVE my eyes. I was on the way to New York, going over my last-minute notes before my broadcast of the 1958 Giants-Colts National Football League championship game, and there it was in the *Baltimore News-Post* — the play-by-play story *written 24 hours before* the game. TV personality Maury Povich, then my college-age assistant, watched me sit up with a start. "Maury," I said, "this is unbelievable. John Steadman has given himself the green light to write the game details even before the kickoff. This is spooky. John's writing who boots the ball, who returns it, who makes the tackle, and where the ball is spotted. The whole game in advance. How can anybody, especially a man of John's reputation, put his neck on the line like that?"

There was no question of the ability of Steadman, the paper's sports editor, to lure readership. The Colts were more than a football team in 1958. They were a religious crusade uniting every Baltimorean who, for years, had suffered the taunts of those who visualized their blue-collar fans as sweaty, beer-guzzling blowhards. The Colts featured tough guys with crewcuts, missing teeth, and battered noses, the legacy of coal miners, truck drivers, and stevedores. Some had sampled the niceties of college life, but few had lingered in the classroom. College was something to be used only for player introductions.

"And from North College, at 290 pounds, No. 76, Big Daddy Lipscomb." Seems that Big Daddy, on his questionnaire, had listed "No College." Someone had added a period after No and the abbreviation provided Big Daddy with an alma mater. The Colts were led by Johnny Unitas, who in 1956 had been a weekend semipro quarterback. It took a phone call and a $6,000 salary to grab him. Raymond Berry was his most accomplished partner. But there were many more: Ameche, Donovan, Moore, Mutscheller, Marchetti. The Giants, too, had players whose fame still shines bright. Names like Conerly and Gifford, Huff and Robustelli, Summerall and Webster. The Giants had tradition and an aura of nobility. Yankee Stadium, New York City, Broadway. Just the right setting for a championship game. And, ironically, it was the Giants' sportsmanship that insured that the game was labeled the greatest ever played. There were no New York alibis in defeat. Just praise and the refrain, "What a game to play in, win or lose."

On December 28th, 64,185 crammed into Yankee Stadium and like good drama, the game built minute-by-minute to a climax. The Colts led at halftime, 14-3, but the game turned in the third quarter when the Colts picked up a first down on the Giants' three-yard line, but couldn't score. Then Charlie Conerly completed a long pass to Kyle Rote, who fumbled on the Colts' 25. Alex Webster picked up the loose ball, was hauled down on the one, and Mel Triplett burst in for the touchdown. The Giants trailed, 14-10, and the crowd roar increased. Just after the fourth quarter began, Conerly hit Frank Gifford on a 15-yard touchdown pass and the stadium exploded. The Giants led, 17-14.

With a little more than two minutes left, the Giants had the ball at their 43, fourth down and inches to go. New York punted, and the Colts had their last chance, taking over on their 14 with a minute and 56 seconds to play. In a race against time, Unitas proved his greatness. His passes dissected the Giants' defense; a final catch by Berry, good for 22 yards, moved the ball to the 13. The seconds were ticking away. Steve Myhra raced onto the field. Nine, eight, seven, the kick was up and Myhra sent the game into overtime. The Giants received the overtime kickoff, but were forced to give up the ball. Unitas methodically led Baltimore to the title — so sure of his play selection that, on the six-yard line, instead of going for the winning field goal, he gambled on a sideline pass that moved the ball to the one. With one final burst of energy, the Colts' line opened up a gaping hole for Alan Ameche, who drove through the game-winner.

I was limp at the end of the broadcast. The emotion was overwhelming. Two years earlier, I had broadcast Don Larsen's World Series perfect game at Yankee Stadium, but that was individual achievement. The Colts were the champions and, of historical importance, had won the first overtime championship game in league history. All this I knew. Later I learned the true importance of the *game*. The television and radio coverage had such a profound impact that the National Football League ascended that afternoon to a new pedestal. Networks, stations, fans, and advertisers clamored for more such heavy drama. NFL-TV football moved from being a game in America to a way of life.

In Baltimore, the outpouring of love was unprecedented in football history. Thirty thousand fans met the Colts at the airport. The sponsor of my Mutual Radio broadcast, the National Brewing Company, put out a highlight record played on newscasts every hour on the hour. The record was distributed as a promotion, and 10,000 copies were gone overnight. Every jukebox in town had my call, "The Colts are the world champions — Ameche scores!" Maury Povich now hosts his own talk show and Harry Holmes, my spotter, is now special assistant to the general manager of the Giants. As for John Steadman, writing his game account before the outcome was known, the incredible happened. Almost everything in Steadman's story proved true in the most amazing feat of prognostication I've ever known.

John's play-by-play vision included such highlights as the tying field goal and Ameche score. To top it off, he concluded his fictional account with the correct final score on the button. Colts 23, Giants 17. The next day, the newspaper used its front page to congratulate him. In Baltimore, the love affair with the '58 champions remained so torrid that when Steadman, in 1988, published his book, titled *The Greatest Football Game Ever*, he sold out his first printing in three weeks. "The marriage between the city and the Baltimore Colts is 30 years old," John wrote that year, "but remains the greatest love affair in sports."
— *Bob Wolff*

THE THING THAT comes to mind about '58 is the great series — three games — that we had with the Cleveland Browns and Jim Brown. We beat them in New York, 13 to 10, in the last game of the regular season with a field goal, and then in a playoff game the next week, 10 to 0. I remember a famous play in that game. [Charlie Conerly handed off to Frank Gifford, who lateraled to the trailing quarterback for the Giants' score.] We had to play another game after we'd beaten Cleveland — the title game a week later against the Colts, who were rested. They didn't have to play an extra week. We did.

I still don't know the better team — just that we didn't have anything left, especially after regulation ended, 17-17. I remember asking Don Heinrich, the backup quarterback, "What do we do now?" Nobody knew. They didn't know that we had to toss the coin again. They didn't know we'd play some more, because it was a championship. The coaches didn't know. Even the officials didn't know. Don said, "I'm not sure what's happening either, but remember we're playing for two or three thousand dollars" or whatever it was — the difference between the winning and losing shares. So we went out on the field and started to play again.

—Pat Summerall

PAT WAS ON THAT "other" team when Ameche scored. I was at the NBC-TV microphone. Bert Bell had a policy of having the announcer from each team in the title game do the telecast. The day before, [Giants' broadcaster] Chris Schenkel and I, as Voice of the Colts, met in Bell's office. Naturally, every broadcaster wants to do the second half — so you toss a coin. I lost, and did the first half. The game ends in a tie — and here's this overtime. It's never happened before, and I get to call it.

They're 8 minutes gone in overtime and the Colts get down to the one-yard line. As they get there, I don't know what's happening. All I see is that NBC's telecast is blank. There had been a lot of people in the NBC booth that day, and I turned around and they were gone. The only people left were Schenk and his spotter, me and my spotter, and the guy cranking the game. Everyone else had disappeared. Panic. What in the world had happened? We learned later that somebody had kicked loose a cable wire. You know, we haven't got any picture.

Our problem was to inform referee Ron Gibbs that we had a technical problem and had to have a time out. But how?

There wasn't the communication to the field there is now. It seemed hopeless — NBC'll miss a classic moment. Then I see this drunk — at least I assume so — run on the field to celebrate the Colts' certain victory. To get him off, Gibbs called time out. When play resumed, NBC had found the loose wire, had its picture back — and everybody saw Ameche's touchdown. It was about a week later I found out that the drunk was a highly-paid NBC executive. He got the game stopped — and I hope got a raise.

— *Chuck Thompson*

WHEN I WON the toss and got the second half — boy, was I delighted. I'd be on network TV when things came to pressure point — you know, in on the kill. Right. How could I have predicted overtime — and having done the first half Chuck'd naturally do that as well? Actually, it was providential because I'd have been a sorry case describing the Giants' loss. Instead, the minute the game hit overtime I knew this would rock America. You'd better see your doctor to see what's wrong if you didn't like this game — the crowd so loud that they shook our main power cable out of its socket. Beautiful! The Colts are about to win, and we're off the air!

I looked at my monitor. We were in commercial, I was to come back in a second, and there's no picture. No communication. So I kept on talking, thinking that somebody'd hear me, and they would get to me and tell me what happened. Fortunately, this so-called drunk came down on the field and delayed action. I don't know whether it was contrived or not. Some say an NBC executive pretended to be drunk. You know, it's not for me to say. It looked a little suspicious — but all in a good cause.

— *Chris Schenkel*

I WAS NBC'S assistant sports director when the cable snapped. Back then, TV hadn't the clout it has now — you couldn't politely ask the referee if he'd mind delaying play awhile. The Colts were in their huddle, ready to approach the line, when out of the crowd along the sidelines comes our friend inscribing a circuitous route headed for nowhere in particular. Thankfully, now the game could not proceed. Our engineers kept working on the cable and suddenly there was the picture again, showing the Colts just as they reconvened their huddle, the drunk having vanished. Nobody at home had seen the intrusion because their screens were dark at the time. And the newspaper reporters were not impressed. Fans often stumbled onto the field. If they had pried more closely, they would have found that this particular fellow was Stan Rotkiewicz, the business manager of NBC News, who doubled as sports statistician. He was an old Roanoke tackle, capable of posing as an errant fan long enough to save the day.

— *Lindsey Nelson*

WHAT'S INTERESTING is the long-term effect of, quote, "The Greatest Game Ever Played." Johnny Unitas, a superstar, was born. The Giants had household names in New York, and all of a sudden they were household names nationwide. It didn't hurt that the game was played at Yankee Stadium. The effect was to sell the television people — "Hey, this is big-time stuff" — which soon [1962] led to the first big TV deal with CBS.

I remember being asked by Wellington Mara as negotiations began if I knew what was going on. I was working for CBS while I was playing. [CBS sports head] Bill MacPhail and [1960-89 Commissioner] Pete Rozelle were friends of mine — a very closed fraternity — and I knew talks were underway. I told Wellington, "I really don't. I just know it's going to be a lot of zeroes." He smiled and a few days later they announced the deal [$9.3 million for two years, the first package to include all NFL teams]. The money seems small now, but it was huge then.

A little later, Wellington said to me, "I hate to see this kind of money come into the game. It can't help it." He was a prophet. And it stemmed largely from '58.

— *Frank Gifford*

IN 14 YEARS with the Browns, I did seven title games. Among them was Otto Graham's last game as a professional. The Browns beat the Rams in Memorial Coliseum [38-14, December 26, 1955, before 85,693] and Otto passed for two touchdowns and scored two. In '56, I did the Giants over the Bears, 47-7. 'Fifty-seven, the Lions beat the Browns, 59-14. In 1962, Packers 16, Giants 7, in New York on a bitterly cold day. The next year, Bears 14, Giants 10. My last two were '64 [Browns 27, Colts 0] and '5: Green Bay 23, Cleveland 12, in Jimmy Brown's final game.

'Sixty-three was historic due to a broadcast I did from Wrigley Field to 15,000 people in McCormick Place and a couple other theatres in the Chicago area. The NFL had never had "closed-circuit"; the idea came when people couldn't get tickets to the game. So began their first-ever coverage — and my color man was Bill Osmanski, one-time Holy Cross running back who later starred with the Bears. And, boy, had he prepared — had all kinds of notes. We started and within a few minutes a call came from Pete Rozelle that the people in McCormick Place were making so much noise that we couldn't be heard. Our producer told me, "Ken, forget trying to do the game like you do on television. Do it like a P.A. announcer — that's all the crowd can hear."

So I start saying, "[Bill] Wade carries — tackled by [Sam] Huff," and so on. I didn't mind — but poor Bill Osmanski didn't get a chance to talk during the whole time we were on the air.

— *Ken Coleman*

I CAN STILL see Dutch Van Brocklin and Chuck Bednarik literally seizing the 1960 Eagles' team and taking it to the title. The entire year was a sensation difficult to describe, but it was something you could almost touch. Some magical force seemed to take effect, until you sensed the Eagles were destined to win.

Anyone at the NFL title game [Eagles 17, Packers 13] can still see Bednarik atop Jim Taylor's chest at Franklin Field, refusing to let him up as 60,000 people roared off the final seconds. Bednarik had become their spiritual leader because he played both ways, at center and outside linebacker, in some big games. For him to make the final play of the year's biggest game was appropriate. It also almost defied belief.

I don't remember exactly what I said then, but I do remember recalling the train ride from Washington to Philadelphia after the final 1958 game when the Eagles finished with a 2-9-1 record. Buck Shaw, their coach, was sitting with a number of us in the dining car and he said, "Look around you and remember these faces. You probably won't be seeing 90 percent of them next year." At that same moment, the Green Bay Packers were coming home from their final game with a 1-10-1 record. Two years later, both of them played for the NFL title.

— *Jack Whitaker*

IN 1960, VINCE Lombardi took the Packers down to New Orleans for their first exhibition game of the year. It was my debut on their broadcasts, and a typical August day in New Orleans — temperature 95, humidity the same. The game was played in City Park Stadium which must have been the breeding ground for every mosquito in the bayou country. About an hour before game time, they fogged the field and all of the mosquitoes decided upon a sojourn in the press box. It's a little disconcerting to be eaten alive during a broadcast — but the thing that bothered me the most was that every time I'd open my mouth to talk, six mosquitoes would fly in. Most important, only four would fly out.

— *Ted Moore*

ANY BROADCASTER will second the adage, "Being there is twice the fun." I can still see many of Jim Brown's great days against the Eagles when I was their broadcaster. He was unforgettable. I saw O.J. Simpson in some games and *he* was unforgetable. Both provided the kind of special moments that don't happen every day. I still remember Tim Brown opening the 1961 season in Philadelphia by running back the opening kickoff 100 yards for a touchdown against the Cardinals. That era itself was special. Every time Tim touched the ball he was exciting. To have it happen in the very first game, on the very first play, with all the excitement coming off the Eagles' [1960] title, made the moment incredible. Football interest that season was at an all-time high in Philadelphia and I always have thought that as Timmy raced down the field he carried 60,000 fans at Franklin Field emotionally on his back.

— *Jack Whitaker*

IT'S STILL HARD to believe. Six quarters. Two teams from the same State — the Dallas Texans and Houston Oilers — in the '62 AFL championship. The weather in Houston was awful, wind off the Gulf. I knew passing would be tough, and kicking tougher — and we [Dallas] had the worst kicking statistics in the league.

The Oilers had won the first two AFL titles, but we're ahead at halftime, 17 to 0. Abner Haynes had rushed for over 1,000 yards that year, and this day he scored twice. But the Oilers came back, and with six minutes left tie the game, 17-all. I was just glad to make it to overtime. We get there, and I start thinking about our kicking game — we'd had trouble punting all year. I wanted that 15-miles-an-hour wind at our punter's back. So I go over to Abner, our team captain, and say, "If we win the toss, we don't want to receive. We want the wind. If they win the toss, we want to kick to the clock [the direction of Jeppesen Stadium the wind was blowing]. Abner, we want the wind."

We were still talking when Bob Finley, an official, interrupted. He's ready for the toss. Abner said, "Coach wants to talk for a second." Finley said, "Abner, get out here or it's fifteen yards."

He obliges, and shakes hands with the Houston captain [Al Jamison]. The referee [Harold Bourne] flipped the coin in the air. "Heads," said Abner. The referee said, "Heads, it is." Abner says, "We'll kick to the clock." The ref then told Haynes he had the choice to receive or defend.

Abner says, "We'll kick." Houston says, "We'll take the wind." Abner just said it wrong. Soon as he said the word "kick," the Oilers automatically had their choice of which side of the field they wanted. Talk about the best of both worlds: Houston got the ball *and* the wind. It was a mistake you don't like to make. But what can you do once it's made? We go into second overtime, and get inside their 20. We weren't much better at kicking field goals than punting. Our kicker, Tommy Brooker, didn't have great range or consistency. We held our breath on field goals that year. Especially this one. After they called time out, Brooker got back into the huddle. "Boys, it's over," he said. "We've got it" — and he did. Neither of those teams still plays in Texas — but they still talk about that game.

— Hank Stram

THE MOST FRUSTRATING game I ever televised was the 1963 championship. The Giants had a near-perfect team, but lost to the Bears, 14-10. It was the end of an era, what with age and the need to rebuild. [In 1964, they fell to 2-10-2.] We had Y.A. Tittle at quarterback. The Bears had Billy Wade. But Y.A. got injured in the first half, couldn't throw off his foot. Had a horrible day — five interceptions. The Giants had a policy. If a player hurt, like, his ankle, they'd never shoot him up — no needles to ease the pain or numb him. At halftime, Tittle virtually begged the Giants to give him some novocain. Their doctor said no. To this day I believe that if Tittle had just a little pain shot, he'd have gone out and the Giants would have won. Sometimes it doesn't hurt to be a little flexible.

— Chris Schenkel

WORD ASSOCIATION ON those marvelous Browns. Gary
Collins said about Paul Warfield — both receivers — "He's the
only guy who can change directions in mid-air." The week of
the 1964 title game, Collins started talking about Frank Ryan,
our quarterback, who could be erratic. "If he's even a little
accurate," Gary said, "I can beat their left cornerback all day
long, anytime." The game was scoreless at halftime. Then Lou
Groza hit a long field goal, and things opened up. Gary got his
wish — three touchdowns from Frank. Some people may not
know about Groza. What a pity. He was one of the greatest
field goal kickers — straight-away, not soccer-style that became
popular later. He was also an all-pro offensive tackle. Lou told
me that after he stopped playing tackle his anxiety increased.
He'd walk the sideline wanting to help — but now kicking was
the only way!

Bill Willis played middle guard on defense, and was so quick
getting off the ball that Paul Brown had to warn officials. "Don't
call offsides because he's in the backfield," he told them. "That's
how fast he is." He had company in Warren Lahr. Warren had
been a running back at Western Reserve University and then
Paul made him into a cornerback. Just a few of the reasons the
Browns were really football's first dynasty.

— *Ken Coleman*

I BROADCAST THE famous game when Jim Marshall ran the
wrong way. [On October 26, 1964, the Vikings' defensive end
picked up Billy Kilmer's fumble and began running — toward
the *Minnesota* goal line.] George Mira threw the ball to Kilmer,
who got hit, dropped the ball, and Marshall picks it up. Maybe
it was the angle, I still don't know, but he starts running toward
his own goal. The minute he picked it up, I knew he was in
trouble — and said so on the radio. He crosses the line for a
safety, throws the ball up in the air, Bruce Bosley of the 49ers
comes up to congratulate Jim, and then it hits him. He's run 66
yards for a 49ers' safety. All those years [1961-76] with the

Vikings, and that's what people remember. Life can be unfair.

— *Lon Simmons*

I WAS DOING THE Ice Bowl [December 31, 1967] on CBS with Frank Gifford, Ray Scott, and Tom Brookshier. We went to the stadium, and it was 15 degrees below zero. I borrowed a stocking cap from Elijah Pitts. I looked like the wrath of God. Gifford was standing there as though it was a summer afternoon. I said, "Don't you want a hat?" He said, "Nah, I don't need one." I said, "You're tougher than I am, man."

— *Jack Buck*

VINCE LOMBARDI IS alleged to have said, "Weather's in the mind." The last drive at the Ice Bowl was the greatest triumph of will I've ever seen. [Behind, 17-14, Green Bay moved 68 yards in the last five minutes to beat Dallas, 21-17. The winning score: Bart Starr's sneak with 13 seconds left and no timeouts left.] Everybody was miserable. The temperature was minus 13, and the wind chill, minus 40. Players' hands were like stone. But the Packers never made a mistake. Never dropped a pass, never fumbled. When Bart and he conferred along the sidelines in their final time out, Lombardi could have sent the game into overtime with a field goal. Instead, he said, "Let's get the people out of this miserable weather. Let's go home." Only Bart knew that the other backs were not going to get the ball. The sneak shocked his teammates. Afterward Lombardi was told that some of the Cowboys had frostbite. "Losers get frostbite," he said.

— *Ray Scott*

THAT GAME HAD problems I never faced before — or since. For a championship game, every space in the press box is utilized. As we had to breathe, the window began steaming up. We sent over to a nearby filling station for two cans of windshield defroster, and one crew was assigned to wipe the window so we could see the field. As the game progressed, our supply of defroster began running out. Toward the end of the fourth quarter, I was looking through a square foot of clear glass to broadcast the game. The rest of the window was frosted over. When Starr sneaked over for the winning touchdown, there were nine guys peeping through that square foot of clear glass, and when they let out their cheers the whole field disappeared from view. It sort of gives the term "broadcasting hot air" a whole new meaning.

— *Ted Moore*

I DID THE ICE Bowl for CBS. The analysts, Frank Gifford and me, each spent a half in the booth and another on the sidelines. Everything about that day is frozen in memory — literally. I woke up in the Northland Hotel and was told it was 13-below. I put on everything I had, and it still wasn't enough. I got to Lambeau Field, and the Packers' Boyd Dowler let me put on his warmup jacket under my coat. The field was rock hard, and I found myself wondering what if I were playing today. My last game as a player had been here in 1961, when the Giants lost the championship to Green Bay [37-0]. It was cold then, but nothing like now. I didn't know how they did it. It was brutal.

The irony is that the cold helped create maybe TV's most all-time famous shot. Many times we've seen the head-on shot of Barr Starr's winning score. What people don't know is that it was an accident caused by the weather. During the last timeout, we figured Starr would fake a run and roll out Dowler's side. So the director told cameraman Herman Lang to expect a rollout to the right. Well, Herman couldn't move his camera. It was frozen. It had to stay on Starr, who went into the end zone behind Jerry Kramer. If not for that, there might never have been Kramer's book, *Instant Replay*. Great book — amazing day.

—*Pat Summerall*

JACK BUCK AND I almost died together coming out of Green Bay after that '67 championship game. I chartered a twin-engine plane to Chicago so we could get home for New Year's Eve. From Chicago, we were going to take separate planes. We took off in about 20 degrees below zero, and my door toward the front part of the plane flew off. Jack and Tommy Brookshier were in the back of the airplane. The sun was going down. We were losing the light, and I suggested that maybe we'd better get this sucker on the ground. Fortunately, the pilot was local and knew a landing strip that had lights on it. We got that thing on the ground just before its controls literally froze up on the inside of the plane. I thought we had lost Buck and Brookshier. We've talked about it many times. None of us have a right to still be here.

— *Frank Gifford*

I'LL NEVER FORGET how the door was open by a foot. Gifford was in the front seat. I had my arms around him. Brookshier was shooting scotch out of a rubber cup into Gifford's mouth. Gifford grabbed a hold of the handle and the armrest, undid the handle, and pulled the armrest out of the door. Now the door was really open. The pilot said, "I can bank the plane and close the door but I don't know which way to do it." I said, "Let's not do anything." We landed in New Holstein, Wisconsin, and start heading for the woods. I said to Brookshier, "When we hit, lean forward a little." He always remembers that. We closed the door, stopped about 50 feet from the woods, went to Chicago, and celebrated New Year's Eve. Trust me. I celebrated.

— *Jack Buck*

CHAPTER

7

DOING WHAT COMES NATURALLY

DEFENSE

The cry of "DEE-fense!" arose at Yankee Stadium, on a frozen tundra, in the 1956 title game. For years, the glamour boys had been offensive kingpins. Now, new names surfaced — Grier, Katcavage, Big Laddy Lipscomb, Bob Lilly — who forged defense's Horatio at the bridge.

Once, Ted Williams said, "When you're a block from a baseball park and hear the crowd roar, someone just hit the ball. It's exciting — and always involves the offense." Not so, the NFL. Baseball's defense is passive — football's, active. It can force fumbles, turn errors into points, and level a guy from here to the nearest hospital.

Williams hit .406 in 1941. Dallas' Doomsday hit people. Also, the Rams' Fearsome Foursome, Minnesota's Purple People Eaters, and Pittsburgh's Steel Curtain, football's answer to SDI. "People say how beautiful pro football is," said Dick Butkus. "Maybe, but it's violence that sells."

He, and it, made "DEE-fense!"'s stronghold of enthusiasm a springtime of possibility. No longer were defenders Backdoor Johnnies. Now they lit the stage — knights defending their realm, and hoping to expand it.

THERE HAVE BEEN many great confrontations in pro football history. You think of Jim Thorpe — and George Halas trying to tackle him when they played in the 1920s. In my era, you remember Jimmy Brown, number 32 of the Browns, and Sam Huff, number 70 of the Giants. It created the cry of "DEE-fense! DEE-fense!" wherever the Giants played. The defense started with Steve Owens when he was [1931-53] coach. He had the umbrella defense in the defensive backfield, with Emlen Tunnell and Tom Landry. The Giants' defense of the 1950s was really the first to capture the public imagination. There's the story of Chuck Conerly coming on the field after a change of possession, and Sam Huff calling out to Charlie, "See if you [the offense] can hold 'em now" — because the Giants' defense was doing so well.

— *Chris Schenkel*

IN 1958, THE Giants went through a stretch in the middle of the year where we couldn't score. The only thing we did was kick field goals. We were in Buffalo to play the Cardinals, and somebody asked me how it felt to be the whole offense by myself. There was some good-natured joking — a definite sense of, "We've done our job. Now you do your's." Way before "60 Minutes," CBS had a show titled "Twentieth Century," and in 1960 they aired "The Violent World of Sam Huff." That kind of publicity you couldn't buy for the NFL — but the Giants' defense did.

— *Pat Summerall*

ED SPRINKLE OF the Bears was a very tough defensive end. This one day, Bob St. Clair is blocking him except for one play, when Sprinkle nailed the 49ers' running back, Joe Perry. In the huddle, Perry says, "Bob, don't touch him. Let me take care of Sprinkle myself." He runs the ball, and at the play's end St. Clair looks over. There are a couple of Perry's teeth, lying on the ground.

— *Lon Simmons*

GEORGE CONNOR WAS the Bears' middle linebacker and the first Notre Damer to make it both to the collegiate and pro football Halls of Fame. One year, we went to San Francisco and Monty Stickles, who'd also gone to Notre Dame, whacked a couple of Bears pretty good and got away with it. Well, Moose decided that he would take care of Mr. Stickles and the next things you know there's Mr. Stickles being carried off the field. We go down to Los Angeles and a guy named Bob Boyd was killing the Bears with a slant pass. He'd slip over the line of scrimmage and the Bears couldn't defense him. Well, the next thing you know Mr. Boyd is being carried off the field. The topper came against the Packers. The Bears were about to lose the game unless they could recover the onside kick. So they kick off, Veryl Switzer of the Packers took it, and Connor hit him. The ball went one way, his body went another, and his helmet went another — we thought it was his head. The single greatest tackle I've ever seen.

— *Jack Brickhouse*

WHEN WOODY HAYES was coach at Ohio State, his motto was run, run, run. The line was that he liked his players to pass only in the classroom. Which brings me to a story told by John Steadman, the sports editor of the *Baltimore News American*. Art Donovan, the Colts' great lineman, has denied it — but his heart isn't really in it. This year, Jim Parker was the Colts' top draft pick — All-American, later became a Hall of Famer — but he didn't know much about pass blocking. How could he? He'd played for Woody.

Jim reports to camp in Westminster, Maryland, and he's having a terrible time. So John Sandusky, then the Colts' offensive line coach, put him head-to-head with one of the great pass rushers of all time, Gino Marchetti. Arty sees this going on and tells his buddies, "Let's watch, this could be fun." Coach Sandusky puts Jim Parker in his stance. Marchetti takes his stance. The ball is put between them and as Sandusky lifts the ball they move. The first time, Marchetti got by him — no trouble. The second time, Parker thought, "I'll get even" — he moves one way and Marchetti feints the other.

By now, Parker is peeved — he's going to get a piece of Marchetti one way or the other. Gino knows it, so as they put the ball down and Sandusky picks it up, he gets up on Parker's shoulders and leap-frogs over his head. Parker turned around and looked at Sandusky and said, "Coach, what do I do now?" From the sideline, Arty Donovan is supposed to have said, "Applaud."

— *Chuck Thompson*

IN 1963, THE Bears won the title at Wrigley Field by beating the Giants — which sort of got even for the '56 championship game I did for NBC. [The Giants bombed Chicago, 47-7.] This day had a lot more excitement. Bill Wade pushed over two touchdowns at quarterback. Giants' quarterback Y.A. Tittle was pummeled by the Bears. The key came early. With the Giants ahead, 7-0, their great end, Del Shofner, dropped a cinch pass in the end zone.

Nobody was guarding Shofner but Bears' defensive back Davey Whitsell. This play has never been talked about, but Whitsell confirmed it not long ago. Davey realized that somebody had missed an assignment and Shofner was all alone in the end zone. Fortunately, there was some ice on the field. Even better, Whitsell did some fast thinking of his own. He did the only thing he could do — yell, "Ice! Ice!" Amazingly, Whitsell distracted Shofner just enough so that he looked to see that he wouldn't trip and fall. It caused him to drop the ball and the certain touchdown that would have made the score 14-0.

Dave Whitsell. The Iceman Saveth.

— *Jack Brickhouse*

FRANK NUNLEY WAS a great [1967-76] linebacker who was also a great stoic. They used to call him "Fudge Hammer" —

he looked like the Pillsbury Doughboy — but as tough as they come. Nunley would get gouged, kicked, beaten up — and he'd never tell anybody. One day, 49ers' cornerback Jimmy Johnson gets a forearm across his nose. It's broken, Johnson gets knocked out, then comes to. He looks up in the sky and there's Nunley standing over him. "Get up! Don't let 'em know you're hurt!" he screams at Johnson. Jimmy says, "My nose is broken — I'm sure going to mention it to *somebody*!"

— *Lon Simmons*

FOOTBALL IS A serious sport, which explains why the men involved need a little humor. One weekend I went to Pittsburgh to a Steelers' game for CBS-TV — and as usual, picked up a copy of Saturday's paper to get ready for the next day's game. I see this story by Al Abrams in which he quotes Pittsburgh's great tackle, Ernie Stautner, blasting his own fans. Stautner said the fans shouldn't get on the team when it was playing poorly, because things would get better. Then he suggested that owner Art Rooney move the franchise away from the fickle fans.

A story like that guaranteed a reaction, and it came the next day. The CBS booth at Forbes Field was located beside the runway where the Steelers came out onto the field, and like most teams they had a guy who led them out. Stautner was the Steelers' — and when CBS gave the signal, Ernie took off. Not surprisingly, the minute he was in sight the fans began to boo. I have never heard a sound to match the booing Ernie got. He ran with his head bowed until he was halfway across the field, when he turned to talk to his teammates. He then found he was talking to the wind. Some *team*mates: They were back in the runway. They had left him on the field to face the hecklers alone!

— *Chuck Thompson*

ONCE IN A WHILE you hear about guys who are drafted first and don't make it. Each club has stories about high draft choices who bomb in spite of college records and scouts' advice. Want to know the single greatest drafting achievement any club ever had? In 1965, the Bears drafted 1-2 Dick Butkus and Gale Sayers. Can you imagine a better team than that? Bill George more than anyone else molded middle linebacker on the defense as we know it. He was tutored by George Connor. Joe Schmidt and Ray Nitschke and Sam Huff played it beautifully — all supermen. But few will argue that Butkus refined the role — the best-ever middle linebacker. Here's to guys who prove scouts right.

— *Jack Brickhouse*

BIG DADDY LIPSCOMB was an outstanding defensive tackle. He was as big as any that played back then [1953-62] — maybe 6-foot-6 and 280 pounds — and a delightful guy to be around. Once, the Colts were on the West Coast to play the 49ers and then the Rams — we stayed in California about 10 days — and they put us up in a really nice place called Ricky's Studio Inn in Palo Alto. Each day ended with a burger and beer routine for all the players and coaches. You had to be there, but we didn't talk much football.

After the meeting one night, I heard a fuss downstairs. I went down and right behind the main restaurant which by then was closed there was a huge fish tank. They offered fresh trout and other fish — and so Big Daddy decided he was going to pick one out of the tank. I truly wish you could have seen the mess. Water all over the place — walls, ceiling, the floor — and three or four of his buddies soaking wet and laughing their heads off.

In the midst of this, I walk in and behind me comes John Unitas. He says, "Big Daddy, *what* are you trying to do?" Big Daddy says, "Just trying to fish." John said, "Maybe I can help you." Unitas steps over to the tank, Daddy steps aside, and John looked at the trout going back and forth. Then he reached into the tank and grabbed one and handed it to Daddy. Daddy grabbed that fish and looked at John and everything got quiet. Finally, he said, "John, how'd you do that?" Unitas looked up at Big Daddy with that crooked grin and I'll never forget what he said. "Daddy, it's easy. All you have to do is know the pass route."

— *Chuck Thompson*

Y.A. TITTLE WAS still with the 49ers as we played in Baltimore. The Colts had this great defensive line, and they KOd Tittle — knocked him out of the game. John Brodie comes in, and the 49ers are driving for the touchdown. John goes back, the receiver's covered, and he runs for five or six yards. He's tackled, but he keeps struggling, and up comes Big Daddy Lipscomb. He blasts Brodie, who then gets up looking for someone to hit. He sees Lipscomb, and thinks better of it. Lipscomb scowls at him. "When Big Daddy plays, quarterback, he don't run."

— *Lon Simmons*

AFTER THEIR '58 victory over the Giants, the Colts went to their first College All-Star Game and again Big Daddy had a line I've never forgotten. He was always a little garrulous. That was especially true when he wanted to show who was boss. The College All-Stars had a talented back, Nick Pietrosante, from Notre Dame. He started on a sweep away from Big Daddy and apparently it got jammed up on the other side and Big Daddy, trailing the play, made the tackle. I'm told that he then reached down and grabbed Pietrosante by the wrist, pulled him up on his feet, and said, "Kid, if Big Daddy can catch you, you ain't never gonna' make it in this league." The record book shows that Pietrosante played for the Lions for a number of years. Still, one hell of a line.

— *Chuck Thompson*

IN THE EARLY '60S, Big Daddy got traded from Baltimore to Pittsburgh. The 49ers are playing the Steelers, and Lipscomb makes a bet with Brodie — "six bits that I get [tackle] you six times." The first half, Big Daddy's on the warpath—four tackles, the bet's won. But it isn't — Brodie gets taken out of the game at halftime. Afterward, Big Daddy comes into the 49er locker room, sees Brodie, and slaps down six bits. "I don't think it's fair for them to cheat by taking you of the game," he says. He paid up, then went out and made some other quarterback pay.

— *Lon Simmons*

A FINAL BIG DADDY story. His sudden death [in 1963] shook our town. It was stated that he had an overdose of drugs. That made some players suspicious, because the punctures in Big Daddy's arm were all in the right forearm, and Big Daddy was right-handed. Be that as it may, he met an untimely death. That night, a man named Bill Neil took the team doctor, Dr. Irwin Mayor, to go and identify the body of Big Daddy. The team doctor was at least in his late 70s. He wore impeccable clothing, three-piece suits, nice white shirts, a perfectly tied tie. Didn't have a hair on his head. Rimless glasses, very bright, a first-class gentleman. He also never under any circumstances would say a vulgar word. I didn't even know he had a sense of humor until Bill Neil told me a story. He had identified Daddy's body as it lay there in the slab. To say the least, Daddy was big in all departments. He's laying there with all his maleness and this very soft-spoken doctor turned to Bill and pointed to Big Daddy. "Bill," he said, "would you believe that I've got one just like that?" Bill turned and said, "You mean to tell me you've got one just as big?" The doctor said, "No, just as dead."

— *Chuck Thompson*

SKIP VANDERBUNDT was a linebacker who in his rookie year played the Bears. He's going down for the opening kickoff, and Dick Butkus is on the kickoff team. Butkus misses a block and is rolling around on the ground, and starts making these growling noises, like a cave man, a maniac. Skip says to himself, "What have I gotten myself into?" Some game — some Butkus.

— *Lon Simmons*

IN 1981, WE were playing the Giants. Our scouting reports said that their rookie linebacker had great speed and strength, but over-pursued. We get down near the goal line, and coach [Joe] Gibbs calls for a bootleg. Lawrence Taylor runs right by me. I must have been smiling. I was pretty fast and there was nobody near me. All I could see was empty field to the goal line. But Taylor reversed himself and started chasing me. About five yards downfield something hits me like a truck. Lawrence reached out, earholed me, and threw me to the ground. The amazing thing was that he comes over to me, helps me up, and then this rookie says to me, "Don't ever do that again. You embarrassed me." He was serious. I knew right then this guy was different.

— *Joe Theismann*

IN 1987, I read a column in a suburban Cleveland paper. It said that because of all the youngsters in camp, don't be surprised if the Browns look to trade some of the veterans who still have value. The last line was that defensive lineman Bob Golic may be among them. From that, people thought I was going to be traded. The next week, I went to a luncheon with Doug Dieken, and I was wearing black pants, a white shirt, and a gray tie. Dieken said it looked like I was dressed to go to the Raiders. All of a sudden, the rumor was that I was getting traded to the Raiders. Sometimes you're better off in jeans.

— *Bob Golic*

WHEN I ARRIVED in '52 from USC in New York I was an offensive running back — but Kyle Rote was there, so the Giants switched me to cornerback. I learned a lot about football that helped me later on offense. Number one, defense wins football games. Number two, you get paid more on offense. Soon I wanted to move back to offense. When I did in 1954, I knew how vital defense is. Go back over the years with the Dolphins. They've got the best offensive machine ever put together. Have they won the big one yet — and with maybe the greatest quarterback [Dan Marino] of all time? They throw for 400 yards a game. But if they win the Super Bowl, it'll be the defensive unit that does it.

I often wonder why Giants' fans took to our defense in the '50s. I think it's because they grasped the game and knew the players who didn't change year in and out. They didn't change on third down. They stayed in the game. Today, it's like a fire drill. Players coming in, out — and when they're not coming in, coming out, they're moving to Dallas or another team. For many years — fortunately, the NFL's growth years — good teams stayed intact. Lombardi at Green Bay — maybe four players turned over. Browns and Colts, too. You knew the people involved, what position they played, and what that position was about.

Today you talk nickle, dime, four-three, three-four, rush zones. Unless you're an avid fan, it's hard to understand. I'd like to see less change legislated by the competition committee. Then people'd again be aware of what is happening on the field — not just a tremendous manipulation of talent and people. Maybe we'd have the same sort of magic of the '50s and '60s defense.

— *Frank Gifford*

ONCE MY MOTHER and father were driving me home from a football game and I was curled up in the back seat. Every time I moved, something hurt. My mom looked back and asked if I wanted an aspirin. I said, "No, I just want to enjoy this for a little while." My thinking was that anybody could play this game healthy. If I walked off the field feeling totally beat down with nothing left, then win or lose, at least I felt I did everything I possibly could for my teammates. If I walked off the field feeling good, I started doubting myself. During the game if I got a bruise or felt an injury coming up, like a sharp pain in my thigh, I began saying to myself, "OK, the game is starting." Don't get me wrong. I didn't like the big injuries.

— *Bob Golic*

I'VE BEEN broadcasting for quite a while, but I remember how it was when I retired as a defensive back. There's uncertainty. You have "instant options." When you're an athlete you're always hearing some guy say, "When you retire, come see me; we've got something for you." Ninety-nine percent of the time it doesn't come true. They've forgotten about you. The people who were telling Beasley Reece that are telling it to some guy now — and when he retires they'll tell it to the next man.

The first week I was out of football, it was tough for me to motivate myself to even work out. All my life I'd been working toward a goal — the next training camp, the next game. Now there was no goal, just an abstract struggle to stay in some semblance of shape. The first week after the Bucs cut me [after 1 and 1/2 years, following 6 years with the Giants], I nearly went crazy. I belonged to a jogger's club. Three or four of us met at 6 in the morning and ran. That made it worse. I was up at 5:30 and had the whole day to try and figure out what to do.

So I became "Mr. Mom," working around the house, doing cooking and cleaning or getting angry with myself. It was a traumatic change. Finally, I called my father. He told me that if I didn't have these feelings for a few days, something was wrong with me. If I wasn't doing what had been so much a part of life for so long — ever since the eighth grade — I should be worried. Beware of "instant options." Even as a player, get ready for the day when the cheering stops.

— *Beasley Reece*

I LANDED A role once as the head executioner in the Cleveland Opera production of Puccini's *Turandot*. I might have been worried if I had to sing, but they told me the only way they were going to let me perform is if I kept my mouth shut. I loved it — what an awakening. I'll bet you never knew that us linemen are really cultured people.

— *Bob Golic*

NINETEEN EIGHTY-SEVEN was my second year hosting "GameDay" — and Tom Jackson's first season with ESPN. About five minutes into watching a game, there's a hard hit. Tom goes, "Wow, look at that hit!" I said, "That's what you did for 14 years. What do you mean, wow?" He said, "Yeah, but what a shot!" He was like a little kid — which is what I am, too.

— *Chris Berman*

LEAVING FOOTBALL — not hitting people — was hard. They say when you die you have flashbacks of your life. The last couple days before retiring I had flashbacks of my career. It's like I was dying, because it was my life. I knew I'd miss my postgame state of total exhaustion. Then came the tough thing: the search for something comparable — that's legal.

— *Bob Golic*

CHAPTER

8

SHOW ME

THE ANALYST

Instant replay began, in 1963, at the Army-Navy game in Philadelphia. It soon went uptown, to the pros, and to the advantage of the analyst. The play-by-play man had been a Rubik's Cube of actor, writer, producer, director, salesman, censor, and cameraman. Now the color man took precedence — drawing, defining, and deciphering what the picture showed.

The great TV teams balanced first downs and explanation. Ken Coleman and Warren Lahr. Curt Gowdy and Paul Christman. Dick Enberg and Merlin Olsen. John Madden and Company — which, at times, seemed to be the world. Technology helped make football exquisitely second-guessable and seem composed of sudden, dramatic starts.

The actor Robert Young said, "I feel myself being drawn to television like a man in a canoe heading for Niagara Falls." Many Americans wouldn't mind if, say, Paul Maguire were in it drawing x's and o's. Slow motion, stop-action, or instant replay: The screen becomes the blackboard, and Professor Analyst explains.

THE ANALYST BEGAN to become popular when pro football became more popular. The x's and o's that people didn't quite understand were explained on radio and TV. Al DeRogatis had been an All-American at Duke and an All-Pro with the Giants — and was the first analyst I worked with on Giants' radio. We'd go to team practices, and sit in on meetings planning the defense or offense for next Sunday's game. Sometimes we knew what to expect. Al would know a certain play was coming up, and predict it. There's nothing like perspective before its time.

— *Marty Glickman*

NO ONE CAME close to DeRogatis. Early in 1972, while we were doing a Dolphins' game, he told me they had a chance to be an all-time great team, not because of [Bob] Griese or other stars, but their offensive line. All Miami did was finish 17 and zip. Once, we were doing the Steelers-Bengals and [Cincinnati quarterback] Kenny Anderson was closelined by [Pittsburgh defensive back] Mike Wagner. Al said immediately that he had been around football a long time, but that was the most vicious hit he'd ever seen. He said Wagner should be tossed out of the game. The next Sunday we went to Pittsburgh. I got a call from NBC in midweek that we would have bodyguards because Steelers' fans were furious at Al. We got the security, but it meant nothing to Al. He was too busy looking at the field.

— *Curt Gowdy*

I WISH MANY analysts would shut up at least once or twice during a game. I think that 100 percent of them feel compelled to say something at the end of the play. It'll be first and 10. They hand it off the tailback. They'll run into the line. Second and 10. Can't you just shut up until the next play?

— *Jack Buck*

PAUL CHRISTMAN WAS an opinionated man. Early in our AFL days some of the owners tried to fire Paul and me. They called Joe Foss [then-AFL commissioner] and said we were too honest, that we didn't build the AFL up enough, that we didn't say it was better than the NFL. We went to ABC and said, "Look, we're not going to say things we don't believe. Are we going to be harassed by these owners?" ABC said no. They told Joe Foss, "These guys work for us, not for you or the league." So we were in trouble eight or nine years before tell-it-like-it-is stuff came along.

— *Curt Gowdy*

WHEN I WAS doing the Jets, one of their former players became the analyst. He came to the first game, and had six pages of hand-written notes. I looked over his shoulder before the game and thought, "Oh, I hope he doesn't try to force all that stuff in." After the game, I complimented him. "You really did a great job." He said, "I was awful." I said, "What do you mean?" He said, "Look." He'd hardly got through the first page. I said, "That's the reason you were great." He said, "What do you mean?" I said, "If you tried to use all that stuff, it wouldn't work." In football, you have to do 100 percent homework, and maybe you use 10. The problem is that you don't know which 10 you're going to use — because you have to react to the situation. And it may not be what you have on page 3 or 4. It may not be there at all. So there it is: My 10 percent rule. If you use more than 10 percent of your homework on football, you'll louse up the game.

— *Merle Harmon*

PAT HARMON OF the College Football Hall of Fame figured out that I had 58 different color experts in my years of broadcasting. To me, the expert commentator is important when he talks about something that amplifies what you see. He needs to go behind the fact — why the quarterback fell, how he hurt his knee — something you didn't notice. The replay shows it, and it magnifies what he said. I don't like today's format — play-by-play talks, then analyst on replay. In my time, we had more freedom — less technology, but more time to interact.

People kid me, "You could do your own thing because people had nobody to compare you with." I say, "Yeah? They could compare me with Curt Gowdy or Mel Allen." Today, the analyst doesn't have that problem.

— *Chris Schenkel*

OTTO GRAHAM WAS great at anything he did. He played the trombone in his father's high school band. He played basketball for Northwestern and was an All-American football player. Then, a Hall of Fame quarterback with the Cleveland Browns. Next, my color analyst in 1964 and '5 when I broadcast the Jets' games on WABC Radio.

Otto had a great sense of humor. I'd kid him, "Did you ever think of going back to coach?" He'd say, "No way." I said, "Come on, what about the NFL?" Every time his name would surface for an NFL job, Otto said, "Forget it. They'd have to make me an offer so ridiculous I couldn't turn it down, and nobody is going to make it." In early 1966, I heard on the radio that Otto had just become the Redskins' coach. I said, "That can't be." I remembered what he had said and I believed him. So I sent him a telegram: "You deserted me. Why didn't you say that you didn't like me? Coach of the Redskins? How could you do it?"

I got a telegram back and he said, "They gave me a ridiculous offer — so I took it." Great guy. Would be a smash broadcasting now.

— *Merle Harmon*

SAM HUFF CALLED me well after he was done playing football. "Can you get me a job in broadcasting as an analyst?" he said. "I miss football. I don't feel at home when I go out on the field, not being part of the team or the game." Fortunately, there was an opening on the Giant broadcast team. Sam worked with me for one year, then moved to Washington, where he still does the Redskins. He wanted to be part of the game, and he is.

Working with men like Sam taught me a lot about current

intricacies. When I played ball with the Jersey City Giants — the NFL Giants' farm team — there was only the single wing, no T-formation. We went both ways. Now they don't. Certainly, the analyst should know football. He should be able to express it, naturally. He has to have a clear voice. But the single most important thing is to love the game — because he can project that feeling as he talks about what's taking place. Football's not just x's and o's. It's emotion. Like Sam, the bext analysts want to be associated with the team, and the game itself.

— Marty Glickman

MERLIN OLSEN WAS the number one analyst at NBC for many years with Dick Enberg until he was replaced by Bill Walsh. CBS then picked him up — wanting, I think, to show NBC that Merlin was still one of America's most popular people, which was true: Only he could do both football *and* FTD commercials. I'll never forget December 22, 1991. We were in Dallas to do the Falcons and Cowboys, and the night before the game he told the production crew and myself that this was going to be his last game. He enjoyed being a television analyst, but it was time to move on.

Merlin said, "Dick, please don't tell anyone from CBS I'm retiring. Just acknowledge that fact at some point towards the end of the game." So that's what I planned to — at his bequest, no hoopla, just a fond farewell. The next day, Dallas leads by a big margin and there were eight minutes to go. I say to my producer, "We ought to get into Merlin's leaving." And he says, "No, let's wait until closer to the end." We get to five minutes on the clock and all of a sudden the Falcons start to rally. The two-minute warning comes and the Cowboys have the ball and they're leading comfortably. Again I start to say, "Merlin, this is going to be your last game."

My next words were going to be, "You've been a credit to the broadcast world," when the Cowboys fumble and the Falcons recover. Now the crowd gets anxious because Dallas needed to win to make the playoffs. The Falcons have the ball and they're throwing it downfield to Deion Sanders — then an Atlanta wide receiver and defensive back — and the crowd is going crazy and so am I, trying to honor Merlin and not doing it well. "Merlin, you've been with NBC and worked with Dick Enberg," I say, then it's, "First down at the 35. No-huddle offense and the Falcons are at the line of scrimmage." Next, "Merlin, many years a great Hall of Fame lineman." Then, "30-yard pass down to the 20."

Dallas finally won, 31-27 — great game, exciting finish — and I couldn't have cared less. What bothered me is that it was such an awkward way to salute this icon. I called the play, which I had to, but didn't do Merlin justice. We just got into it too late. Sometimes football can be frustrating.

— *Dick Stockton*

IN THE EARLY '80S I did play-by-play with Bob Trumpy. Trump has the best ex-athlete's voice I know of — it's better than 95 percent of all broadcasters — but even more, he's opinionated, he never backs off. Even if you had the better argument, he'd stay in there. We never got mad at each other — just came at most issues from opposite sides of the ball. In 1981, Richard Todd of the Jets got upset at some criticism by a reporter of the *New York Post* — then, finally shoved him into his locker. Trump said he agreed with Todd: "You can only take so much criticism, and after that a reaction is justifiable." I disagreed — anger may be justified, but not violence. He said, "Bob, you don't understand the pressures of playing in the NFL." I said, "Disproportionate rewards, disproportionate pressures."

— *Bob Costas*

I'M ASKED IF the better technology today — the producer in the ear, slowmo, skycam and rest of it — diminishes the broadcaster. I never felt that way. Instant replay is the greatest invention in sports history. It tells grandmothers, kids, the knowing or unknowledgeable fan, what happened. Why that play didn't work, or why it did. Let's see it again — there, see. See that block on that defensive end. It's a great educational tool. I think it's created more interest in sports than anything, and the interest has drawn the big bucks from television. It's made the color man the star. Ralph Kiner used to say, "Home run hitters drive Cadillacs." Today, it's the analyst.

— *Curt Gowdy*

ANOTHER TRUMPY TALE. We're doing a Jets' game. Richard Todd is their quarterback. Trump says, "It's tragic that every time Richard Todd is going to release the ball he gives it away by patting the ball with his left hand." In other words, Todd was unintentionally telling the defense that he was about to pass. I said, "Uh, Bob, maybe tragic overstates it." He said, "It *is* tragic." I said, "Does that leave any room for, say, a famine, or air crash, or earthquake, or tornado?" He said, "I don't care what you say — it's tragic." Just then, Todd happens to throw an incompletion. I said, "On third and seven, the pass falls incomplete — and now, tragically, the Jets must punt."

— *Bob Costas*

IT'S AMAZING THE variety of people you team with over the years. I have worked with quarterbacks Roger Staubach, Len Dawson, John Unitas, Terry Bradshaw and Dan Fouts, all Hall of Famers, and linemen such as Dan Dierdorf and Randy Cross. I have worked with linebackers such as Wayne Walker and Matt Millen. Coaches? Hank Stram and John Madden, who worked with a lot of announcers in his first years with CBS. The interesting thing is the different approaches these analysts took. Coaches looking at the big picture. Quarterbacks looking at receivers and the passing lanes. Defensive people looking at the line of scrimmage to see how to stop the running game. Offensive linemen looking at pass protection. Old habits die hard. I'm glad they do.

— *Dick Stockton*

IN THE MID-70S, I retired as a player — 32, and here I am, washed up, what do I do? My wife was, shall we say, succinct. She told me to get off the couch and make myself useful. She was an actress, and had her agent arrange an audition on a local New York show called "Sports Extra." I got a job as a reporter, worked my way to co-host, then got a call in 1980 from CBS. I've been an analyst and sideline reporter since. When you do football as a sideline reporter you're a three-headed monster. First, I'm part analyst, especially as a former player, because you've played the game. Second, part entertainer, trying to create a flavor of what's going on in the stands or on the field. You have to remember that if people are bored they're not going to listen. Finally, I'm part reporter, there to observe what's happening and why. Here's the strategy. Here's what to look for. The key is the balance you have to strike — because it's wearability. Take a homecoming queen. Yes, it's nice to interview her, but you have to go beyond. Do that, and you serve the audience. Don't, and you find another job.

— *John Dockery*

MY FIRST PARTNER at NBC was Cris Collinsworth. Our first game was Notre Dame-Michigan at South Bend in 1992. It ended in a tie, and Lou Holtz was criticized for running the clock out at the end. NBC is the Notre Dame network, and Cris and I got blasted by some for favoring Michigan. By the second game we were under a microscope. By the third game we're in Lou's office, and we sense hostility. Notre Dame's coach isn't pleased with the Notre Dame announcers.

Cris has an aw-shucks manner which blends a sharp tongue and homespun humor. We're talking to Lou and Cris says, "What about your offensive line? I don't see any holes." Cris means that it doesn't have any weaknesses. Lou and I think that he means the line isn't *opening* holes for the backs! So Lou says, "That's it" — he went crazy, stomped off. End of interview. I said to Cris, "What are you thinking of? Why are you saying the line's lousy?" He said, "I didn't. I said it's great." I said, "That's not how we took it." So he gets mad, thinks a little more, gets madder, and starts after Holtz. By now, Lou is in the bathroom, so Cris follows him in, and there they have the Great Urinal Debate. They're arguing, shouting, then start to calm down. It was an interesting place for a clearing of the air.

— *Tom Hammond*

FOOTBALL ON television is an analyst's medium, because of how far the game has come from a technical point of view. Unlike other sports, the football analyst is extraordinarily significant because it is such a replay-geared sport. What makes a good one? You start with entertainment value — showing the viewer something he doesn't know and get out in time for the next play. Knowledge: Seeing many things on the same play. Bill Parcells is back in coaching, but he did a year with me in the booth and was terrific. When he sees a play, he maybe sees 30 possible things that he can say. He's looking at it as a coach, at the defensive end and the offensive situation. He's looking at 30 game films. He's editing in his own head what makes sense to the viewer, and what will keep the viewer glued. To assimilate all this is really difficult. Not many do it well.

— *Marv Albert*

MOST COACHES HAVE their own TV shows. You prepare, go in, and answer questions from a host or audience. Best of all, you're in control. When you enter television, there are a hundred people involved in the production — and you don't control a thing. Most disconcerting is that what you'd hear from the production truck wouldn't coincide with what happened on the field. The director'd say, "Watch No. 65, look at his eyes" — and then No. 65 got knocked on his butt. You don't even *see* his eyes. What do you talk about then? Coaches take their chalk and talk about what you see — no interference to wade through. That's why I liked radio — you have your producer, engineer, statistician, play-by-play, and you. Five guys. You look at film, you talk, you *do*. It's like coaching — a little easier to control.

— Hank Stram

CRIS'D START SAYING things off the bend. I was always bailing him out — he called me his Voice of Reason. One day we're doing a game at Municipal Stadium in Cleveland, and it's a rout. People are starting to leave. The stadium's almost deserted. Cris says, "This looks like Opening Day for the Indians" — this is when they weren't drawing flies. Then he gets out his telestrater, and starts drawing exit routes to the airport! Later, he literally had to apologize to the City of Cleveland. What a decade. First, Cris, and then they lose the Browns.

— Tom Hammond

NOT ALL THE stuff a sideline reporter does is war and peace. Once, I found the "Pigeon Man," a Brigham Young fan who celebrated each touchdown at home games by releasing pigeons strapped beneath his chair. Another time, I learned about dinosaur bones stored under BYU's Cougar Stadium. The archeology department showed me where they were, and our camera recorded them for posterity. Who says football doesn't have any skeletons that are buried? I love pro football, but the college sideline is populated by more colorful characters. At Notre Dame, you might have four Heisman winners within 20 yards and each has something interesting to say. The NFL keeps the sideline more antiseptic. They like things tidy. Remember that the coaches were dead set against sideline reporters. So what I try to do is peel back the cover a bit and show the personality. It'll come in time — even in the NFL. It will also *take* time.

— John Dockery

AT NBC I'M on the sidelines, trying to tell you what 15 cameras can't. I'm there to give you inside stuff, augment the pictures, give you instantaneous reaction when you want to know — who's hurt? What happened? Why did the officials rule the way they did? That's why it annoys me what we are *not* permitted to do. Football has a lot more restrictions than other sports. Say you're on the sideline. You talk to a coach or player, or move outside your area, it's like you've breached national security. We're not there to steal x's and o's, or transfer state secrets. Say George Allen was coaching against Lombardi. They knew who the enemy was — *each other*! Too many people today think we're the enemy. I've never known an announcer who dropped a pass or tackled an open-field runner. So to the coaches, players, and league, lighten up. We're just there to do our job.

— Jim Gray

MY FIRST YEAR was Fox' first year [1994], and my partner was Anthony Muñoz. He had retired as a great offensive tackle shortly before — which led to a reaction I can only liken to what I've heard about Joe Namath, being too young to see him play: The football people fell all over him in the production meetings we'd attend. These meetings include coaches from the home and visiting teams — and they couldn't do enough to get him to *un*retire. Before the meeting, the coach would say, "Anthony, would you come back to play for us right now?" He wasn't joking. We'd watch some tape. A coach would say, "Offensive line — we need help. Anthony, you sure you don't want to play?" Part of him wanted to. Part of him loved what he was doing, and stayed.

Our first game was Carolina against Atlanta. The Falcons' coach was a terrific guy named June Jones. But what I remember is how one of his defensive coaches refused to talk to Muñoz before the game started. A Carolina assistant, Jim McNally, had formerly coached him — and this Atlanta assistant said that Anthony would take what he told him and sneak it to back to McNally! Can you imagine? He thought that Anthony Muñoz

— now a broadcaster, desperately wanting to make good —
would jeopardize all that by betraying a confidence and telling
what he knew to a former coach. Amazing!

This was my first look into the difference between football
— and baseball and basketball. I'd heard stories of the paranoia of other coaches — their secrets, mistrust, don't confide in
anyone, worse than the CIA. Now I saw what they mean.

— *Thom Brennaman*

IN 1995, I worked with Anthony for Fox, and I had never been
around anyone so well-liked. An 11-time Pro Bowler, he was an
even better person than player. We were at an Eagles' practice
one day and Ray Rhodes stopped practice to talk to Anthony for
a minute. Up in Green Bay, Reggie White stopped what he was
doing during practice to hug Anthony and relive old times. We
were in Cincinnati, and Anthony had the entire crew over for
Christmas dinner. We get there, and see presents on the table
for everybody — Anthony's idea. Just a spectacular guy.

Even Anthony can't stop coaches from being superstitious.
During their [1993-96] playoff run, Green Bay won 27 of 28 games
at Lambeau. The only game they lost was Opening Day 1995,
and guess who did it? Anthony and myself. Maybe we were
somewhat of a jinx — at least that's what coaches think and,
believe me, they remember. In 1995, Anthony and I worked
two of the first three Carolina games and then got another Panthers' assignment. Their coach, Dom Capers, was the first to
tell us, "Hey, we're 0 and 2 with you guys. I don't know if we
want to see you again." P.S. The next year, Carolina won 12
games, made the playoffs, and made the NFC title game. I hope
that Dom has forgiven us.

— *Kenny Albert*

OUR FIRST YEAR at Fox, Anthony and I were down the totem
pole. We got the also-rans — did about four Arizona Cardinals' games. Late in the year the Cardinals go into Washington.

Buddy Ryan was their coach, and he'd been very fair to us. He comes into our production meeting, about 6 o'clock at night, and he's got two Cardinals' hats. Our producer, Roy Hamilton, said, "Who are they for?" Buddy says, "For my pals" — Anthony and me.

Buddy keeps his hats. We start talking and the topic of the no-huddle offense comes up — the kind that Anthony anchored when he played at Cincinnati. Keep in mind that Anthony is a very religious person. Buddy says, "That god-damned no-huddle's never done a thing against our 46 defense." Muñoz sits there, doesn't say anything, I can see he's turning pink. Buddy goes on: "Oh, shit, I don't think I've ever allowed a touchdown to that rinky-dink thing." Muñoz sits there. Buddy says, "What a horse-shit way to play offense."

Boom. Muñoz explodes. "Buddy," he says, "weren't you the coach of the Eagles in '88?" Buddy sits there — he's made a tremendous mistake. He's riled Mr. Muñoz. "As I remember, Buddy, we were the the Number One offense with our no-huddle. Didn't we score 28 points against your Philadelphia team?" Buddy's turning red. The righteous Anthony is on a roll. "Buddy," he says, "weren't you the coach of the '89 Eagles?" Then he talks about teams who scored a lot of points against their 46 defense. Absolute silence in the room.

Buddy doesn't say a word. Just gets up and walks out. If he'd stayed there five more minutes, Muñoz would have strangled him — which says a lot. Anthony is so gentle it would take an act of God for him to hurt anybody. We never did get our hats.

— *Thom Brennaman*

THE ANALYST'S ROLE has changed because of the equipment. When I started as an analyst, you saw whatever the director chose to show. You saw a play run. You might get a shot of the coach on the sideline. You said so and so threw a pass, and so and so caught it. You had no tools to work with. There was no instant replay. The game was over in two hours and 45 minutes. You didn't have a chance to go back and look at a play again, talk about whether it was a zone defense or man to man, whether the quarterback threw to the wrong guy. Then came better cameras, with more experienced operators, who knew the game almost as well as we do. Above all came instant replay. At Fox, our director has a meeting with his cameramen each Sunday morning to make sure they know what our analyst wants to talk about that day — which guys are playing well, which aren't. With so much equipment now to help the analyst make his point, the analyst's role is bigger.

— Pat Summerall

DURING MY TENURE at NBC I hooked up with Joe Namath on several games. I remembered him as Broadway Joe when he played for the Jets — long hair, the lavish lifestyle — but he turned out to be an extremely nice guy. We went down to New Orleans to do a game. My wife Julie and I had dinner with Joe and his wife Debbie and Joe's long-time agent, just a wonderful time. It had been quite a few years since Joe played but the reaction was still unbelievable when people saw him in a hotel or getting into a cab. They were constantly stopping him for autographs and telling him how much they loved him. The guys of this magnitude are incredible to be around — like rock stars. The only athlete I've been around who had a similar reaction was Muhammad Ali.

— Mel Proctor

MY FIRST YEAR AT NBC, I had a new partner every week. My first partner was Namath, and I was amazed at how fans were attracted to him. I don't just mean folks old enough to have seen him play — but teenagers, twenty-somethings too young to remember him as a player but who were wowed by his charisma. His life had completely changed. He admitted to the stories of the past, but now he was the gentlest, kindest guy, no wildness, no drinking. Once, he was advising Jeff George in George's rookie year at quarterback. Namath said, "This is a bad team, and you can develop bad habits on a bad team. But if you keep your mechanics straight, you'll be fine." So George says to him, "You blankety-blank, who are *you* to tell me what to do?" I couldn't believe it. Who was *Namath*? He was just trying to help, and he gets abused in return. He didn't say anything, just walked away. Says a lot about some players today — how little they know about the greats — and even more about Broadway Joe.

— *Tom Hammond*

I DID ONE GAME with Namath in Indianapolis — Colts-Patriots — and Joe was so recognizable. He brought 18 or 19 pages of notes to the game — like the Chiefs' Len Dawson, he saw the whole field — and like Dawson, he treated me like an equal and a peer. But what knocked me out is that I remembered Joe from his hell-raising days. I get into Indy on Friday, we finish Saturday night at 8 with our production meeting, and I'm dressed to go on the town. I figure Joe'll go with me — hey, he's No. 12! He says, "I'm going to bed, guys, that's it." What? I asked the production people what was going on: They said, "He went to bed at 8 last night, too." Broadway Joe, we hardly knew ye.

— *Kevin Harlan*

IN 1996, I WORKED with Tim Green, who has written four books and went to law school while with the Falcons and is now a sports contributor for "Good Morning America." A real intelligent guy and part of a week that will always stand out in my mind. Jacksonville was playing Carolina, and both of us had friends chuckle that we were stuck with a lemon — two expansion teams only a year old. Thirteen weeks later, each team played in the championship game. Tim and I had the last laugh. Right now that lemon tastes pretty sweet.

— *Kenny Albert*

MY MOM WAS a schoolteacher, and my dad a systems analyst. Each Monday they went to the library, and came home with grocery bags of books. We read — and I was voracious. The first book I remember reading was *The Three Musketeers*, by Alexander Dumas. I liked it so much I tried *The Count of Monte Cristo*, which I liked even better. Later, I was an English major at Syracuse — but at eight, I knew what I wanted to do. I wanted to play in the NFL, and I wanted to write. People point to incongruity — what a difference between playing a violent game and writing novels. I view it as an opportunity: Like broadcasting, you marry the up-close and distant. Maybe that's why my favorite era is the Victorian novel — I like how they plumbed the psychological depths of their characters. The focus is on their experience of life — and isn't that what analysts try to relate each Sunday?

— *Tim Green*

EARLY IN MY broadcast career a player came up and said, "What did you say about me losing weight?" I said, "What do you mean?" He said, "Somebody told me you said I should lose ten pounds and I'd be a better player." I said, "I did not. I said you should lose *twenty* pounds and you'd be a better player." I get less of that now that I've been around a while and players get to know you. But you can't let it bother you. Hey, that's your job. You say things, and somebody won't like it.

— *Matt Millen*

WORKING THE NFL is working a Super Bowl every week. Now that we're doing [1996-] "Monday Night Football," Matt and I feel the big-game sense every time. Millen is an NFL junkie and a John Madden disciple: By his own admission, he sees so many things on the field that he has a hard time saying all the things he wants to say at once because he wants to say everything, *now*. That shows how bright he is about football — not surprising since he played linebacker with four Super Bowl

champions and has been nominated to the NFL Hall of Fame.
Every place Matt went he won a ring. Either he was smart
enough to pick the right team, or he had a hand in winning.
My money's on the latter.

— *Howard David*

PAUL MAGUIRE GOES to all the pre-game interviews where,
you know, we talk with the coaches and maybe six players from
each team. But he never takes notes — not one. The only thing
he brings to the game is his flipcard. He's marvelous at strategy, has a great sense of humor, but usually leaves story-telling
to play-by-play guys who *have* taken notes and therefore know
the background of the players. This one Sunday Paul is telling
a story and I'm just amazed. He talks about a player and the
obstacles the man's overcome — it's heart-rending, detailed.
Only one problem. Paul had the wrong player.

— *Tom Hammond*

WHEN TNT GOT the NFL franchise, I was assigned to the studio and my partner was Ken Stabler — "The Snake." When I
learned we'd be teaming up, I got a paperback copy of his life
story. Great read — better life — a natural guy, just good folks.
We'd be watching games, and Snake'd hobble into the studio
about 2 o'clock on Sunday. "I'm playing hurt today, E.J.," he'd
say. I never knew if it was because of his bad knees or because
he'd had a tough night. He then proceeded to straighten me
out. "I don't know what time I got in, but the newspaper hit me
in the head."

— *Ernie Johnson, Jr,*

I WORKED WITH many CBS analysts — Ken Stabler, George
Starke, John Robinson, Dan Jiggetts, Randy Cross, Hank Stram.
Stabler taught me the body language of a quarterback — whether
his confidence was waning, or getting his game together. The
coaches' perspective was global — breaking down the game.

Robinson showed me why Emmitt Smith was so good. One, the offensive line so beat the defense that by the time he touched the line of scrimmage they were two yards back. Two, as Smith approached the line his feet were parallel, planted — not one after another like most guys. At CBS the analyst drove the broadcast. They'd tell you before the game about their story-lines. It made it easy to set them up during the game — because I knew where they were coming from. I'd played basketball, not football, prior to CBS. The analysts were my learning curve.

— *James Brown*

SOMETIMES I THINK analysts are put on this earth to keep life from being dull. I worked with Bob Trumpy for two years during the time that Art Modell moved the Browns from Cleveland to Baltimore [as the Ravens]. Trumpy hated it — thought it betrayed a great city — and said on the air that he wished Baltimore nothing but stormy skies, muddy fields, and cold hot dogs. The next year we go — where else? — to Baltimore to do a game, and as we arrive the papers and talk-show hosts are going crazy. People had thousands of "Dump Trump" signs. During timeouts, they turned around, looked at the booth, and started jeering. The whole game you heard chants of "Trumpy Sucks." Nice stuff. At game's end, four armed policemen escorted us from Memorial Stadium. Remember that the Ravens *won* the game. You'd think the fans would be in a generous mood. If they'd lost, I might not be here to tell this story. Not to mention Mr. Trumpy.

— *Tom Hammond*

CHAPTER

9 REVOLUTION

AMERICAN FOOTBALL LEAGUE

Nineteen-sixties America was grand and awful, stirring and infuriating — its divide embracing sex, race, religion, and pro football. On one hand — the Establishment, august and stony — a.k.a. the National Football League. On the other, the American (some said Almost) Football League. "The NFL wouldn't expand, so *we* did," said owner Ralph Wilson of the AFL charter Bills. The NFL meant Vince Lombardi — power-sweeping opponents like Patton storming Germany. Its foil seemed outlaw, even alien, more UFO than AFL.

In Oakland, the high school field was named for an undertaker. Billboards urged fans to "follow the Raiders." Said *The New York Times*: "It's hard enough to find the Raiders, much less follow them." The Broncos wore horizontal socks. The Patriots changed homes yearly. At the Polo Grounds, pigeons outnumbered New York Titans' fans. Aptly, players wore names on their jerseys: Who *were* these guys, anyway?

Amazingly, the AFL survived: TV became its life-preserver. The leagues fought, then agreed to merge — Main Street and Aquarius. On January 12, 1969, the AFL won its first Super

Bowl. In July, men first touched the moon. People still debate the greater miracle.

IN THE EARLY 1960s, when the NFL got so attractive, it figured that somebody else would crash the party. That's always been its story — always competing. It looks so good that every wealthy guy wanted to get involved with it, because it's a sport, it's a team, I own them, kind of a macho thing.

Harry Wismer was a great salesperson and a good announcer — not terribly accurate, but that didn't matter. He started the AFL [as Jets' nee Titans' owner] in competition with the NFL and enlisted people who couldn't get into the NFL — like Ralph Wilson, still owner of the Bills. There was Lamar Hunt, still owner of the Kansas City Chiefs — then, the Dallas Texans. Bud Adams owned the Oilers. Wayne Valley had the Raiders, before Al Davis took them away. A determined group.

They went to ABC and said, "Hey, we'll give you the stage and stars you need." They went out and struggled. Then they went to NBC, a huge network with money, and brought Sonny Werblin into the picture [as new Jets' owner]. They were good, and the time was right. But they only made it because of television.

— *Frank Gifford*

YOU KNOW HOW much it cost for a franchise in the American Football League in 1960? Twenty-five thousand dollars. If you had $25,000, if there was a franchise available, if you knew the people, you could get one. In those days, those owners used to walk around with money — I'm talking about stacks of hundred dollar bills. They would try to get someone off by the side that they were trying to sign and wave that money in front of him. Bud Adams down in Houston did that because everyone was vying for the top players in the country. And they talked in the most eloquent language possible — cold, hard cash.

— *Jack Buck*

THE EARLY AFL was a bandaid operation. The Patriots had to fly to Denver. They start their flight in Boston, fly into Buffalo, and pick up the Bills. The Pats got off in Denver to play the Broncos. The Bills, meanwhile, stayed on the flight and flew to their game in Oakland. Imagine the NFL allowing that today. There were eight AFL teams — and two, Buffalo and Boston, were on the same plane. If the plane crashed, there went the league. Billy Sullivan owned the Pats, and his players stayed at hotels with a $6 room rate. Even that was too high — so Billy told his players, "Don't mess up the beds, or turn down the covers." Then he tried to get a rebate. Harry Wismer had his team fly into road cities the very *day* of the game — anything to cut costs.

I'll never forget New York flying into Dallas for a game with the Texans — and they're taping players on the plane an hour before kickoff. Today, most players could buy the tape. Heck, they could buy the plane.

— *Van Miller*

MOST AMERICANS thought that AFL players came from Upper Slobovia, and that NFL players came out of the colleges. They just wouldn't accept the AFL. Paul Christman, my ABC broadcasting partner, didn't want to do it. "That league is nothing," he said. "I don't want to lower myself." I talked him into it, and we started doing the games. The Raiders played at Frank Youell Field and the Oilers at Jeppesen Stadium in Houston. Both were high school fields. You might say, "How did the AFL finally make it?" Through owners who stuck together, put their money up, and kept signing good players. Year by year, the league got better. To me, it's one of America's greatest success stories.

— *Curt Gowdy*

IN 1961, THE Bills went to Boston on Thursday for a Friday game at B.U. Field — and as we're traveling we learn about a hurricane alert going up the Eastern Seaboard. The next morning,

Dick Gallagher, the Bills' G.M., and I are at Billy Sullivan's office — the Pats then had their headquarters at the Kenmore Hotel. Billy talks about the hurricane, and says, "I'm going to postpone the game. We'll play on Sunday." I told him, "You can't do that — you've got eight thousand season-ticket holders expecting a game." First, he threw me out. Then, he postponed the game. We stayed over till Sunday. Talk about the AFL's lack of luck. Friday night, 78 high-school games were played in the Boston area in beautiful weather; the hurricane never got near Massachusetts. On Sunday, we kicked off in a monsoon. In the early AFL you took your choice — and usually paid the price.

— Van Miller

FENWAY PARK WAS a home site of the Patriots when they were the Boston Patriots. One day I covered Gino Cappelletti's 100th game in a nor-easter. The wind was blowing 60 miles an hour — and at the end of the game the only thing left of the flagpole and the flag were shreds. The rain was coming sideways and I had to stand behind the booth on the back of a chair with two spotters holding my spotting boards down. Those early AFL parks had some tiny booths. Even later, the booths at the Orange Bowl in Miami were so small I could hardly squeeze into them. When I worked with another big man like Lionel Aldridge or Willie Davis, there was no room for anybody else. Memories? I worked with many color men. Paul Maguire is a great character and I have hundreds of stories I could tell about him and most of them you couldn't or wouldn't want in print. Sort of like the early AFL.

— Jay Randolph

THE EARLY AFL had some prestige teams. One was San Diego. In '65, we [Buffalo] played them there for the title. There was all that propaganda about what they were going to do to us. They had the horses — Lance Alworth, Ernie Ladd, Keith

Lincoln, Paul Lowe. Then when Billy Shaw got knocked out of the opening kickoff it pulled the team together — that sounds strange but it's true — it made us realize again it was going to be a tough afternoon. I'll always remember Harry Jacobs and John Tracey with eight minutes to go in the game, yelling for the defensive unit to shut 'em out. Final score: 23 to nothing, Buffalo. All together: "On any given Sunday..."

— *Paul Maguire*

WHEN THE EARLY AFL teams went to the West Coast, they'd stay there three weeks and play Oakland, San Diego, and Denver. That way, you'd save airplane money. One year, the Bills had a big win in Oakland and [owner] Ralph Wilson threw a party for the team at the Fairmont Hotel. He invited a friend of his, Frank Tompkins, American Airlines vice-president — and Tompkins, in turn, invited fifty of his stewardesses. The next morning, trouble: A writer, Jim Peters, described the party in print in the *Courier-Express* and how the fifty stewardesses were mingling and dancing with the players. The Bills were still on the West Coast preparing for the next game and didn't know about Peters' piece — until the phones started ringing. And ringing. And ringing. You can imagine what the players' wives and girl friends thought about fifty stewardesses with their guys! When the road trip ended, you've never seen so many big men bringing so many expensive gifts back to Buffalo for their women. It's safe to say Jim Peters was not on their Christmas card list.

— *Van Miller*

AT THE TIME, the AFL had enormous problems in other cities. But not New York — and it encouraged the league — New York being the world's media center. At the 1964 World Series, I got off the subway and, walking down the steps, looked at a building across from Yankee Stadium. A huge sign hits me: "Congratulations, Yankees. Come see us next year at Shea Stadium. New York Jets." That was Sonny Werblin's hype. The next year, he signed [Alabama quarterback] Joe Namath and [Notre Dame's] John Huarte, who never really played — but so what? In one week, they sold enough tickets to the subway alumni to pay Huarte's salary. Soon the Jets, like the Giants, were packing their park. Each Monday the *Daily News* ran a big picture on the back of both crowds. Two teams playing, same day, both sellouts. Did the AFL have a future? It did — blooming in New York.

— Merle Harmon

IF THE NFL REPRESENTED wonderful tradition, the AFL represented hope. That's why I felt the Chiefs could beat the Packers in the [1967] first Super Bowl. I thought we could go to them and throw in front — that is, throw short at first and gradually go deeper. People forget that we were in the game until the third quarter. We were doing the things we do well. We're only down, 14-10, and driving. Then Willie Wood runs an interception back 50 yards to our four — it changed the personality of the game. That put us 11 points down and we had to deviate from our plan. Everything blew apart. From then on, it was throw, throw, throw — and if you did that against Green Bay, forget it. I didn't think there were specific differences between the NFL and AFL. No one game could be a criteria to measure both leagues. Later, people talked of parity between the leagues. Forget that game's final score [35-10]. I thought we had parity then.

— Hank Stram

I LOVED THE OLD Rockpile [War Memorial Stadium, the Bills' 1960-72 domicile]. The seats were close, the sightlines tremendous. There was a wonderful intimacy, and charm. But it had terrible facilities. In the two-level press box there was one cruddy old toilet. The locker room was so crowded you wouldn't put a high school team there. Some Bills' fans still bemoan leaving War Memorial. The problem is money. You'd have had to spend $5 million to fix it up — and that would have just been to condemn.

— *Van Miller*

JERRY KRAMER WAS with me at halftime of Super Bowl III [January 12, 1969, Jets *v.* Colts, in the Orange Bowl]. I was doing radio, and Jerry had gone up to Fort Lauderdale to visit with the Jets and do some tapings. Kramer played for Vince Lombardi, and before Super Bowls I and II Lombardi's players were sequestered. Kramer comes into the Jets' hotel and finds them out by the pool! So Jerry said to me at halftime [Jets 7, Colts 0], "I'll tell you one thing. The Jets have set back preparation 20 years." The next year, Kansas City put the stamp of approval on the AFL by beating Minnesota in the Super Bowl. Then people realized there was parity. Some tale — this upstart league finally plays with the big guys and helps creates the biggest event in the world.

— *Merle Harmon*

I WAS BLESSED to have been around in the back rooms during draft days — and to have heard about owners or scouts taking players and keeping them on an airplane until they signed, or hiding them so that the AFL couldn't find the NFL, or vice-versa. In many ways, I thought the AFL did a better job than the NFL. I still do.

— *Dick Enberg*

CHAPTER

10 SOMETHING WONDERFUL

LOMBARDI AND GREEN BAY

Vince Lombardi was a 1930s guard on Fordham's "7 Blocks of Granite." At Green Bay, he turned granite into steel. His 1959-67 Packers won five titles in seven years, swept the first two Super Bowls, and made the "G" on the helmet sport's marque label. Their creed, "Run to Daylight"; symbol, the power sweep, a modern version of the old single wing off-tackle play; Voice, Ray Scott, playing language like Jascha Heifetz did a violin.

Lombardi thrived by making the complex simple. "He treats us all the same," said tackle Henry Jordan, "like dogs." He made men of boys, and stars of Taylor, Hornung, Nitschke, and McGee. In 1961, the Packers got a break. Commissioner Pete Rozelle persuaded Congress to pass a bill exempting football from monopoly charges. Rozelle put all teams in a single package, sold the rights to CBS, and shared them equally. The step buoyed small-market teams, and parity on the field.

Most Lombardi breaks were self-induced. Green Bay became Titletown; Lambeau Field, akin to Lourdes. On September 3, 1970, Lombardi died, of cancer, at 57. Today, the NFL championship trophy bears his name.

TOM LANDRY AND Vince Lombardi were both Giants' assistant coaches when I played. Landry wasn't emotional. On the opposite end was the guy who was very emotional and was the greatest teacher I think I ever was exposed to — not just in football but in life.

I remember my first meeting with the Giants [1958]. We were training in Salem, Oregon. Everybody went home in the off-season in those days. So this was homecoming. Most of the guys had just finished their first practice. You had met the new people, and people who'd been there before. Everybody is still saying welcome back as an assistant coach starts calling roll. People were talking. He couldn't quiet the group. Then, this gentleman walked in and cleared his throat. The room went silent, and I said to the fellow next to me, "Who the hell is that?" He said, "Lombardi," and added, "You'll find out soon enough."

From that moment on, you never had such a feeling of this is a guy I want to follow. If he tells me to run through the end of Yankee Stadium, I will.

— *Pat Summerall*

IN 1956, THE Giants beat the Bears in the championship game by forty points. They'd forged a great team, and we thought they'd be invincible for years to come. Then, in '59, Lombardi left us, moved to Green Bay, and built an empire using the same philosophy he used in New York. Get quality people — Fuzzy Thurston, Paul Hornung, a Bart Starr — and you have a winner. There was just something about the Packers and Lombardi that — well, Ray Scott and I did those [1961 regular-season and '61-62 title] games. And he felt so sorry for me, because we lost them all.

I remember the 1962 championship game at Yankee Stadium. It was horribly cold [13 degrees; wind of 40 miles an hour], and we were out in right field with no protection. Maybe Lombardi wasn't bothered, but I'm shaking by the first quarter. Bud Palmer, another sports announcer, always sat in the box behind me. He sees me shaking and tells my spotter, "Give me Chris' coffee." He put brandy in it, and I sipped a little bit, but it got cold and tasted terrible. Ray was so bundled up he couldn't reach his handkerchief. He had a slight cold, and had mucous coming down. It was so cold the mucous froze on Ray's lip.

When the game ended, I went back in the Giant locker room, and they made me go to a mirror and look at my face. It was blue. I'd taken the coffee with me and it was frozen — the brandy, too. I told the players, "You thought you were cold, look at this." Packers-Giants — it meant Lombardi. It's still fun to look at their tapes. And I do, when I get the chance — inside.

— *Chris Schenkel*

PEOPLE TALK ABOUT the Packers' famous power sweep. Actually, Vince started it in New York before he left in 1959 for Green Bay. In New York, he had Gifford running the ball, and [Alex] Webster and [Mel] Triplett blocking. Lombardi knew when he digrammed the sweep that it would take us five or six hours or however long he felt we needed to assimilate that play. We knew that if we did it Vince's way, it would work. He knew how long the guard's step should be when he was pulling to lead the sweep. If he took a longer step than this, he'd trip over the quarterback — and Lombardi knew how long in inches that step should be. He'd tell the quarterback, "You've got to get your left foot out of there, because the guard's coming out with his right foot. And his first step is going to be eight and a half-inches long. If you don't get your foot out of the way, the sweep won't work" — that kind of detail. Nobody knew football like Lombardi. Nobody has presented it like him to this day.

— *Pat Summerall*

IN 1958, THE Packers won one game. The franchise turned around only when Lombardi arrived. He ran everything — even the announcers. He asked somebody who did the games with me. They told him that in 1957 and '58 Johnny Lujack, the

Heisman trophy winner and great Notre Damer, and Hall of Famer George Connor. They'd both played for the Chicago Bears. Lombardi explodes, "No more Bears!" — which meant no more Bears. So I started teaming with Tony Canadeo, the great Packer member of the Pro Football Hall of Fame. When Lombardi first got to Green Bay, he said, "I'm in command here." One of the understatements of our time.

— *Ray Scott*

THE GIANTS OF the early '60s always thought they were the Packers' equal. It's like two great thoroughbred horses in a match race. They're even, until one makes mistakes. The Giants did. You can talk about the cold weather at Green Bay and New York. I don't know if it made the difference. There was a magic about that man. I married a girl of Italian descent, Fran. She had blue eyes. The Maras thought I was marrying a nice Irish girl. Vince found out her maiden name was Italian, and from then on I could do no wrong. I would come to Green Bay after he'd left us, and play golf with him on Saturday before the game. He and his wife Marie were very close friends. Tough, but an incredibly good executive and coach. Who beat him? Nobody. The tides of life ran out.

— *Chris Schenkel*

LOMBARDI WAS THE greatest motivator and genius at handling people that I have ever known. That was his secret — and the values he convinced the majority of the players to adopt. The bottom line was that the team was the most important item, not the individual. He convinced players that if the team triumphed, individual rewards would follow. I was at Lombardi's home after each home game and had a chance to ask him why he did this and why he said that. He never complained about officiating or weather or injuries. I asked him why, and he said, "Look, I don't want any player to think in terms of why we lost the game except by what he saw in the mirror." Almost all of the men who played for Lombardi were successful in their later business and personal lives. Once, when I was sure he was in a good humor, I said, "I think you're the most gracious loser I have ever known and the most miserable winner." He looked at me and said, "They [the players] don't need me to tell them when they lose. It's when they win — they get fat-headed. *That's* when I get on 'em."

— *Ray Scott*

I DID 19 YEARS of the NFL on CBS, and got to know Lombardi well. Vince was amused by the fact that of all the stuff I did over the years, it wasn't the NFL on CBS, or college football per se, that people knew me for. It wasn't the [1962-78] New York Mets. It wasn't [Mutual's 1974-77] "Monday Night Football." It was the years I re-created Notre Dame games for the C.D. Chesley Network. I remember once doing a Packers' game in the '60s at Milwaukee, and I went out for a morning walk with Lombardi. We came back to the Pfister Hotel and some kids see us, and one yells, "Hey, here comes the Notre Dame announcer!" For once, Vince was overlooked. It didn't happen very often.

— *Lindsey Nelson*

HE IS MORE IN my thoughts than anyone I have known in sports. Dave Robinson, a great Packers' linebacker, and I were at the Hall of Fame in Canton not long ago. He said, "I know you knew him very well, but let me tell you what the real Lombardi was like. Remember the [January 1, 1967, NFL title] game in Dallas where the winner went to the first Super Bowl? The Cowboys had the ball in the closing seconds and were at our two-yard line." I said, "Of course I remember. I was call-ing it!" [The Packers won, 34-27, intercepting Don Meredith on fourth-and-goal.]

Dave said, "You may remember that I blitzed Meredith and forced him to throw off his back foot when he wasn't ready. Don put it up for grabs and Tom Brown picked it off. When the game was over I was in the locker room and saw Lombardi coming toward me. I figured he'd tell me what a great play I'd made. You know what he said? "You weren't *supposed* to blitz!" I was shocked. Later, he congratulated me — after all, I'd helped get us to the first Super Bowl. But what stuck in his mind was that I'd departed from the game plan! He wanted to make his point.

Lombardi was kind and thoughtful — and arrogant and insulting. He was anything he wanted to be. Looking back, I believe that he never said or did anything unless he had a purpose. He achieved legendary status — and that status has been transferred to Green Bay. You go up there and see Lombardi Avenue, Hornung Street, and Packerland Drive. When babies are born at Bellin [Memorial] Hospital, they're often sent home wrapped in Packers' green and gold. Kids attend Vince Lombardi Middle School. It's like a time warp. Vince still hovers — football's Banquo's Ghost.

— Ray Scott

I'LL NEVER FORGET the day before the Ice Bowl in December 1967. Lombardi did a massive interview with Dallas and Green Bay media. At the time I was new to the Dallas area, but I'd arranged an interview with him. Then he had second thoughts, and told Chuck Lane, the Packers' PR guy, "I'm not going to do it." The reason he gave Lane was that he didn't have a coat and tie. I told Chuck, "I'll give him mine." Finally, he agreed to the interview and we talked — primitive, optical sound. I remember what he told me: "Don't worry about the weather. We've got a grid system that will not allow the field to freeze." The next day, virtually every player froze to death. Maybe he was just setting me up.

— Verne Lundquist

IN JANUARY 1967, both CBS and NBC simulcast the first Super Bowl between the Packers and the Chiefs. It was the first and, I am sure, only time two television networks have broadcast the same game. Frank Gifford and I spent a half each on the sideline and in the booth for CBS — but what I remember is that when the second half began NBC missed the kickoff because they were interviewing Bob Hope on the sideline about his next special. Someone at NBC decided to send some guy down to the Packer sideline and ask Lombardi if he'd mind kicking off again. You can imagine the kind of reception that guy got.

— *Pat Summerall*

IN 1988, I had the chance to work with Jerry Kramer, the ex-Packer guard. One night in Houston I sat in the hotel bar listening to him reminisce about Vince Lombardi — and I can still remember Jerry telling me that playing for his Packers was the most satisfying thing he'd ever done. He'd done a number of things since playing ball — mining, undersea diving of some sort. Nothing could compare with Lombardi. Sometimes football never lets go.

— *Mel Proctor*

IT'S THE EARLY 1990s. I'm working Detroit at Green Bay with James Brown. Our CBS team flew in Friday morning. It's 30 degrees below, and we're told it'll be at least that cold Sunday. I get a brainstorm. I tell James and our producer that we should do our segment for "NFL Today" in a slightly different way. They look at me as if the cold has snapped my brain. By Sunday I've won them over. I open by saying, "Welcome to lovely, balmy Green Bay. It's 32 below, but if you're here long enough it's not bad." I'm wearing long underwear — but the viewer only sees my Hawaiian shirt. I switch to James, who's in a lounge chair, has sunglasses on, and is being fanned by several young ladies. Lombardi would tell you: It's like the Ice Bowl — mind over matter.

— *Randy Cross*

BEFORE ANY GAME you have a production meeting where,

among other things, you interview the upcoming game's top players. In 1994, our last game was the Bays — Green at Tampa — as it turned out, also [Packers' receiver] Sterling Sharpe's last NFL game. He had injured his neck and doctors told him to give up the game. Today, Sterling does a great job on ESPN — but back then he treated the media like a leper. You couldn't imagine him behind the mike. So much for imagination. The meeting starts, and we interview Sterling and another player — some guy named Favre — and are we surprised. We go two hours and it's a comedy routine — the last thing you'd expect. One thing that I do on the pre-game is the "Fox Watch," where James Brown does what they call a whip-around to all of the stadiums. That day, we went to the parking lot where the Packer fan club is cooking bratwurst — 3,000 cheeseheads in Tampa Stadium! That's the thing about small towns like Green Bay. Small towns can surprise you.

— *Kenny Albert*

AS A KID I was a Packers' ballboy and hung around with Bart Starr Jr., Tiger Devine, Dan's son, and Zeke's son, Steve Bratkowski. We'd take Packer footballs in the golf cart, cross Oneida Street in Green Bay — you felt so special. We worked on the field all day, then went to St. Norbert College, and ate with the players at their camp. It was hero-worship — like the rest of the town. There's a passion in Green Bay unlike any in the world. That made losing tough, but now the love's flowered — you see the full-fledged mechanism of what it is to be a Packer fan. It's the stadium and natural grass, the ghost of Lombardi on the sidelines, it's Starr in the Ice Bowl, and the fans — not the corporate luxury suites, but the Joes up in Nosebleed Heaven. When the Packers won Super Bowl XXXI, I knew people who took out bank loans to go to New Orleans, guys using retirement funds. If need be, every American ought to use funds to see Green Bay once. The folks up there have their job, their family, and their team.

— *Kevin Harlan*

WHEN MY PARTNER, Ron Pitts, and I go to Green Bay, it's like his homecoming. Ron grew up in Buffalo, but his dad, Elijah, played there — so he's like the prodigal son. The first time I went to Green Bay [1994] was my first meeting with Mike Holmgren. He loved to talk about his Harley-Davidson, so we asked, "Can we follow you around?" No problem — Mike was like a proud papa, glad that somebody would take time to showcase the Packers, who weren't yet the class of the league. We go around town — Mike's on his cycle, everybody's waving — and ever since then you're pleased for him. You haven't lived until you've experienced the Packer fan. If Fox said to me, "We're putting you at Lambeau Field for the whole season," I'd say, "Hey, man, no complaints. I don't care how tough it is to get home to Phoenix, deal." I'd do it and I don't care if they went 16-0 or 0-16. I've broadcast football, baseball, and basketball, and I'm here to say: Green Bay is the best place on earth to do a sports event.
— *Thom Brennaman*

A STORY ABOUT football's good, bad, and ugly. In terms of good vibrations, you couldn't beat the 1997 title game at Lambeau Field. Beforehand, a cameraman told me, "Look, little lady from Los Angeles, we're going to outfit you right." He gave me boots, socks, hats, foot- and hand-warmers — I looked like Nanook from the North. The week before, the Packers had played the 49ers at Lambeau in the rain — the worst conditions of my 15-year career. This day was indescribably cold. Yet when the Packers won and they opened the stadium so that more fans could join the crowd inside for the trophy presentation — by then, you didn't *feel* it. It was surrealistic — the weather felt so natural — an unbelievable merging of relief and pride. They'd done it. The title was back where it belonged. You knew there was not another place on earth you'd rather be watching a football game.

Juxtapose that to the bad and ugly. It was December 1990 in Buffalo. The Bills were about to beat Miami [24-14] to clinch the Eastern Division title. About two and a half minutes were left, and I was on the field shooting standups for that night's "SportsCenter." My producer had shot the 1986 World Series at Shea Stadium, where fans got violent, and he sensed trouble. "Let's do this in one take," he said. "I'm getting you out of here." We did, and suddenly hundreds of fans swarmed on the field — the drunks, the bare-chests, a swell of emotion, people taking down goalposts. I was standing in the tunnel, and police had some fan by his hair, dragging him bleeding along the ground. For the only time in my career I was scared. Buffalo's mayhem *v.* the love-in at Lambeau. It shows the two sides of the NFL — and the passion it creates.

— *Andrea Kremer*

I LOVE GREAT stadiums in football. RFK Stadium was wonderful. It was small and you had to duck your head to get into the booth and it was rickety and wooden and old — but when the fans would yell and you sang, "Hail to the Redskins," the booth would shake and you'd think this is how it ought to be. Arrowhead is good in Kansas City. Giants Stadium has an ideal booth and perfect sightlines, which is true in all the new stadiums. Then, there are places such as Tampa Stadium where you're high and far away from the action. All well and good, but there is nothing like Lambeau. I'll never forget the [January 4] playoff game I did there in 1997. Sleet, horrible weather, and how many no-shows? Exactly three [attendance, 60,787]. Lambeau is what the NFL is all about. It comes from the Lombardi era. It's green and oval. You have your Cheeseheads. The place is always packed — and the devotion is amazing. I've never done a game at Notre Dame, but I'm sure it's similar. The tradition. The exhilaration. Nothing rivals Lambeau — and I grew up in New York.

— *Dick Stockton*

I SPENT THREE weeks at Green Bay in late 1996 and early '97. Everywhere on TV and the papers, pennants, waiters dressed in green and gold. After a while, you get burned out. One night I came back to my hotel, tried to sleep, couldn't, and got up and closed the drapes. I look out the window and there's a neon sign, "Go Packers." In Wisconsin, you can't escape it.

— *Andrea Kremer*

MY DAD [Packers' president Bob Harlan] and I have a wonderful relationship. The first radio game I did was at 15, and I came home and my dad had about three pages of notes. He'd been a writer with UPI, and he listened to my game like my biggest fan and toughest critic. That's why I loved what happened in 1996-7. [Green Bay won the NFC title, then beat New England, 35-21, in Super Bowl XXXI: its first title since 1968.]

Dad was the first non-Green Bay born-and raised-person to head the Pack. He got the team back on top and did it behind the scenes. He put sky boxes at Lambeau, hired [general manager] Ron Wolf and Mike Holmgren, built the Don Hutson Training Center. I'll never forget the day dad reached the zenith of his profession. The Super Bowl was in New Orleans, where, in 1986, the Bears had won it with my brother, Brian, as their PR director. It's 1997 and after the game we leave the Superdome. Traffic's gridlocked and Brian says, "When we won it, we walked back to our hotel. It's a nice night. Let's do that now." We did, and it was a huge tailgate party. Everything's a sea of green and gold. Suddenly, someone says, "Hey, there's Mr. Harlan," and forget Brian and me — dad is mobbed.

We're at the outside of the circle, and at its center are people hugging dad and saying the same thing, "Thank you," "This is so wonderful," "We're so happy" — as close to a Frank Capra movie as you get in the 1990s. Finally, we got back to the Fairmont Hotel and a giant NFL party: They've got a parade with dancers, bands, and at the end the Packers' equipment manager with the Vince Lombardi trophy. If you see a better story than the Packers, call me collect. *That* I'd like to see.

— *Kevin Harlan*

FORGET THE COWBOYS. Green Bay is America's Team. Around the country I'm amazed by the support. At road games, thousands of people wearing green and gold. I live in Minneapolis, and bars show Packer games. NFL Properties says that they're the hottest team in jerseys and jackets sold. A lot has to do with the setting, the mythology. The Packers are the quintessential small town. Green Bay has 95,000 people. No NFL city is anywhere near that small. It's the only community-owned team — people own stock from all over Wisconsin. Want a ticket? There's a waiting list of 29,000 — people sign up their babies for a 45-year wait. To America, the Packers won as pro football was emerging — its first TV dynasty. Millions grew up hooked on Titletown USA. When the Packers return from road games, win or lose, people still put on the porch lights to show support. When snow hits, people get shovels and clear the field. It's like [receiver] Robert Brooks says, "There's an aura, and you can feel it in the stadium. It's like you're back when Lombardi was here. Only the names on the jerseys have changed." So little in life stays like it was. What makes the Packers special is that they have.

— *Ray Scott*

CHAPTER

SEASONS IN THE SUN

GREAT DAYS/YEARS II

Plato said, "Before we talk, let us define our terms."

Take football. To some, it denotes Joe Namath. No. 12 wore white shoes, espoused free sex, and threw a football as nimbly as Robin Hood used a bow. At the other end, it also means the man who ran the ball better than anyone has, or is ever likely to. "That Brown," said a rival. "He says he isn't Superman. What he really means is that Superman isn't Jimmy Brown."

So, too, for great days and/or years. Which do you prefer? Super Bowl III, Hail Mary, and the Immaculate Reception — or the Sneakers Game of 1934, Ice Bowl of '67, and game coining "sudden victory." (Christmas Day 1971: Dolphins 27, Chiefs 24, in double overtime.) *Each* means football — then, and now.

PEOPLE STILL recall the "Heidi" game. The Jets were playing the Raiders in November 1968, and the Jets were leading when Oakland scored two touchdowns in the last minute to win. Just before they did, somebody pulled the switch at NBC's headquarters at 7 o'clock Eastern Time and went to the special, "Heidi." As the little girl was going up the mountain, holding her grandfather's hand, the Raiders achieved their miracle finish which only fans on the West Coast saw. The rest of the country was shut out.

This was an American Football League game at a time when it was still considered, you know, subpar to the NFL. "Nobody cares about the AFL" was the conventional wisdom. Then they pull the plug and over 10,000 protest calls blow out the lines at NBC. The uproar was so huge I got called back to re-create the two last-minute touchdowns. I'd left the booth when an assistant starts yelling, "Gowdy! Gowdy!" He says, "Here are the earphones to the truck." I pick them up and the truck says, "Look, uh, uh, uh." I do the re-creations and they played it on "The Today Show" next morning and all day long. "Heidi" turned out to be the greatest publicity the AFL ever got.

To this day the "Heidi" game is one of the all-time lowlights or highlights of sports television. Since then, nobody has ever cut a game off.

— *Curt Gowdy*

BACK THEN, PRIME time in the East began at 7 p.m. NBC had spent tons of money hyping the movie. It looked like the Jets had the game locked. So NBC elected to cut away, because they wanted to get "Heidi" started on time. Who cared if they cut into the game? They wanted to beat ABC and CBS' prime time shows.

Afterward, I go down in the dressing room after the game — and everybody's heartbroken. We still don't know what happened. I was doing Jets' radio. I had no idea NBC had cut away. About this time, [coach] Weeb Ewbank's wife, Lucy, called him in the dressing room to congratulate him on winning titles in two leagues — the NFL [1958-59 Colts] and AFL. "It's great!" she said. Lucy hadn't switched to radio when NBC-TV pulled the plug. Weeb said, "What are you *talking* about? We lost." Lucy couldn't believe it. Neither could NBC. Even today, nobody remembers much about the game, but they know it involved "Heidi." What was the "Heidi" game? Well, that was the "Heidi" game.

— *Merle Harmon*

IT WOULD HAVE been fun the next morning to be at NFL headquarters in New York. They'd say, "How could they have done this? Look at all the phone calls, all the mail, that we're getting." I bet, though, that there was a point soon after when they said, "This really tells us something. We've got ourselves a monster sport that people really care about." They did, and people do.

— *Dick Enberg*

BIGGEST UPSET I ever broadcast in sports was the Jets beating the Colts in Super Bowl III. The Packers had won handily the first two Super Bowls. Just before game time, the Jets were 20-point underdogs. Baltimore won 15 games that year, and lost only once — and the Jets beat them. Go figure. Joe Namath bragged all week, "Don't take the points, bet on us. I'll guarantee the win." Before the game, Al DeRogatis predicted the Jets would win if they gained over 100 yards on the ground. Matt Snell gained over 100 himself [121], and they won, 16 to 7. At halftime the Jets are leading, 7 to 0, and I was up with Al in the booth. I said, "Al, we may really have something here." He says, "Curt, I told you." Great call — amazing game — biggest upset, by far.

— *Curt Gowdy*

IN 1969, THE Packers and the Steelers hooked up in a wild game at Pitt Stadium, which the Packers won, 38 to 34. I took a friend of mine up in the broadcast booth with me. After a Steeler touchdown, we were in a commercial break when he excused himself to go to the men's rom. While he was gone, the Packers regained the lead by returning the kickoff for a touchdown. Later in the game, the Packers were behind again and my friend —

Fred, let's call him — decided that he had to visit the men's room once more. Again, the Packers scored on a long punt return. When he returned, we started feeding him lots of coffee — just in case the Packers needed his strange powers again.

— *Ted Moore*

I'VE NEVER HAD a week like the week preceding Super Bowl IV. I'd been with the AFL since the start, and this would be the last championship game between the two leagues before they merged. That alone meant pressure. We're getting ready to play the Vikings when word breaks of a gambling investigation into seven pro football players who supposedly had a relationship with a gambler — and one of them was Len Dawson, our quarterback! Not a word was true. The reports were unfair, not only to the player, but to the person I knew. Very unfair, and cruel. Len barely slept a wink all week. We get down to New Orleans for the Super Bowl, and the night before the game Ed Sabol of NFL Films comes up. "I need a favor," he says. "What?" I say. He says, "Let me put a live mike on you." I couldn't believe it. "You don't think this has been a tough enough week? Why me?" Ed says, "[Vikings' coach] Bud Grant isn't that expressive. Second, I think the Chiefs have a chance to win. Even better, Hank, you don't use profanities." I said, "You're damn right I don't."

The next morning I went for a morning walk with a friend of mine who was a priest. You always need all the help you can get. Anyway, we won [23-7]. A key was moving our line so that tackle Buck Buchanan lined up across from their center, Mick Tingelhoff. Buck weighed about 280, Tingelhoff 235. That's the kind of matchup I liked. After the game, my wife and I and kids went out to hear Al Hirt, had dinner at Brennan's, and then went back to the hotel and saw the game again on television. It hadn't changed from the original. I still liked what I saw.

— *Hank Stram*

I MUST HAVE a thing for long games. In 1962, we played a six-quarter game in the AFL championship [page 67]. In 1971 comes the longest game in NFL history. Back then, the NFL rarely played games on Christmas Day. This broke tradition, and how. We were playing the Dolphins in a playoff game, and *what* a game. *It* lasted six quarters — over 82 minutes — and unlike '62, we lost [27-24]. You remember the people. On one hand, our Ed Podolak had 350 yards rushing, catching, and on kick returns. On the other, Jan Stenerud, the Chiefs' great field goal kicker, missed a chance to win for us in the last minute of regulation. For him, it was a breeze [32 yards]. We thought it was all over. I think everyone in the stadium, maybe including the Dolphins, thought it was over. Jan just didn't miss from there — except this time he did by inches. I couldn't believe it. I even raised my arms.

In overtime, Garo Yepremian kicked the field goal which beat us. For Christmas Day, we didn't feel much like celebrating.

— *Hank Stram*

I SHALL NEVER forget the 1972 playoff game between the Raiders and Steelers. The Immaculate Reception catch or no catch that Franco Harris made. I was doing NBC's pre- and post-game "Sperry-Rand Report." I watched the replay — we had three angles — and I must have watched it 40 times after the catch was called and I honestly couldn't tell from any view whether he caught the ball or not. After the game, Roy Hammerman, my NBC producer, and I went to the airport in Pittsburgh to the United Airlines lounge. We were having a little libation when in walks Raiders' coach Al Davis, dejected as you might think.

Al said to me, "Jay, was it a catch?" I said, "Al, I must have looked at it 40 times and I can't tell." We visited for awhile and then got on our planes. I got home late that evening and the phone rang early the next morning. My wife answered it and came into the bedroom and said, "Jay, Commissioner Rozelle is on the phone." I got on and said, "Good Morning." He said, "Can you tell me exactly what you told Al Davis yesterday afternoon in Pittsburgh?" I said, "The only time I visited with him was in the United lounge and he asked me if I thought it was a catch and I said, 'Al, I looked at it 35 or 40 times and I couldn't tell.'"

The Commissioner said, "Well, he has quoted you to all of the West Coast papers and it's now on the UPI and AP wires that you said it wasn't a catch." I said not true — I couldn't tell. Obviously, Davis took that to mean I didn't think it was a catch. I might have been in hot water except that thank goodness Hammerman was there to corroborate what I said. Whether Franco caught that ball or not, I'm not sure even Franco knows.
— *Jay Randolph*

A COUPLE SUPER Bowls stand out. The first one I hosted was in 1976 in Miami between the Steelers and Cowboys. We had lost power until about 10 seconds to air, and they were prepared to go with Lindsey Nelson hosting the show at a hotel position. Then someone found that a little AC plug was out of the wall, and they plugged it in and away we went. The other one stands out for a different reason — up in Detroit [San Francisco *v.* Cincinnati in 1982 at the Silverdome in Pontiac, Michigan]. The cold weather outside made it a surreal setting when you went under the bubble for the game. After the game, I had told off-camera personnel that when [President] Reagan came on the phone, I wanted to make sure there were no flacks in between so he could talk to Joe Montana. I could hear the director screaming to the White House over the phone: "I've got to have the president; we only want the president; give me the president." There was this pause, and this familiar voice said, "Young man, this *is* the president."
— *Brent Musburger*

POLITICIANS LOVE FIRSTS. How about the Patriot-Dolphins'

Snowplow Game — December 12, 1982, in Foxboro. This was a strike-shortened season, and the day typified the year — lousy, snow and wind, the artificial turf in awful shape. In the second half, John Smith kicked a 33-yard field goal to give the Pats a 3-0 victory. But Smith had a little help from a guy named Mark Henderson. Henderson came from the state prison and worked at the stadium on weekends. He was out of jail on work release, and was clearing snow from the field with this plow — actually, a big brush like the kind they clean the street with. Before Smith kicked, out comes Henderson to sweep the field exactly where the ball was to be placed! Made the kick easier — and Smith hit it through. I've talked to Don Shula, and he felt that [Patriots' coach] Ron Meyer bent the rules by having the field cleared. It's still maybe the most bitter defeat of his career. Later, the NFL reprimanded Meyer. Big deal. The Pats won.

After the game came the hullabaloo — people saying it was illegal for Henderson to sweep the snow. When Henderson's criminal release came out it was blown into a tremendous story. Blown is the proper word. I'm still shivering from the cold.

— *Jay Randolph*

PEOPLE ASK ME how I handled the pressure of big games. First off, you had to be a little mentally deranged. Maybe that's why I handled it well. That's never been a big problem for me. I remember coming down to the end of that [January 1982 AFC title] game with San Diego that put the Bengals in the Super Bowl. The fans were going crazy, throwing paper on the field, doing things like that. We were in the huddle and a sheet of newspaper blew right in with us. I decided I'd pick it up, tear it up, throw it around like the fans were throwing it around. But the sheet I picked up had a big picture of me on it, so I just passed it around and said, "Hey, guys, you ever seen a better looking fellow than that fellow pictured right there?" I can't tell you what they said.

— *Cris Collinsworth*

IT'S HARD TO replace a good quarterback in any franchise. It's even harder after Terry Bradshaw led the Steelers to four Super Bowls in the '70s. There was the expectation that I'd do the same. What I remember is not just that it didn't happen: I remember the year that gave false hope that it would.

In 1984, I'd had reconstructive knee surgery over the winter. There was doubt that I could come back. So the Steelers traded for David Woodley, who started, floundered, and was benched. I got the shot. We beat the 49ers at Candlestick — their only defeat while winning the Super Bowl. We won the Central, went to Denver in the playoffs and won a game no one thought we could, then went to the AFC title game in Miami and held our own for a half before Dan Marino shot out the lights.

All of a sudden, fans are saying, "Hey, this is the Steel Curtain all over again." But they forgot we only finished 9 and 7. We were overachievers who in talent weren't comparable to the '70s' teams, quarterback included! Come '85, and I had injuries, was up and down, and stayed that way the rest of my Steelers' career. Moral: If you're a fan, think with your head as well as your heart.

— Mark Malone

WHEN YOU TALK about memorable games, you darned near have them every week. That's what I like about broadcasting. Every week is different. One year, you do a game that doesn't look like much — the Carolina Panthers at San Francisco — and you think, geez, Sam Francisco is a defending Super Bowl champion. The Panthers are a new team. And the 49ers are going to blow them out because they're so good. Then, lo and behold, the Panthers beat the 49ers. You know, like wow, I didn't think that would happen. I think if I had to look back, the most fun year was 1985 and the Chicago Bears. The Bears were down for so long, and Chicago has great fans. Finally, it gave them a chance to say, "How 'bout them Bears." For so long they'd hear, "The Bears are no good." And the fans'd answer, "I know they're no good, but I'm a Bears' fan." So to see them win it all was fun. There was Jim McMahon and the Fridge [William "The Refrigerator" Perry] and Walter Payton and Richard Dent and Mike Singletary. Mike Ditka was the coach. They were playing those games in snow and cold weather. Soldier Field. The Bears for the championship. Dick Butkus standing on the sideline watching his old club.

If you don't love *that* football, you just don't like football.

— *John Madden*

NEVER HAD I heard the Bears' fight song played or sung in late January until 1986. There just hadn't been a reason to play or sing it at that time of the year. The Bears changed all that when they crushed the Patriots to win their first Super Bowl. They did it in the 70-degree warmth of the Louisiana Superdome and I couldn't help but remember that 11-degree day of December 29, 1963, when the Bears beat the Giants, 14-10, to grab their last NFL title in pre-Super Bowl days.

I got the feeling that somewhere up there George Halas was smiling as his grandson, Bears' president Michael McCaskey, raised the Super Bowl trophy ironically named in honor of Halas' old nemesis, Vince Lombardi. Mike Ditka was one of my favorites as a Bears' tight end, so I loved watching him coach what may have been the best football team ever. I was broadcasting the Bears when Ditka got $5,899 as his share of the '63 title money. He probably would like to be around if they ever have a Super Bowl where each winning player gets $100,000 and each losing player gets nothing. But don't ask me to referee it.

— *Jack Brickhouse*

THE GAME I remember best from my football years at NBC was the Broncos-Browns, January 2, 1987. This was for the AFC title, and we were live in Cleveland. It's already famous as The Drive — John Elway taking the Broncos 98 yards in the last four minutes to beat the Browns — an amazing performance. But it was football as it ought to be even before Elway went berserk. Our makeshift studio was right on the field. It's 10 degrees, snow flurries, the wind blowing off the lake. We did the pre-game show — already, it was overcast, I was wearing a parka, and yet it felt so perfect — this is *football*. Just before I went to commercial to turn it over to Dick Enberg for the play-by-play, I said, "Who needs domes? Who needs artificial turf? It's cold. It's dark. It feels right. And it's for the championship of the AFC. Next."

— *Bob Costas*

I'M ASKED WHAT I remember about my years watching or covering football. Lynn Swann's great catch in the Super Bowl [X] against Dallas. The Dolphins' perfect season [17-0 in 1972-73]. But the topper was The Drive. Ninety-eight yards. The last couple minutes. Cold and dark in Cleveland. Eighty thousand roaring to knock you down. I was there, and knew it was special at the time. It's historical today.

— *Jim Gray*

I'VE DONE FOOTBALL for CBS for 12 years, and I come back to the game where the unimaginable kept happening. Super Bowl XXIII. The 49ers beat the Bengals, 20-16. Montana takes 'em 92 yards in the last three minutes. Jerry Rice is the MVP [catching 11 throws for a Super Bowl-record 215 yards]. John Taylor grabs the winning pass with 34 seconds left.

Before the game I'm testing a wireless mike to make sure the antenna picks up our signal. What I don't know is that NFL Films has wirelesses on about 90 people — or that somehow they and CBS've been given the same frequency. When we turn on our mike, it blew NFL Films' signal off the channel. [Films' president] Steve Sabol's got a ton invested in this game — and now he can't even use his mikes. We both couldn't use the same frequency at once, so we decided that CBS'll only use our

wireless on the field until the players come out and are introduced — then it's the NFL's turn. Five to 10 minutes before
kickoff, I'm in the press box — Steve's using the frequency —
and our anchor, Brent Musburger, says to me, "Jim, I don't want
to alarm anybody. But I swear I just heard Sam Wyche giving
the Our Father."

Wyche was the Bengals' coach, NFL Films had miked him
giving the pre-game prayer, and we could hear every bit. None
of us knew what was going on. By now, *we* could have used a
prayer.

— *Jim Hunter*

THE INFAMOUS RIGHT doesn't refer to Pat Buchanan. It's
Scott Norwood's 47-yard field goal attempt that would have
won the 1991 Super Bowl. Instead, it drifted more right than it
should. The Bills earlier had dominated the game. The Giants
controlled the second half. Enter Norwood, who was asked to
answer a near-impossible prayer. I know that 47 yards is 47
yards — but football people say that when you kick on natural
grass it adds about five yards to the difficulty compared to artificial turf. I'll never forget looking down at the sideline and
seeing all the Bills' players, coaches, and staff holding hands as
if in prayer when the kick occurred. Afterward, I went into the
locker room for the post-game, and Norwood answered every
question. That's why I was so happy the next day as we got a
police escort from Rich Stadium to the steps of city hall in
Niagara Square. The square almost filled with people. The
people chanting for Scott Norwood. How close it was — but
how sweet it seemed.

— *Pete Weber*

ANOTHER SUPER BOWL XXIII pre-game story. Brent's up in
the booth and I'm down on the field, where, as usual, the NFL
is doing a spectacular pre-game show. As Brent throws it to
me, a guy is standing about three feet in back of me — Rocket

Man, who has an astronaut jetpack attached to him and who chooses this exact moment to blast into space. I'm the only guy in the stadium who didn't see him, but I certainly heard him — Rocket Man was so loud he drowned me out. Terrific. Brent now has to tell America why we were going to hear Jim Hunter and why we aren't. By this point, I'm five years older than when the pre-game started.

— *Jim Hunter*

REMEMBER THE NOTORIOUS drop by Ronnie Harmon in the end zone in the 1990 playoff game at Cleveland? It cost the Bills the game — the Browns won, 34-30 — but may have spurred them to later success. Success until each Super Bowl.

Four straight seasons — 1991 through '4. Four straight Super Bowl defeats. First, the Giants, 20-19. Then, Washington, 37-24, with Thurman Thomas forgetting his helmet — the one Super Bowl where the Bills lost their poise. Next, the Cowboys — turning nine turnovers into a 52-17 romp which would have been 59-17 had Leon Lett not showboated and Don Beebe streaked down the right side of your screen and stripped the ball away before Lett waltzed in with a fumble return. A year later, the Bills lead, Thomas fumbles, the Cowboys recover and go in to score.

To lose four straight Super Bowls you have to *make* them first. Likely, no team will do it again — especially in this era of the salary cap because balance can shift so quickly. I've broadcast all major sports, and working with football people is different. They only have one game a week. They live with losses for too long — and don't get to enjoy wins long enough. The problem is what the Bills have had to live with — losing the so-called ultimate game. Duane Thomas, interviewed by Tom Brookshier after losing a Super Bowl [V], said, "If this is the ultimate game, why do they play one again the next year?" Wait 'til next year, he was saying. Buffalo, take heart.

— *Pete Weber*

WE COME NOW to the Super Bowl XXIII post-game — amazing on its own. There are a couple minutes left, and it looks like the Bengals will win. [With 3:20 left, a 40-yard field goal gave Cincinnati a 16-13 lead]. The way it works is that you make a decision which locker rooms you're going to visit before the game ends — that way, you beat the players down there and get your cameras set up. Brent Musburger was going to the winners' locker room, and I the losers' — so with a couple minutes left he heads for the Bengals' room. I go to the 49ers'.

Then Mr. Montana begins his act. I should have known better. They score in the last minute; now, it's San Francisco who's about to win. So off Brent and I go — running, bumping into one another, shifting rooms before the game ends. The teams come in and begin the most dramatic Super Bowl post-game of all time. It was rumored this would be Bill Walsh's last game as 49ers' coach, but he didn't want to announce it yet. So when Brent asked him whether he was retiring, Walsh started to cry. Then they go to me, with Sam Wyche at my side, and *he* starts crying. Keeps saying, "34 seconds, 34 seconds" — all that kept him from winning. I'm thinking, "What do I do now?" He's still crying, so I led him into how he saw that last drive by Montana: "All we needed was one play, and we couldn't stop him." Walsh crying. Wyche crying. I'm almost crying. For crying out loud.

— Jim Hunter

I'M IRISH, SO it's apt that my greatest memories lie at Notre Dame Stadium. Both were in 1989 between Notre Dame and Southern California and both came in the tunnel the teams share when coming into and leaving the field. The first was at the end of pre-game warmups. The Notre Dame players were in front of the tunnel entrance, giving USC two options: Go around, or through, them. Notre Dame didn't let them through — at least, not easily — and a fight broke out. Even [coach] Lou Holtz was knocked to the ground. I was nearby with a cameraman, and as I reported the fight I said I thought Notre Dame had started it with its formation. They didn't like it, but so what? They were trying to psyche USC out — make your opponent tiptoe around you, block the path to his own locker room. At halftime, USC leads, 17-7. Both teams go through the tunnel to their locker rooms, and USC starts to mockingly sing the Notre Dame fight song. I heard this, and said on the air, "Not a real good idea by USC." I was right. Notre Dame comes back to win. Sometimes *you* can't win unless you remember that you're there to inform your audience.

— *John Dockery*

THE MOST MEMORABLE game I ever did was the [1992] week after Dennis Byrd was partially paralyzed, which got a great deal of national attention. The following week, the Jets, a very overmatched team, played in Buffalo — and they said they were dedicating the game to their teammate, Dennis Byrd, who was watching in the hospital. Paul Maguire and I did it, and the Jets somehow dramatically defeated the Bills in Buffalo [24-17]. You saw players crying on the sideline. You saw tears during the game. And you knew that Dennis was on their minds. It was a tough game to broadcast because I knew what was going on. Dennis was listening with his wife and family — and I wanted to make sure that I was saying the right things. Since then, Dennis has walked and come a very long way. Anyone who says that emotion isn't a big part of football ought to really think again.

— *Marv Albert*

I'VE DONE A lot of pro football, but it's a college game I remember. September 1992, at South Bend. Notre Dame had just tied Michigan, 17-all. Notre Dame had the last possession, but Lou Holtz called two running plays in the final minute. The home crowd booed Holtz for doing what mankind hates: playing for the tie. I fought my way down to Coach Holtz, and talk about pressure: NBC was paying Notre Dame $7.5 million a year to do its games. Maybe people expected cream-puff questions. No way. I had an obligation to the people at home. So I ask, "What was your thinking late in the game?" The question was balanced. It gave him breathing room. He said he'd run the ball because he was trying to learn Michigan's coverages. I didn't believe it, and said it looked like he was playing it close to the vest.

That set him off. He was enraged, said he was trying to win, it's easy to second guess, said, "Read my lips. I wanted to find out what the coverage was." Sarcastic, sure, but you can't let that throw you. I asked, "But couldn't you have found out the coverage as well by throwing the ball?" That did it. My guest left and he was livid. A couple days later, Coach Holtz called to apologize — not necessary, but nice. I think he'd agree: Fluff is for cakes, not football reporters.

— *John Dockery*

IN THE '93 wild card game between Houston and Buffalo I was working with Pat Haden — insightful, a Rhodes Scholar, a very bright guy. The game is already legendary. Bubba McDowall had just intercepted a pass two minutes into the third quarter to give Houston a 32-point lead. Recently, I listened to the tape and had to laugh: "Buffalo's down, 35-3," I'd said, "and nobody's leaving Rich Stadium. They're expecting a miracle." Pat replied, "They can expect a miracle all they want — this game is over." So much for prophecy. The Bills came back and won in overtime on a Steve Christie field goal. I remember Frank Reich, leading the way as a backup quarterback. Buffalo scoring touchdowns. The place rocking. The lead shrinking from 32 to 25 to 18 to 11. Then, a touchdown pass to Andre Reed. Pat saying, "Unbelievable," and saying it so emphatically I started to laugh. As I listen to the tape it's even funnier — although not to Houston! Just history being made — and knowing we were part.

— *Howard David*

SOMETIMES WHOLE YEARS are memorable — like 1994. I remember Ron Pitts, Buddy Ryan, and 8 to 5. My first game with Fox-TV was Ryan's first coaching the Cardinals. They lost, and got beat the next Sunday, 31-0, at Cleveland. A lousy start, and for Buddy it got worse. That year, I worked with Ron, former defensive back with Green Bay and Buffalo whose father, Elijah, played in the first two Super Bowls with the Packers. September comes and we go to Green Bay, where Ron had grown up. He comes out of the tunnel to the field which everyone always talks about — and people go nuts. After the game we almost missed our flight because Ron was signing so many autographs in the parking lot. We had to pull him into the car just to make the airport.

Later, Ron and I worked Atlanta at the Rams, and the score was 2 to 0 at halftime. The Rams add a field goal and it's 5 to 0 before the Falcons score a late touchdown plus a two-point conversion to lead with a couple minutes left. The next night I'm watching "Monday Night Football," and see a graphic that ours was the first 8-5 game in NFL history — the two-point conversion having been added that year. So far it's *still* the only 8-5 game. Not a bad year to have in your first year in the league.

— *Kenny Albert*

EVERY YEAR PRODUCES a Cinderella team. Look at the '95 Colts. What a wonderful story to be around [Coach] Ted Marchibroda. To see his team of non-quitters — led by the biggest non-quitter of all, Jim Harbaugh — knocked down, get up, pull off miracles right up to the last play in the AFC championship game [January 14, 1996, at Three Rivers Stadium, *v.* heavily favored Pittsburgh]. Harbaugh throws this Hail Mary pass in the end zone. It gets batted around and lands in the stomach of Aaron Bailey, who's lying on the ground. If Bailey holds it, the Colts win the upset of all time. Instead, they lose, 20 to 16. Sometimes you can't write the scripts, which is what separates the NFL from most prime-time TV. You never know the finish.

— *Howard David*

PEOPLE ASK ABOUT pro versus college football. A lot of the great games I've done are college. Cris [Collinsworth] and I did the Orange Bowl when Nebraska won its first title. Or that immortal '93 Notre Dame-Boston College game [B.C., 41-39]. I walked out thinking that football, not B.C., won. Having said that, college ball is more difficult to broadcast. More players to keep track of. They're unfamiliar, in school a short time. Pro football's got the athletes, great skill, the popularity. College has the enthusiasm and the history. I never go to South Bend without thinking of Knute Rockne. I think how he designed Notre Dame Stadium. He wanted it to be a downscale version of the University of Michigan — made a trip to Ann Arbor to see it for himself. He wanted seats up-close, the sidelines narrow to keep away hangers-on. The first time I went into the Notre Dame locker room, I got chills. College or pro? I like 'em both.

— *Tom Hammond*

I WORKED THE last game played by the Cleveland Browns. It was December 1995 — Cincinnati at Cleveland Stadium. It was common knowledge that Art Modell was moving the Browns to Baltimore. The team was leaving, and the fans were mutinous. I've seen the wave done before, but not until today did I see fans waving chairs, rails, and other metal. It was so bad that when the Bengals began driving toward the Dog Pound [disorderly/uproarious fans in the stadium's open end], the officials had the teams trade sides. They were worried about what the fans might do. Sure, the NFL has said Cleveland will get a new team. It'll be called the Browns — sort of a MacArthur, "We will return." But it will never be the same. The real Cleveland Browns died that day.

— *Randy Cross*

CHAPTER 12

OH, WHAT A NIGHT

MONDAY NIGHT FOOTBALL

For years, CBS and NBC aired the NFL on Sunday afternoon. In 1970, ABC became a new keeper of the flame. "Monday Night Football" forged pro football as the athletic Holy Land, the violent light that led — fusing prime-time pageant, a pastiche of darts and recollections, and made-for-TV narcissism.

"Monday Night" treated you like a guest — its beat garish and intoxicating. "You could be a casual fan, viewing Sunday as something to take or leave," said Frank Gifford, "and view Monday as command performance." It began in a time when events were called "happenings." It became a flagship and then institution — the landmark sports series of post-World War II America.

Today, Giff, Al Michaels, and Dan Dierdorf key the still-running hit. How to forget Dandy Don and Cosell, Howard later wrote, "as in Cosell"? One would no more try to reverse the sands of time.

IT'S APPLES AND oranges — "Monday Night" and other games. This was Monday night — entertainment — prime-time, baby — and those three guys kept 'em entertained. Most of the time

Howard and Don were going at it. Meredith would put him down, and Cosell would come back. The other guy's calling the play-by-play, and trying to survive. The three trained bears.
                                                                — *Curt Gowdy*

PETE ROZELLE HAD trouble trying to sell a Monday night football series. They had tried prime time TV football in the late 1960s. It really had not done very well. Pete went to CBS and NBC, and they had full schedules. So he approached Roone Arledge at ABC, which was getting a test pattern rating in prime time. They had nothing to lose. I was in on the ground floor, because Roone asked me to come over from CBS in that first year of 1970.

I couldn't do it. I was under contract. So I talked to Roone more as a fan than participant. Roone said he wanted a three-man booth, and asked me about Howard Cosell. I said, "Don't be ridiculous." Even then, Howard was self-caricature. It seemed ludicrous to even think of him on football. But Roone wanted an identity — football on ABC Monday night. Who better than a guy you loved or irritated you to the point that you wanted to kill him? He knew that Howard would generate media interest. I don't think he realized that there would be the chemistry between Howard and the guy I suggested, Don Meredith. If he did, he's even more of a genius than I think he is.

Middle America loved it instantly. Here was this arrogant New Yorker, with his "I'm more intelligent than you are" delivery that Meredith could just puncture a hole in. All he'd say was, "Aw, come on, Howard" — and America would say, "Did you hear what Don said?" Actually, Don said nothing other than what everyone wanted to say. Howard thought ex-athletes in the booth were ridiculous. I think he would have liked to be the host, the play-by-play announcer, and to have played the game. I often felt more like a resident psychiatrist than a play-by-play man. Don and Howard had their dialogue, and tried to include me in it — while I was busy trying to maintain a sense of sanity.

It was a rebellious age. When "Monday Night Football" started, some of what we did on the air reflected that. It was a rebellious announcing group. Howard pontificating on the rights of this, or that. Using it as a social forum for his social sermons — and he had a lot of them, whether or not they pertained to the game. Fitting, really. A lot of "Monday Night"'s furor had little to do with what happened on the field.

— Frank Gifford

PEOPLE WONDER WHY I left "Monday Night" [in 1974]. The Humble Howard and Dandy Don routine was something like — well, it was a routine. After four years we'd gotten to the point where if Howard said something, people would expect me to say something else. It was like two stand-up comics — you can anticipate what the other one is going to say. Anyway, I never felt I was Danderoo.

— Don Meredith

I'M CONSTANTLY ASKED about the greatest game ever on "Monday Night Football." As I think back over the plus-400 games I've done on Monday night, and throw in others that we used to do on Thursday and Friday and Sunday nights, one stands out — Houston's 35-30 win over Miami in 1978. Earl Campbell had 200 yards rushing [199]. Bob Griese must have thrown for 350 yards [349]. It was back and forth. The night, also, that on our show the song, "Love You Blue," was born.

The rest is a collage. The night Joe Theismann broke his leg in Washington [November 19, 1985]. The great [1994] game between Kansas City and the Broncos. In the twilight of his career, Joe was Joe and Joe was fabulous — speaking of the one and only Montana. A patented last-second drive, time running out, he throws a touchdown pass, and on the last play wins the game [31-28].

Incredible things, and not always in the booth. John Lennon died on a Monday night on December 8, 1980. We were in Miami, and got the news from New York. Howard loved obituaries. He couldn't wait to go with the story — but I wouldn't let him, because I couldn't believe that what had happened, happened. Finally, we broke the news that Lennon had been murdered. Just another thing that I will always link with "Monday Night."

— *Frank Gifford*

I'M PROBABLY IDENTIFIED with "Monday Night Football" — but to this day what's mentioned most to me is the United States hockey team's Gold Medal in the 1980 Winter Olympics. [Upon the Wonder of Lake Placid, Michaels said: "Do you believe in miracles? *Yes!*"] You didn't have to like hockey, or even follow the Olympics all that closely. The game transcended sport.

For one thing, the country needed a boost. Hostages were being held in Iran, inflation was rampant, the prime rate 20 percent, the Cold War at its coldest. And here we were opposing the world's best hockey team — really, professionals. The Soviets had beaten the NHL All-Stars the prior year, and now were meeting our amateurs — a bunch of kids out of college and minor-league rejects who beat the best hockey team in the world, and did it in America — unforgettable, and never to be duplicated.

This was before cable television and *USA Today*. We're in Lake Placid, New York, which might as well be Siberia. We don't have local TV — just a grainy picture from Albany, some weak radio stations, and two-day late papers. These kids stage the most incredible sports upset in history and have no idea what they'd done. It took several days to get out of Lake Placid and find that they'd taken the spirits of two hundred million Americans and sent them soaring at a time when the U.S. was near despair. I can't imagine anything that could come close.

Saying that, each Monday night we try.

— *Al Michaels*

IN 1984, GIFFORD, Meredith, and O.J. [Simpson] did "Monday Night." We were in the Orange Bowl in mid-season. The booth there is pygmy — and if you're five-six, you had to bend over and somehow truncate yourself to even get in. I remember Giff and Meredith struggle mightily to bend their knees. Both were in severe pain — as players, the game really tears you up. I made the observation, "I guess middle-age bodies aren't made to play football at this level." Meredith made an acute reply, born of sad experience, that showed why he was great: "The *human* body," he said, "isn't meant to play football at *any* level."

— *Jim Lampley*

"MONDAY NIGHT" IS a different breed. For one thing, half-time usually comes at your bedtime. You're used to going to sleep, and you've got to play another 30 minutes. Your rhythms get mixed up, but it's worth it — you're on center stage. One Monday night we go to the Astrodome. The Bengals usually didn't have much luck there — but this Monday it's close. At halftime, the offensive and defensive teams huddle by themselves, then come together just before the second half. Our offensive team is to one side of the locker room when all of a sudden we hear Hank Bullough, the defensive coordinator, screaming up a storm. We found the reason when we got back together. A rookie defensive player had put himself in the front row, listening to Bullough, and proceeded to fall asleep — out *cold, asleep,* at *halftime,* on *"Monday Night Football"*! Forget that it wasn't too smart to be in the front row as you're sleeping. Worse is the unbelievability. We had enough adrenaline to fill a balloon, and this guy's asleep. It takes all kinds — but maybe not *his* kind.

— *Anthony Muñoz*

THE BEAUTY OF "Monday Night" is that it's one of the few things on TV that is live. "Monday Night" is also prime-time. It's under the lights, a surreal atmosphere to begin with. Even if you're not a football fan, you know the history of "Monday

Night." Lennon's death made me remember another night in California — we were doing the Rams — when Lennon was there with the future President of the United States, Ronald Reagan. They were going to be our halftime guests, and Reagan had his arm around Lennon, looking down on the football field, explaining the game to this guy who didn't have a clue. Lennon was there trying to sell a record — Reagan, because he liked football. Here were two people, totally apart in every way possible, brought together. Things happen on "Monday Night" — not always with the game.

— *Frank Gifford*

O. J. HAD BEEN retired from football for, maybe, five seasons when he and I did an '84 game in New Orleans. By this point Frank and Meredith were room service-types. After the game, they'd go back to the hotel. But Juicy and I were still young enough to make the circuit — so we got into a stretch limo and off we went for the bars. We got caught in traffic on Bourbon Street and then somebody recognizes O.J. They start rocking the car — I through they were going to turn it over. We had thirty guys with their hands on the car. Finally, we gave up and came out, and O.J. spent 45 minutes signing autographs. I can't think of any player with that kind of impact — especially a *retired* player. I've often thought back on that night — what a fishbowl he lived in, and at what cost.

— *Jim Lampley*

ON "MONDAY NIGHT," we have designated responsibilities, but part of the reason for the success of the meld is that we aren't totally defined by those responsibilities. I'm not confined to, "Second-and-six, Smith runs for three; third-and-three." I can offer analysis, prod, say things to provide jumping-off points. On the other side, once my colleagues are talking, unless it's such a critical play that I have to jump in to give the call, they're free to finish their thought even if they run over into the next play. There's by-play, a conversational approach. But you can't take it too far. There has to be some structure and discipline. A line must be drawn. But it's almost innate, a feel. There's a rhythm, a beat to it that plays out like a song. Sure, you'll hit a few bad notes over the course of a game, but we're judged by the whole — how we were over three hours.

— *Al Michaels*

THE CHIEFS WERE pretty bad in the years after I started broadcasting in '85. Then, Marty Schottenheimer took over. They got good, sold out, fans started the tomahawk chop. Which brings us to "Monday Night Football." You're not on "Monday" if you're awful — so the Chiefs had been absent about eight, nine years until they played Buffalo at Arrowhead in 1991. They won, 33-6, but I remember a call, not the score.

The Chiefs scored on a long play and I said, "He's in for a touchdown" — then, dragging it out, "Oh, baby, what a play!" We used it on the highlight show, but I didn't think about it until we're driving home. I'm listening to a call-in show and a caller asks if he can say something. The host says yes, and the caller backed by a chorus of drunks says — all together now — "Oh, baby, what a play!" Pretty soon merchants start printing T-shirts, "Oh, baby, what a play." The Chiefs begin putting it on the scoreboard. Advertisers start using it. A car dealership runs ads, "Oh, baby, what a sale!" I enjoyed it, of course. I guess "Monday Night" brings out the ham in broadcasters, too.

— *Kevin Harlan*

HAVING DONE "Monday Night" for more than 25 years, never missing a game, and playing another 12 years with the Giants, I feel an importance to the National Football League, the players, and ABC. "Monday Night" gives ABC one night of prime time that we don't have to program to win. We've been in the top ten for many years among all prime-time shows. More importantly, it's a special night. The players who play that game will tell you that. When I arrive at the stadium a couple of hours before the game, we do the tease — Hank Williams, Jr. is fed into it — we talk to the players and coaches, and we soak up the moment. Anywhere between forty and sixty million people. Under the lights, all live. If you're blasé about this, you've got a problem.

— *Frank Gifford*

IN 1987, I DID CBS play-by-play. Kenny Stabler was extremely anxious to get started as an analyst. Terry O'Neill, our executive producer, hired the Snake as my analyst — interesting, since Terry grew up in western Pennsylvania, was a big Steelers' fan, and Stabler had such classic games against them with Oakland. Terry's concerns were: a) would anybody understand Kenny's Southern drawl, and b) could he be trained — that is, clean up his personal life. He had this reputation of studying a game in a bar by a jukebox. Kenny tells them he'll fly right.

Believe it or not, our first game's at Pittsburgh. We're at the Greentree Marriott, which has a reputation as an active bar. We go down for a drink and Kenny is talking with a bunch of Steelers' fans, taking flak and having fun. We're having a good, harmless time when a Steelers' fan walks up and hits Kenny across the side of his head with a full bottle of beer. Huge gash — blood flowing — our producer, Mark Wolfe, takes him to the hospital. Kenny is totally innocent, but we can see the headlines in next morning's paper: "Stabler Hurt In Bar Fight."

All night we stay up for damage control — keep it quiet. We know that if word gets out, it's the end of Kenny's broadcast career. Next day, we do the game and he has a giant black bruise and gauze on the gash — 16 stiches. Wolfe shoots Kenny in full profile so you never see the cut. New York asks him why, he makes something up, and nobody was the wiser — till now.

— *Jim Lampley*

AFTER A GAME, Al, Dan, and I leave together, usually just the three of us in a limo. We'll have a beer and talk to unwind. As many games as I've done, there's still an elation, the kind you feel after a performance. Sometimes it's special. With or without articulating it, we know when we've done absolutely the best job we could have done and that honestly, no one could have done it better. It's the same feeling — minus the bumps and bruises — I used to have after we'd won a big game. Everything I'd prepared for, everything I'd worked so damned hard to do, had happened.

— *Frank Gifford*

A THREE-MAN booth is most difficult in a highly competitive game because everyone wants to say something. There are times between plays when Al wants to add something but feels crowded because he knows Frank and I will be staring at him, wondering what the hell he's doing. On the other side of the coin, when a game goes south the three-man booth is a real plus. It affords us a much better opportunity to go into what some would call our entertainment mode. We can talk about other subjects, other ideas, whatever, to try to hold our audience. That's what we're paid to do — and three in the booth is key.

— *Dan Dierdorf*

IN THE EARLY days, there was some criticism about Monday night, because if you go back that far you'll remember that used to be P.T.A. night. It's no longer P.T.A. night. They moved it to another night. We still get letters from people who have Monday night parties. Down in Nashville, a group goes to a farm, sets up camp, gets a generator, and has a party each Monday night. It's the night reserved by a lot of people to stay home — male and, yes, female. We like to remind viewers and sponsors that we've got a high percentage of women in our audience. Because I think it's a good night — the wife or the girlfriend, heck, they know that the old guy is sitting there with them watching television, and if you sit back and listen, you might enjoy, too.

— *Frank Gifford*

ONCE, WE WERE getting ready for our publicity pictures. Gifford says, "Three blind mice." Howard says something about, "Hurry up. I've already blown my lunch with the Olympic boxers." I smile into the camera. "It's amazing what happens in America."

— *Don Meredith*

CHAPTER 13

PASTURES OF PLENTY

OFFENSE

Imagine that Johnny Carson is hosting "The Tonight Show." Ed McMahon says, "Bronko Nagurski. Sammy Baugh. Emmitt Smith. Jerry Rice." Carson, as Carnak, answers, "Who are men that caught, threw, or ran the ball?" However you may like to see linebackers crush heads, there is no trick to note that offense has reaped the headlines of the NFL's first 70-something years.

If you like scoring, the names alone spawn existential pleasure. Grange. Hutson. Unitas. Elway. Like a baby, pro football learned to walk, run, and finally pass. Single-wing. Shotgun. T-formation. Today, the West Coast offense. If defense was crucial to winning a title, offense keyed the NFL's becoming the apple of the electronic eye.

Before 1933, the passer had to be at least five yards behind the line of scrimmage to throw a forward pass. That year, the owners approved rule changes — among them, moving the goal posts, changing hash marks, and deeming passes legal if they originated *anywhere* behind the line. "We hoped the new rules would open up the game," said Papa Bear. "The record shows that we were right." Below, Voices recall how right George Halas was.

FRANK GIFFORD WAS the first leading man, so to speak, in the National Football League. He came out of Southern California, an All-American and number one draft pick, and played two ways that first year — defensive safety man and offensive halfback for the Giants. He was handsome as a movie star — a football player who was everything that every mother and father wanted for their son. Intelligent, great athlete, nice guy. Although he was not the spokesman for the National Football League, in effect he was.

— *Marty Glickman*

PEOPLE TALK ABOUT great quarterbacks like Unitas, Namath, and Marino. In my book, Number One was Otto Graham. In college, he was a single wing tailback — ran as well as threw. He played on the Northwestern baseball team and later for Rochester in the NBA. He was a great golfer, but his love was football. Otto played in the All-America Football Conference from '46 through '49. The Browns went into the NFL and he won there from 1950 through '55. In 10 seasons, each time his team was in the title game. The defense would say, "Let's get that ball back because Otto will think of something." He could throw long and feathery or short and hard — whatever was necessary. He ran the quarterback draw as well as anybody and he wasn't all that fast — just a step faster than the guy trying to tackle him. If the bottom line is winning, Otto is the best of all time.

— *Ken Coleman*

NORM VAN BROCKLIN was a great quarterback. He was also a little volatile. I've heard a story attributed to Van Brocklin and I'm not sure it's total fact, but here is how it goes. Norm's daughter came home from college for the Christmas holidays, anxious for the family to meet her fiancé. Norm was delighted to see her, and hugged his daughter and held her in the air, then put her down so she could greet her mother. Then, Van Brocklin looked in the doorway. There stood a young man whose appearance turned Van Brocklin off because he had hair that hung down to the middle of his back. "Young man, go get a haircut," said Norm, and shut the door. A half-hour later the fiancé came back. Mother and daughter were still furious about his abrupt dismissal — but guess what? The kid had gotten a haircut. Van Brocklin started beaming, and placed his hands under the visitor's armpits and carried him across the threshold. "Young man," he is alleged to have said, "you're going to be all right."

— *Chuck Thompson*

I BELIEVE THAT I'm the only person to see every [1957-65] game that Jim Brown played for the Browns. He played hurt sometimes. The only time that I remember him being out of a game was once in New York when he had a concussion, and came back and played the second half. Naturally, you remember the long runs. But what stands out is what he'd do with five minutes left, the Browns up by seven, have the ball, and Brown runs out the clock. He'd go four, then six, 14. Eighty thousand-plus in Cleveland Stadium knew he'd get it. So did the men on the other side of the line. I'm not trying to demean the achievements of people like Walter Payton and Gale Sayers. It's just that Jim was special. He weighed 228 pounds, but had a 32-inch waist. We had two world class sprinters — Bobby Mitchell and Ray Renfro — who did the hundred in 9.8, 9.9, and Brown could stay with them. Paul Brown never ran the three of them in the 40-yard dash because he said, "They'll kill themselves to win it, and I don't want any hamstring pulls." It was amazing. They talk about best this, best that. Jim Brown was the best, period.

— *Ken Coleman*

JOHN BRODIE CAME up with great lines. When Dick Nolan was coaching, he wanted Steve Spurrier to play quarterback. So Brodie got pushed into the background, and didn't play too much. Detroit is killing the 49ers at Kezar Stadium, 30-0, about

two minutes left to play. John hasn't played a down. Nolan
tells John to go into the game. Brodie said, "What do you want
me to do — go for the win, or the tie?"

— Lon Simmons

JOHN UNITAS WAS the greatest quarterback of all time. Many
years after he retired, he and I appeared at a fundraiser for The
Cystic Fibrosis Foundation. It was there that I got a look into
what made Unitas tick. John and I were drinking a beer and
yacking about our golf game when a guy came up and interrupted our conversation. He said, "Unitas, I've hated your
guts all my life." John looked at me and I shrugged my shoulders and said, "I don't know who he is." So John turned back
and looked at the guy, and he said, "In 1958, I was 10 years old
and you broke my heart." He was referring, of course, to the
Colts' victory over the Giants in the sudden-death championship game. John looked at me and I could see the grin starting.
He turned back to the gentleman and said, "Believe me, sir, it
was my pleasure."

— Chuck Thompson

BROWN WAS ONE of those people that when you met him in
his civilian clothes, he didn't look that big. But when he started
taking the shirt off, he was all muscle. I don't know if he even
had to work that hard at it — no weight lifting or anything. But
he never had a down game. And I think everybody remembers
how he would get up after being hit, and amble back to the
huddle like he was not going to make another move again.
Nothing seemed to ruffle him. He didn't get mad, but even.
One Sunday the Browns beat the Giants, and afterward Jim's
face around his eyes was all puffy. Later, when we got together
to tape his weekly TV show, I asked, "Jim, I couldn't get over
how you looked — what's going on?" He said, "When we got
down into the dirt part of the infield, some of the Giant linemen
threw dirt into my eyes. They wanted to get me mad enough to

get in a fight and get thrown out of a game, but I wouldn't go for it." Then he looked at me. "I'll tell ya' one thing. If it ever happens again, I'm going to kill 'em — a one-time shot. Never again will anybody go after my eyes." Maybe the Giants were listening. No one ever did.

— *Ken Coleman*

I STILL REMEMBER a downtrodden Jack Kemp being waived by the Chargers for $100 in the early '60s [1962]. The Bills claimed him — they needed a quarterback — but Jack didn't want to come here. He's a great skier, and hoped that Denver would claim him. Instead, he winds up in Buffalo, disconsolate. So what happens? Buffalo gives him two AFL titles [1964 and '65] and, when he retired, a ticket into politics. He winds up being a U.S. Congressman from Buffalo. That leads to the vice-presidential nomination in '96 and, who knows, maybe the presidency itself some day. Not a bad reward for coming to Buffalo. Even if its skiing's not Vail's.

— *Van Miller*

PROFESSIONAL ATHLETES react in different ways to winning and losing. Unitas was a man who never took the game home. Once the game ended, if he lost he didn't want to think or talk about it. Just go to work on the game ahead. One year, the Colts played the Rams late in the year. If they didn't win, they'd miss the playoffs. They didn't win and I'm in the clubhouse after the game, staring at my shoes. I didn't want to make eye contact with the players — let's face it, they're hurting. So I'm leaning against the wall with my head down when John walked by, reached over, and with his finger underneath my nose picked my head up and made me look straight at him. He never said a word — just looked at me and then walked to the shower. It was classic Unitas. Game's over. You can't win it now. Let's win the next one. Usually, he did.

— *Chuck Thompson*

JIM BROWN AND I owned what I would politely call a bil-
liards parlor in Kent, Ohio, with several other Browns' players
like Dick Schafrath, Gary Collins, and Gene Hickerson. I once
had the chance to play the legendary Minnesota Fats, who was
the character that Jackie Gleason played in the movie "The Hus-
tler." Fats was nowhere near as good as Willie Mosconi. For
the opening of our parlor Willie came down for an exhibition. I
happen to be a pretty good pool player, so I played him in 150-
point straight pool. I like to say I came in second. By a wide
margin. We practiced at separate tables and obviously Willie
had been watching because instead of lagging for the break, he
said, "I'll break" — which he'd never do if he was playing a
professional.

He broke and sank the front ball in the triangle in the side
pocket, sank four more balls and then — believe it or not — the
man who once ran over 500 balls, missed. I ran off the rest of the
table and the announcer said, "At the end of the first rack, Mr.
Coleman 9, Mr. Mosconi 5." Sadly, before we finished Mosconi
ran up streaks of 89 and 149 balls. Jim was there. For our TV
show we taped highlights, and Willie asked Jim to do a trick shot
where you put a handkerchief over balls in different locations
and then hit the object ball as the rest go flying into pockets.

Jim is stoic, but he'd never played pool. So he couldn't get
over it when he hit the ball as instructed by Mosconi and they
all flew into pockets. Later, he told me, "You know, when you're
a professional athlete everybody thinks you do everything well.
I don't know how to shoot pool but that was a thrill." I recall,
too, what he said about our TV show. "When I started, I'd rather
be looking at the front four of the Rams than that red eye in that
camera." That's the thing about the truly great. Deep down
they know what they can do — and what they can't.

— *Ken Coleman*

LEAVING THE HUDDLE, Brodie always walked with his head
down to the line of scrimmage. Dick Nolan was always after

him to keep his head up. We're playing the Jets, and John goes back, throws a pass that goes through the receiver's hands, and gets intercepted. Brodie comes over to the sidelines and looks at offensive coach Jim Shofner. "Well," he says, "at least I kept my head up."

— *Lon Simmons*

COOKIE GILCHRIST WAS a flamboyant bruiser, about 6-foot-2, 243 pounds, whom the Bills got from the Canadian Football League in '62. Paul Brown tried to get him for Cleveland — can you imagine Cookie and Jim Brown in the same backfield? — but [Coach] Lou Saban beat Paul to the punch and Gilchrist came here. People remember him in the backfield. I remember how he also kicked off. One day he 'bout took three blockers to the hospital on a return. Once Cookie had a promotion at War Memorial Stadium. He bought 3,000 pairs of earmuffs and tried to sell 'em. The problem is that it was 57 degrees. He was a worse poker player than businessman. In those days we traveled in DC7s — and it took forever to get places. So we had seven-card stud games that lasted an eternity, and Cookie'd never drop out. We'd leave Buffalo for the Coast. By the time we hit Chicago, he was already short. You'd lend him money. If it had just been colder for that earmuff promotion.

— *Van Miller*

JOE NAMATH CAME to join the Jets in 1965, and it became a circus. Especially after he made his guarantee that the Jets would win Super Bowl III, he was bigger than life. We'd go into a city and the mobs were just unbelievable. You could hardly get through the hotel lobbies. They had to have security people on the floor the Jets were on to keep people off the elevators trying to get up to see and touch him. Once, the Jets played Minnesota in an exhibition game in Winston-Salem, North Carolina. And they had the police form a line, lock hands, just to get Joe from the dressing room to the team bus. They called Namath an anti-hero. Tell that to his teammates.

— Merle Harmon

RAYMOND BERRY, THE Colts' Hall of Fame wide receiver, was one of the greatest students of pro football I have ever met. Raymond was the first player I saw who used netting under the goalposts as he practiced catching passes. This way, inaccurate or misjudged passes wouldn't get away — and time wouldn't be wasted chasing them. No one spent more time looking at film than Raymond. People don't know this, but he had a good sense of humor. He didn't show it often, but it surfaced once when I heard that Raymond was getting married. I asked if his future bride was a football fan. "I don't know," he said, keeping things in perspective, "but she can run a projector."

— Chuck Thompson

WE WERE AT a banquet one night, and someone asked Brodie why, with all the money he made, the 49ers had him holding the ball for extra points. He said, "If I didn't, it'd fall over."

— Lon Simmons

I'LL NEVER FORGET my arrival at the hotel where the Jets were staying before Super Bowl III. I got out of the cab and was greeted by Earl Christy, a defensive back and special teamer. "Merle," he said, grabbing me, "did you hear what Joe said? Joe said we're going to beat the Colts! We're going to win the Super Bowl!" I said, "Earl, the game's a week away!" — but that's how it was. The Jets were that confident. We'd seen films of the recent NFL title game [Colts 34, Browns 0] and felt that if Cleveland had tried to run, they'd have won. But they didn't: The Colts had this reputation that you'd better not run on them. The Jets ran in the Super Bowl — and that decided the game.

Namath said, "I shouldn't be the most valuable player. Matt Snell should." He gained something like 121 yards, running left, on Baltimore's vulnerable side. Looking at the Browns' film, Pete Lammons, our tight end, said, "Coach, don't show us any more film. We're going to be overconfident." They felt they could beat the Colts on ability — and when Joe made that statement, they thought they'd better back him up.

As we were leaving the hotel to go to the Super Bowl, we were told not to check out of the hotel. We're coming back for the victory celebration. I always wondered if that were really true, or just a way Jets' management could tell the players, "Hey, we believe in you. You are going to win the Super Bowl." Whatever, they did, and we went back to the hotel.

— *Merle Harmon*

ALEX HAWKINS WAS the captain of the Colts' special team, but that's not what people remember. He was also one of the team's most delightful personalities. The Hawk was a great player who, shall we say, was not exactly a stickler for rules — even in college. Marvin Bass was his coach at the University of South Carolina, and he told me that one day a thunderstorm happened and the players ran for the locker room as lightning began to flash. Everybody, that is, except Alex. When teammates yelled for him to hurry and join the others in the safety of cover, Alex reassured them: "Don't worry, it's *me* He's after."

— *Chuck Thompson*

MOST CLUBS ARE lucky to get one great runner. The Bears had two. Thirteen years with the Bears. Twenty-eight Bear records and nine National Football League records. That's nice, but what I loved about Walter Payton was his second and third and fourth effort. His predecessor was Gale Sayers, who in 1968 was nailed by Kermit Alexander in a San Francisco game and his knee was wrecked — not deliberately, just one of those things. He had to have it operated on and was never the same again — not the Sayers who was the greatest broken-field runner ever. The next year, he came back and wanted to get his 1,000 yards rushing, like before his injury — and amazingly, he got it — not with speed, but heart between the tackles. What does this say? Gale's longest run after his injury was 28 yards. And this? The Bears that year went 1-13. For him to get 1,000 yards — four here, five there, his knee always hurting — says all you need to know. So does this: Sayers played only five full years — seven, in all — and still made the Hall of Fame.

— *Jack Brickhouse*

WAYNE WALKER WAS a great linebacker for Detroit. The 49ers are playing them, and Gary Lewis was supposed to be blocking him. The problem is, he wasn't, and Brodie spends most of the afternoon on the ground. So John goes up and grabs Gary and walks him over to Wayne Walker. He says, "Here he is — here's Number 55 — meet the guy you're supposed to be blocking."

— *Lon Simmons*

ROGER STAUBACH WAS a combination of Navy Lieutenant and Captain America. Family man, did his duty in Viet Nam, his image was so positive. What made it amazing was that the Cowboys of his '70s had a lot of the same problems as today — girls and drugs. But you didn't think of that. First, you didn't have the "SportsCenter" reporting of the 1990s. Second, when you mentioned Dallas you thought of this convergence of dignity, All-America, and war hero. Dallas was still enduring the scars of the Kennedy assassination when Roger arrived. He changed that, gave Dallas a reason to thump out its chest. Sportscasters aren't supposed to have heroes. With Roger I plead the Fifth.

— *Verne Lundquist*

A COUPLE OF observations on the position I once played. The offensive lineman is the lowest you can get on the food chain, higher in football only than the guy who hands out jocks. Where does he come from? If you have a little kid who likes to be ignored, who doesn't mind when you hit him, doesn't mind being alone and likes to read, then you have the makings of an offensive lineman.

— *Randy Cross*

FOR ME, FOOTBALL started with family outings to see Paul Hornung en route to the [1956] Heisman Trophy. My father went to Notre Dame. So did my brother. The first game I ever broadcast for the the student station at Notre Dame was Texas Christian University in the fall of 1972. Little did I know that four years later I'd be covering professional football on a regular basis in Buffalo. I'll never forget how accommodating O.J. Simpson was. Inevitably, he would take care of reporters' needs whether it be written quotes or quotes on tape. It's something I will never forget. I say that knowing he's kind of been in the news for other reasons nowadays.

— *Pete Weber*

YOU LEARN A lot from your parents. My dad taught me to play chess and poker and taught me to win. Today, I spend more time at poker. It's tough paying the rent playing chess. My mom taught humility. When I was in the third grade, I outran everybody in the class and won a medal. When I came home, I told mom what a fast dude I was. She said, "Don't brag." I said, "But it's true." She said, "Come with me," and took me outside the house and had dad pace off a 50-yard strip. I was laughing, "C'mon, mom, get serious." She beat me three straight. I swear. You don't mess around with mom.

— *Cris Collinsworth*

I GOT MY START broadcasting at WEEZ radio in Chester, Pennsylvania, a 5,000-watt station, and was able to sign up Widener College to broadcast their football games. At that time, one of their running backs was Billy Johnson. It seemed like he'd score five or 10 touchdowns a game and would grab a punt, start to his right, head back to his left, find a way to keep on going, get to the sideline and sprint 70 or 80 yards to score. Of all the football I've done, it's Johnson at Widener that I remember.

I left to go to Hawaii and after Johnson finished his senior year at Widener and was a small college All-American, I suggested to the director of the Hula Bowl that he select him. I said, "Johnson is the most incredible football player I've ever seen. I know he went to a small school and you usually pick from the football schools, but I think you should make an exception." He told me that the smallest school they'd taken someone from was Rutgers. They wanted to stick with the big names and schools so they didn't take him. Soon after, the World Football League started a team — the Hawaiians. I did their play-by-play and suggested that they draft Johnson. They were a little smarter and drafted him pretty low. He was also drafted by the Oilers and went on to have a great career in the NFL where he picked up the nickname "White Shoes." I should have been his agent.

— *Mel Proctor*

WHEN I CAME to Cincinnati I once raced against a horse. It had something like 120 losses and three wins. I was one of the three. It was a 50-yard race, and they wanted to take a picture of the finish. But the horse beat me by 47 yards. You couldn't have got me in the picture with a wide angle lens.

— *Cris Collinsworth*

SOMETIMES YOU DON'T know how confident and cocky a guy is until you see him in his element. Bo Jackson was a senior at Auburn, and I was working at a Mobile station. At the end of practice, players had to run through cones, sprint thirty yards, then run through more cones. Bo was the anchor man on his unit, and when the runner handed off he was trailing the other team by half a football field. No sweat — Bo was laughing, like no way anyone can beat him. By the time he finished his run *he* was leading by half a football field — and the amazing thing was I got the impression he wasn't putting out! Two things hit home. First, how incredibly fast he was. Second, what fun he had — and that he didn't know defeat. The best way to spur him was to say he couldn't do something. I see him now, and he's bitter, distant. I think he knows what I do — if he hadn't hurt his hip, we'd be calling Bo Jackson the best running back of all time.

— Eric Clemons

I STILL REMEMBER the first day I reported to camp. I saw Kenny Anderson and Ross Browner and Pete Johnson, guys like that. And I said to myself, "Man, if those guys were 6 and 10 last year, I don't think I want to see the Pittsburgh Steelers. Maybe I just better hike this skinny body of mine back to Florida and pick oranges the rest of my life."

— Cris Collinsworth

WHEN STEVE SPURRIER came to the 49ers, we used to have an annual event — our first pre-season game was against the Rams in the Coliseum. Rookie quarterback, going to be nervous, right? Spurrier was supposed to play the second half. We come back from halftime, and I remember my color commentator saying, "Spurrier will be warming up — this is it, big chance, the second half." I looked down and there he is. He isn't playing catch, not warming up. Some nervous. He's spinning the football on his fingers.

— Lon Simmons

I ALSO REMEMBER the day I got in the shower room with the veterans for the first time. Degrading. Insulting. Catcalls. Somebody said, "What the hell's going on? How come one of the trainers is being allowed to take a shower with us?" I mean, it was awful.

— Cris Collinsworth

IT'S 1993. LEN DAWSON and I are doing Chiefs' radio in Miami as Joe Montana gets knocked out and goes to the locker room. K.C.'s getting killed. During a break, Len and I are talking about how lousy they look. We don't know poor Montana is lying on a stretcher in the locker room listening to our live, raw feed. We're not on the air — fans at home can't hear us — but we have wires in the locker room for the post-game and Joe hears us talking and *thinks* we're on. So on our flight home, he goes to Carl Peterson, Chiefs' president, and says, "What's going on? Even our broadcasters on the air are belittling us." It caused a big stink. We had a summit meeting with Peterson, who agreed with us — we'd sucked — and told Joe nothing that we'd said was heard by the fans at home. Ultimately, Joe and I became good friends. He'd see me and my wife at a restaurant and send us wine — we'd do the same for him. Maybe we should drink to being careful in the booth — even when the mikes are off.

— *Kevin Harlan*

I'LL NEVER FORGET how it was going on the field for the first time in a game. I can't tell you everything those defensive backs were calling me. Words mentioned frequently, though, were rookie and mother. They were after me, trying to intimidate me. Somehow, I survived. I guess after a while they figured I was either too deaf or too dumb to know what they were saying.

— *Cris Collinsworth*

I'M A POSITIVE thinker. Maybe that's true of quarterbacks. I don't have time for people complaining that they can't do this or that. Those people are whipped before they start. I'm a guy who believes everything starts with a positive idea. Suppose the guy who started McDonald's had said, "What kind of future is there in fifteen cent hamburgers?" Suppose he decided to invest his money in bow ties or something? Where would he be now? Look, the guy went with the idea and now he's rich.

Positive thinking. My high school coach was a great believer. He'd say, "Don't tell me how big the other guy is, just knock him on his butt." The mind is our most powerful muscle. If you think you're tired, you'll feel tired. If you feel like King Kong, you'll tear people up. I enjoy books on psychocybernetics. Did you know when Jack Nicklaus putts, he envisions the ball going in the hole? Most guys stand over a six-foot putt, thinking about the ten different ways the ball could break — the two grand they'll blow if they miss. Nicklaus just locks himself in mentally and knocks it in. That's why he's won the most big tournaments. It's not his grip. It's his head. Same with a quarterback. You gotta' believe before your teammates can.

— *Ron Jaworski*

IN 1985, I LEFT UCLA and was drafted by the Bills. What made it unique was that my dad [Elijah Pitts] was one of their assistant coaches. It was a little awkward for some people on the team, but not us. It's still football, and you can only make it so difficult. The bottom line is you have to make plays, score touchdowns and win; everything else is secondary. It was kind of nice to be around the family again after four years of school. For most of my three years with the Bills, I lived at home. My dad knew why. He said I was too cheap to live anywhere else.

— *Ron Pitts*

I HAVE A LOT of respect for every player in the NFL. Just to get there is amazing. You have to be the best of the freshmen in high school to play junior varsity. Then you have to be the best on the J.V.'s to play varsity. Then you have to be the best of all the high school kids to get a scholarship in college. Then you have to be the best college player to make All-American, and then to get drafted to go to a pro camp. Then you have to make the team. Plus the things that you have to go through. We see a game and say, "Oh, look at all these players. This guy missed a tackle. That guy made a great play." You forget that they've been getting ready for this since they were eight years old.

They've had to pass a lot of tests and jump a lot of hurdles. Take offense. I don't mean just a running back or quarterback or wide receiver. I like to move things around. One of my favorite players of all time is Nate Newton, the guard from the Dallas Cowboys. Erik Williams, the big Cowboys' tackle. When Joe Montana was playing, he was the best offensive player that I'd ever seen. Emmitt Smith is fun to watch. Barry Sanders, too. Jerry Rice running patterns. You can't just pick one offensive player. I have a tough time picking the best *100*.

— *John Madden*

14 BIG SPENDER

SPONSORS

Long before Madonna, pro football was a material *game*. Coaches, players, and stadia change — but not the need to sell your product. Some marketing plays at 33 rpm — other, 78. All hope to strip money from the customer like Dick Butkus peeled runners from the ball.

The upstate New York town that I grew up in divided loyalty between the Browns and Giants. I can still warble "Mabel, Mabel, Black Label" — Mabel, being the signet of Carling Brewery's major beer. At eight, I was introduced to the opposite sex by the Giants' prosopopoeia — Julie London, atop a piano, singing, "You've got a lot to like with a Marlboro." Disliking cigarettes, I liked what I saw of her.

Until the 1960s, each team sold a separate ad package. By contrast, companies today buy time on a national, not local, basis. Still, the need to hawk is football's First Commandment. Mercedes, Nike, or Anheuser-Busch. Welcome to a sellers' market where the buyers don't complain.

WITHOUT TOBACCO sponsors, television wouldn't have come along as rapidly as it did. Cigarettes did Harvard games in '47 and '48. I had to do the commercials, and never forgot: Lucky Strike means fine tobacco. Later, with the Giants, I got involved with Marlboro commercials. Some of the players did them — Chuck Conerly and Sam Huff — and I was hired to do voice-overs. Many of the commercials starred Julie London — perhaps the most beautiful titian-haired, blue-green-eyed female who ever lived. After I'd done a couple voice-overs, someone noted that I'd never met Julie. This led to a prank played by the ad agency who handled the account. They set up a cocktail party, and all the execs and I walked in. There's Julie. I go over, and instead of Julie saying hello to me, she said something — this was a setup — that I never thought I'd hear out of that beautiful mouth. We hugged and kissed, so I guess the shock value worked.

— *Chris Schenkel*

IN THE 1950s and '60s, one company could afford more sponsor time on your game. In our case, Carling controlled things. We had them for quite some time. People will come up in Ohio — "Hey, Mabel!" Or in Boston, it's "Hi, neighbor, have a 'Gansett" — for all the Red Sox' years with Narragansett Beer.

In 1966, I'd just left the Browns to return to New England. It's Opening Day, very cold, and I had a live commercial during the game. Afterward, I walk into the press box and this fellow from an ad agency in New York says, "I thought you did a beautiful job." I was thrilled — he likes my work. Think again. He meant my *pour*, not *performance*. "You know, even though we warmed the beer, it was cold today," he said. "But you didn't let that bother you — you still got that pour."

A broadcaster got identified with a product, particularly beer — which was good, except if the team changed sponsors. Then the identification hurt, and they'd fire you — *you*, but never Mabel.

— *Ken Coleman*

LINDSEY NELSON WOULD do those [C. D. Chesley] re-creations of Notre Dame football every Sunday. Once, he said, "TV is picture plus captions." Boy, was he right. Cynically, your job is to bring the audience to a sponsor — nothing wrong with that, it's just that you're a conduit. On television, you've got a lot of restrictions. A good analyst has to work with the producer and director — go with their story-lines. You might like to talk about a fullback, but if the picture's on the quarter-back you do the same. Otherwise, one, you make the director look bad. Two, you become irrelevant. That's why I love radio. It's your job to tell everything that's going on. On TV, the picture's the stimulation. Radio, *you* are — or you'd better be — which is why your verbiage is so important. You're more visible on TV, but important on radio. Sponsors be darned, my choice is radio.

— *John Dockery*

FOR MANY YEARS, the Gillette safety razor company was the major sponsor of the country's sports events. Boxing was one of the primary attractions on TV in the 1950s. Advertisers liked it because of the commercial after each three-minute round. I discussed with Gillette hosting another type of show that would also give them steady breaks — competitions in each sport deciding the best runner, kicker, passer, and so on. Had boxing not endured for so long this would have been a replacement. Forty years later it surfaced as celebrity competitions.

I mention this because my newest concept is of a more intellectual nature. How about a pro footballer's spelling bee? I already have the jackpot question. When the Eagles played the Cardinals in the 1947 title game, they had their great ball carrier, Steve Van Buren, passer Tommy Thompson, fullback Joe Muha, and an all-time great center. OK, for the giant jackpot spell the center's name. I'll make it easy — the first name is Alex. Here we go — get this one and break the bank. Raise your hand. No hands raised? Here's the answer. WOJCIECHOWICZ.

I had a few interviews with him for my TV and radio shows.

A gentle man off the gridiron. I was enthralled to hear he was into knitting sweaters. I said if he could get around to knitting one for me I could think of no greater fun than having him pull the wool over my eyes. With that I sign off.

— *Bob Wolff*

WHO'S THE GREATEST agent in the world? The greatest sponsor, too. The only reason I'm with Fox today is that at the Super Bowl my mom just happened to run into Fox Sports President Ed Goren and his wife in 1994 — and she just happened to also have a tape of me doing a game. I guess she just plucked it out of her handbag and she told him, "If you're putting together a network doing football, you can't do it without Joe!" Moms are so objective.

— *Joe Buck*

IT IS SAID that I may have been the first football player to enter broadcasting. In 1937, I was a halfback for Syracuse, which beat Cornell, 14-6. I scored both touchdowns and intercepted a pass. The following Monday, a haberdasher in Syracuse decided to cash in on my success by offering me a chance to do a fifteen-minute sports show on a local radio station. My immediate reaction was to say no, but when he said he would pay me $15 a show, I changed my mind. I was a pre-med student, but I did the show that fall and into the winter and made a great discovery — I liked being on the air. "What a wonderful line of work," I thought, and I've thought the same thing ever since.

— *Marty Glickman*

CHAPTER

15

I LOVE TO LAUGH

BOOTH YARNS

All work and no play make Jack a dull boy. All gravity would make the NFL duller than, say, the Weather Channel. Mention pro football, and it forms an image: Peals of laughter don't make the cut. Yet laugher thrives, born of necessity. NFLers need humor, lest life overwhelm them all.

Laughter lightens, freshens. John Madden, miming vaudeville. Cris Collinsworth, zinging his victim of the week. Chris Berman, mixing moniker and metaphor. Each puts perspective on the NFL's pulp of life. Pro football is *un sport serieux*. It need not flaunt wholly serious men.

"If I could not laugh," said Lincoln, "I believe my heart should break." Football breaks legs, arms, and parts you've never heard of. Below, read how it can lift the heart.

I WAS IN the Army during World War II, and was on the banks of the Elbe River when V-E Day celebrations broke out in Paris. I only wish I could have been there — for I was told it was one of the wildest celebrations in the history of man. Among those taking part was another Army man — one of the best football announcers I've ever heard, the late Lindsey Nelson. Lindsey and the Pulitzer Prize-winning war correspondent, Ernie Pyle, were standing in front of a hotel when the celebration started. Champagne was flowing. GIs partying with anyone in sight, mostly women. Music playing as they jumped up and down on the hoods of cars, grabbing and hugging one another. I was told that in the midst of this ecstasy, Ernie turned to Lindsey and said something that has remained with me all these years: "Linds, any man out there who sleeps by himself tonight is an exhibitionist."

— *Chuck Thompson*

A STORY ABOUT college qualifies for this book because so many of its players made the pros. In 1944, Army had [Doc] Blanchard and [Glenn] Davis. Ed McKeever was coaching Notre Dame because Frank Leahy was in the service. Later, everybody realized McKeever was telling the truth when in the clubhouse speech before the Army game he said, "Fellows, as you know, I'm worried about my father in Texas." Mr. McKeever was ill. He continued, "You know what Notre Dame means to my dad and so I just want you to know what it would mean to all of us if Notre Dame could do a job today." The team got fired up, goes out, and what happens? Army slaughters Notre Dame, 59-0. It's the third quarter, already, 39-0, Army. Marty Wendell, a backup fullback, says, "Well, fellows, if we haven't killed old man McKeever by now he oughta' live forever."

— *Jack Brickhouse*

A FOOTBALL REFEREE gets little attention from the fans unless it's to boo him. Unless he's Tiny Maxwell, a happy-go-lucky man who weighed 300 pounds. In spite of his bulk and stuttering speech he was a tough ref who could settle any argument by the wit of his tongue. One day Tiny and a number of other officials were assigned to officiate a game in Pennsylvania. There was bad blood on both sides and their last game the previous season almost ended in a riot. This return match promised to be a bitter affair, and the officials were naturally worried.

No one wants a game that has a lot of penalties. Fortunately, Tiny had an idea. "Fellows," he said, "we have to show these college kids who's boss or they'll get out of control. So I propose that we penalize the team that gets the kickoff 15 yards on the first three plays." The game started with a frenzied crowd. Minutes later the two teams were a mass of legs and arms on the frozen ground. As they unpiled, Tiny waddled over, picked up the ball and marched off a 15-yard penalty for unnecessary roughness. The penalized team was furious as it lined up for the next play. Tiny lunged into that mass of legs and arms and grabbed the ball — again, 15 yards for roughness.

Tiny now came face to face with the livid coach of the offensive team. He rushed at Tiny, shouting, "Why, you big, blind, stuttering, overstuffed pumpkin. Those boys of mine are playing clean. I oughta' break your neck." Tiny smiled and said, "Stop sputtering and get back to your bench. There's 15 yards more coming up on the next play because of what you just said." Right then, both teams knew that Tiny Maxwell meant business. The rest of the game was 14-karat clean. Later, the same Tiny who could make you thrill and laugh was killed in a car accident. Yet he lives — *truly*, a referee writ large.

— *Jimmy Dudley*

NINETEEN FORTY-FIVE. That team — Notre Dame — against Navy. Eighty thousand people jam that lakefront bowl [Municipal Stadium] in Cleveland. One of the craziest finishes I've ever seen. Frank Leahy was in the service, so Hugh Devore was Notre Dame coach. The score was tied, 6-all, when the Irish quarterback threw a pass and the receiver caught the ball at the goal line. His legs and belt went into the end zone but the upper torso with the ball did not. The receiver hit the ground six inches from the goal line. The crowd, of course, went bonkers. Things got worse when Navy held. The game wound up tied. I'm told that one broadcaster was so excited that when someone asked him, "Who gets the game ball?" he answered, "Let's flip a coin to see if it's a touchdown."

— *Jack Brickhouse*

I DID NOT ONLY pro, but college, football. I broadcast the first football game between Army and Air Force. Yankee Stadium, 1959. I miss those college games. Michigan-Ohio State was a thrill in Columbus or Ann Arbor. I loved the carnival air. It reminds me how in '52 I began doing Kansas University network hoops games and met maybe America's first full-time coach, the legendary Dr. Forrest C. [Fhog] Allen. We'd travel by train. When the players were tucked in, he'd open his compartment door and knock on mine and start talking basketball.

That year his great team of 1951 had graduated. On the '52 team was a guy named Dean Smith. Kansas goes to Louisiana to play Tulane and LSU and its great star, Bob Pettit, with a team one guy called "two bantam-legged roosters, two football players, and a crane." Kansas loses to Tulane, and is a heavy underdog at LSU. I'll never forget the pre-game meal. Dr. Allen was grand at motivating players. "You made bad passes at Tulane," he began. "You gotta' see things happen — improve your eyesight — don't go to movies — rest your eyes. You got to see the lanes — have peripheral vision — see to the right and left." He then segued into a tale about "a great boxer who was briefly heavyweight champion. Could have been even better — but didn't last 'cause he couldn't see the punches coming."

Max Baer was the champion, and Dr. Allen was just warming up. "They kept telling Max, 'You gotta' improve your eyesight to stay as champ — take care of those eyes.'" By now the players are hanging on every word. "They told Max to go to California and lay on the sand and look at the stars. But Max went there and laid the stars and looked at the sand." Suddenly, the kids' mouths opened as wide as their eyes — and they started to laugh and the tension vanished. Doc's medicine worked every time.

— *Merle Harmon*

I'VE BROADCAST football and baseball forever, but one of my yearly treats doesn't concern either. Doesn't even happen here. It's attending the Irish Derby. You drink a Budweiser around the piano and sing some Irish songs. You mix among the people and you learn a lot. The Irish are very relaxed. If you go to buy a newspaper in Ireland, they say, "Do you want yesterday's or today's?" I say, "Of course, I want today's." They say, "Come back tomorrow."

— *Jack Buck*

IN THE 1960S, Texas and Houston played each other for the first time in college football — and in the first game of the season. I was Houston's announcer. One day I got the UT scouting report from Houston's assistant coach, Emory Bellard. I look at it, and see this strange formation. "What *is* it?" I said. What it was was the Wishbone T, with the fullback and the tailback lined up behind the quarterback. Never been tried before. They had a cocktail party the night before the game for the coaches and broadcasters. I see Darrell Royal, the Texas coach who invented the Wishbone, and walk up to him. I describe the formation, and then say, "Tell me about it." He turns white, excuses himself, and goes over to Houston's athletic director, Harry Fouke. "Who's that blond-haired kid?" he said. Harry says, "Harry Kalas. He does our games." Darrell couldn't believe the Wishbone had leaked. If *I* knew about it, hell, the whole *world* did. He leaves the party and they play the game. A 20-20 tie. So much for the biggest secret since the A-bomb.

— *Harry Kalas*

OVER THE YEARS I had a couple trademarks. "Go to war, Miss Agnes!" was something that I'd use when a guy made an outstanding play, or the Colts took the lead. It came from a guy I played golf with who had a few books on putting. He thought he was a pretty good putter. He wasn't. He was also a devout young man, and when he'd miss a putt, he'd say the same thing

— "Go to war, Miss Agnes!" You hear that 15 or 20 times in a round of golf, and it stays with you. Same thing with a friend of mine that used to work with me in football. When the Colts were rolling, he'd kind of rub his hands together and say, "Man, ain't the beer cold!" If a fan heard Miss Agnes, he probably thought, that must have been a heck of a play. And if I said, "Ain't the beer cold!" they knew things were going well. Life's like football, in a sense. Sometimes you use a litle shorthand along the way.

— *Chuck Thompson*

PEOPLE ASK IF you've made booboos. Only one that I truly recall. It happened in 1962 — a record-breaking day. Y.A. Tittle threw seven touchdown passes at Yankee Stadium. Three had gone to Del Shofner, who was very skinny like me at that time. Shofner was covered by a good Redskins' defensive back, Claude Crabb. Y.A. goes back in his classic back peddling and spots Shofner, who was right in front of Pat Summerall and me. Shofner puts a fake on poor old Claude. His feet get crossed, he falls down, and Del goes in for the touchdown. In my excitement, without even knowing it, I said, "Ladies and gentlemen, Del Shofner has just faked Claude Crabb out of his jock." Pat starts laughing. I didn't know I said it. Later, they told me that the CBS switchboard lit up like a Christmas tree — undoubtedly, everyone saying how wonderful it was that I was giving locker room talk on the air.

— *Chris Schenkel*

BROADCASTERS GET mail. Once I got a letter. "Dear Mr. Brickhouse: My girl friend and I are both young, attractive, and unattached. We would like to know how to meet two Chicago Bears who are equally young, attractive, and unattached. Object: throwing a few passes! However, Mr. Brickhouse, it's about as easy to meet the Chicago Bears as it is to defeat the

New York Mets. If no Bears are available, a few, good ol' Chicago Cubs would do nicely. Hey-hey!"

— *Jack Brickhouse*

AT 15, I WAS doing sports on our student station. I was a Packers' ballboy, and during the week I'd sneak up to the press box at Lambeau Field, go in the radio/TV booth, and start re-creating the games. I used the names of Packer players, picked an opponent like the Vikings, and I'm going wild since there's nobody there. I taped the audio of TV games and fell asleep at night to Keith Jackson, Summerall, Enberg. I'd listen to their tapes and talk along with them in my room. I used to imagine mom and dad outside the door, hearing me talking to myself, and thinking, "Poor Kevin, we've really got a problem." I loved description. I'd drive down the road, see a car pass me, and start the play-by-play: "There's a car in the left lane, it's veering to the right, moves past the red Impala, passes nicely into the passenger lane — *touchdown, blue Cadillac!*" It's safe to say I knew what I wanted to do at a *very* precocious age.

— *Kevin Harlan*

DOING FOOTBALL, you're so preoccupied before a game. Once, I went to pick up some books at a store near my home. I passed a shopper on the street, and didn't pay any attention. The woman turned and tugged at my shirt. She said, "Pardon me, I'd like to introduce myself. I'm Jerre Gowdy. Your wife."

— *Curt Gowdy*

I'VE BROADCAST Bears-Packers' games since Year One and only one thing hasn't changed: I never have a good night's sleep in Green Bay the night before. Bears' fans always move into Packerland in big numbers, no matter the team records. Any Bears' fan who has spent the weekend in Green Bay and still finds himself able to go to work on Monday simply hasn't given it his all.

One Saturday night, I was in my hotel room after dinner checking the depth charts. Like most schoolboys in the Illinois-Wisconsin area, I knew the numbers of Starr and Taylor and Hornung like my own telephone number. But a handful of new players show up in every pro game, so you keep checking numbers until kickoff. I turned off the lights at midnight and fell asleep. At 2 A.M. came the sound of loud voices fortified by beer. "Bear down, Chicago Bears," they sang, accompanied by a bass drum and blaring trumpet. Up and down the halls of the second floor they marched, reaching a crescendo when they got to "pride and joy of Illinois, Chicago Bears, bear down!"

Finally, I stuck my head out the door: "Fellows, how about toning it down? I have to work today." From the end of the hall, a drunk screamed: "Hey, ain't you Brickhouse?" I answered, "I am." He yelled, "Brickhouse is a jackass. Hey-heyyyyy." You could hear him all over the place, the word "jackass" piercing the air, and it brought the house down. One by one, I saw doors open and faces emerge to laugh their tails off — the troubadours insisting I join them for a drink. A half-hour later, I was singing, "Bear down, Chicago Bears." It occurred to me that if the Bears' team had this exuberance, they would beat the seven-point spread. Sadly, no luck.

— *Jack Brickhouse*

AS A HIGH-SCHOOLER I went to an all-boys' Catholic school — one of the few in Wisconsin that had its own 10-watt student-run FM radio station. It was my sophomore year, and my dad, who'd gone to Marquette, mentioned that if he had to do it all over again he'd go into radio/TV. This impressed me, so I auditioned for the role of football play-by-play. The nuns and the priests are judging the contestants. They show a film of a previous game on the blackboard, and we talked into a cassette. My turn comes, and I'm doing OK when all of a sudden I see in the corner of the screen a player jumping wildly. I say, "It looks like the Cadets may have recovered the ball since I see

Joe Smith jumping up and down in ovulation." Silence. I guess the nuns and priests found it entertaining — since ovulation or jubilation, I got the job.

— *Kevin Harlan*

I STAND FIVE foot two and three-quarters inches tall — and don't you forget that three-quarter inch. It's always very challenging to do interviews with much taller players. Sometimes I stand on a box to seem taller — no big deal, I don't have an ego, and it's a great conversation piece. One day I'm interviewing Jim Kelly after the Bills won an AFC championship. I ask a question, and he's off and talking. He starts talking about his receivers and runners and then, without breaking stride, ad-libbing, so quick you might even have missed it, almost subliminally, he says, "Andrea, get off that box," and keeps talking. We were doing a two-shot — one camera on Jim, the other on me — and the one of me showed me dissolving in laughter. Boys will be boys.

— *Andrea Kremer*

SPORTS PEOPLE CAN be superstitious. I have a routine I like to follow. I always begin the day of the game with a French toast breakfast in my room. One game in Boston, the room service at the hotel couldn't deliver my French toast and I had to have scrambled eggs. Tell me it's just coincidence that right after the kickoff we lost our audio somewhere between Boston and New York. They told me a phone connection had been mistakenly unplugged. I knew better — it was the eggs. Since then, I tell people that I always check the room service menu before I register at a hotel.

— *Charlie Jones*

OVER THE YEARS the Bears and Packers have battled in the snow. It was on such a day at Wrigley Field that a Green Bay rooter aproximating 300 pounds, warmed by the contents of his flask, held his Packer banner high and bravely paraded back and forth in front of the Bears' rooting section. He was pelted by dozens of snowballs but continued until he had made the rounds. Of such stuff are champions made. Still another year and game at Green Bay brought an incident that tickled George Halas. A Packer Backer stood on the walk outside the Northland Hotel in Green Bay at 4 a.m. on Sunday, lifted a bullhorn to his lips and blared, "Halas, if you're half a man, you'll come down and fight!"

There's a human side of sports, and a humorous one as well. Paul Hornung was a fabulous runner on Vince Lombardi's Green Bay teams of the 1960s. Some years after Miami had won two straight Super Bowls, and finished one year unbeaten, I asked Hornung how the Packers of his era would have fared against the Dolphins. Hornung grinned. "I've already inquired and we would be favored over Miami by 7 to 10 points!"

— *Jack Brickhouse*

WHEN GREEN BAY beat Dallas in the Ice Bowl, I was a member of the CBS crew working the Packers' dressing room. Up to the camera came the great middle linebacker, Ray Nitschke. "Here's the madman of the Packers," I said. I thought it was a compliment. When I was growing up, it was great to be called a madman. Nitschke didn't like it. He said he wasn't a madman and didn't like being called one — the son of a gun damn near hit me. The funny thing is that early in the game, Nitschke couldn't get to [Dallas] runner Don Perkins, so he tried to kick him instead. But he didn't like me saying that in front of a big television audience. Later, I heard that a director in our mobile truck said, "If he punches Brookshier, let's go to commercial."

— *Tom Brookshier*

ONE NIGHT IN 1968, my parents were at home in Chicago, watching the news about the riots in our city about the Democratic Convention. At that moment, cops were chasing me around Grant Park during the convention. My father says, "Hey, that looks like Gregory." People ask who discovered me on television. I answer, "My dad."

— *Greg Gumbel*

IN THE NFL, the networks run the show. When Dallas made Super Bowl V against Baltimore, local radio rights weren't settled until the week before the game. Our Dallas competitor, KLIF, was offered the game for $5,000. They said nope — nobody would listen. So KRLD grabbed them. I was already in Miami to cover the game, and got a call saying would you like to do the color? I said yes, and wound up doing the game from the roof of the Orange Bowl. There I am, flourishing in beautiful 1970s clothes — just kidding — when my notes are washed away by the water from helicopters hovering over the stadium. I'll bet nothing like that happened to Ray Scott doing the game on CBS-TV.

— *Verne Lundquist*

ONE SUNDAY IN the '70s the Cardinals were playing Dallas. The Cardinals had a terrific offensive line. Conrad Dobler was at right guard, Dan Dierdorf right tackle, Bob Young left guard, and Roger Finnie left tackle. Tom Banks was the center. This day, Lee Roy Jordan of the Cowboys was bitching to the referees — and he's pointing at Dobler. Conrad is supposedly clipping and holding and playing dirty. We return to St. Louis, and next day I go into the offices and [assistant coach] Jim Hanifan and the other coaches are looking at film and laughing. I ask what's going on. Hanifan says, "Look at this." They show me the film, and it's our center, Banks, who's gouging. Only Jordan doesn't know it, and Dobler gets the blame. This went on for weeks — good cop, bad cop — Dobler getting blamed while Banks is slashing Jordan. There are two ways to look at this. One, things aren't always what they seem. Two, pro football is so frantic on the field that even refs get confused. Distract them,

throw them off the scent, and you get all sorts of goofy things.
— *Bob Starr*

IN 1973, THE Bears led the Vikings, 10-3, with time running out in the first half at Soldier Field. The Vikings had the ball in their own territory. I nudged my color man, Irv Kupcinet, and blared, "Kup, old boy, it's comforting to know that even if something catastrophic happens the worst the Bears can have at halftime against these powerful Vikings is a 10-10 tie. That's the worst." Seconds later, Fran Tarkenton had passed his Vikings into the end zone for a touchdown, the Bears fumbled the ensuing kickoff, and on the last play of the half Fred Cox kicked a field goal. It was 13-10, Minnesota, and the Vikings never were headed. Me and my big mouth.
— *Jack Brickhouse*

OVER MORE THAN 30 years of doing football I worked with a lot of analysts. I worked one game with Dick Butkus, and I thought that he'd be destroyed before we ever got under way. Dick had worked some radio in New Orleans, but this was sort of an on-the-job audition with CBS. Understandably, he was a little uptight. Most people are when they get into television for the first time. They're afraid of the whole procedure of network television. The terminology is new and different. I remember our producer running down the show, and he started by saying, "OK, we come out of billboard to Lindsey and Butkus." Dick interrupted to ask, "What's the billboard?" If you're new, it's a logical question. The billboard is the announcement of the sponsors. It's where this fellow says, "... brought to you by A, B, C," and so on.

Butkus was appropriately attired that day, I thought, in a leisure suit, open at the throat laid back. But when we stood up for our rehearsal and came out of that billboard to Nelson and Butkus, we heard a scream from New York. Our boss, Barry Frank, let it be known that all of his announcers would wear jackets and neckties on camera, and that they certainly would not wear leisure suits, and put a necktie on that man, now!

Some day, *you* try putting a necktie around Butkus' size 23 neck. He didn't have a necktie. Nor did we find one in the CBS booth — so we went next door to the press box. The visiting team was San Francisco. At a home game in San Francisco you may not find a necktie, either. You might even find a stray without shirt or shoes. But on the road it is different. The 49ers' publicity director, George McFadden, was wearing a necktie. We asked if he would lend us the tie, and George said yes.

Our final problem was that the collar of a leisure suit is not made to be encased in a necktie. When we got the tie around Dick's neck it looked as though the whole arrangement had been devised by Rube Goldberg — and it might explode the first time Dick took a deep breath. It didn't, and we survived the broadcast. All of which proves that ties are not for everyone — and that there is only one Butkus.

— *Lindsey Nelson*

IN THE YEARS the Colts were in Baltimore, I heard stories that men of the cloth had little plugs in their ear, and a transistor radio in their pocket, when the team was on the road so that they could keep abreast of what was going on. To use a terrible pun, it was like adding one religion to another.

— *Chuck Thompson*

IN 1974, TWO Cardinal roomates — Jim Hart and Jim Bakken — had a show on KMOX in St. Louis called "Arm and Leg." Bakken went on a three-week vacation, and I was asked to substitute. I had no idea what to do. I walked in, sat down, the red light flashed, and out it came. The people at the station told me I was a natural. I guess they meant it, because next year I was on the show with Jim Hart, and Jim Baaken was out. I felt bad for Jim, because I really wasn't trying to move him out, but sometimes these things happen. It reminded me of a Conrad

Dobler story. At the time, Dobler was second string, and the guy ahead of him forgot his chinstrap. So he comes running to the sideline and says, "Dobler, let me use your chinstrap." Conrad just stands there with his arms folded across his chest. Finally, a coach comes along and screams, "Dobler, get in there." Conrad goes into the game and never came back out. The other guy lost his job. So now I have adopted a couple of philosophies: Never take three-week vacations and never forget your chinstrap.

— *Dan Dierdorf*

BLOWOUT GAMES are deadly for an announcer. You have to fight the temptation to get cute. In 1977, I did a game for ABC and Utah State. In the second quarter, BYU led, 28-0. The final score was something like 65 to 6. Almost the entire crowd had left by late in the game. Then our director, Joe Aceti, focused a camera on a lovely old lady sitting alone, covered with a shawl. It was a beautiful nostalgic picture — but I couldn't leave well enough alone. The minute I spoke I wanted to retrieve my words. "See that lady? She was eighteen years old when this game began."

— *Verne Lunquist*

BROADCASTING ISN'T all glamour. In 1978, I got an Acapulco assignment to cover cliff diving. It started with no luggage on the carousel at the airport when I and my wife Linda got in. Then the cab, an old clunker, broke down. Next was a tram that was supposed to take us up the side of a mountain to our cockamamie hotel. The tram stalled on the way up, and we had to be rescued. We were relieved to reach our hotel room. Then we opened the door. The first thing we saw in the room was a rat. Let's put it this way: When it comes to events, I wasn't going to cover that baby again.

— *Al Michaels*

WELCOME TO THE trip to hell. In the '80s, I was working for NBC Radio and teamed with former Raider and Colt Dave Rowe.

We were scheduled to do a game in Seattle on Sunday afternoon. The night before, I had a basketball game in Chicago so Dave was to meet me there Sunday morning. When I arrived at O'Hare airport to meet him, all flights to Seattle had been canceled because of fog. The closest we could get was Portland — but because of the people trying to get to Seattle, all the tickets were sold out. We went to an American Airline sales representative. He said, "No way can I bounce any passengers." We then went to people waiting for the flight to Seattle and tried to bribe them if they'd give us their seats. That didn't work either. In a panic, we went to United Airlines and finally found a sales rep. who understood our plight. We get a couple of people off the Portland flight and Dave and I got on. Whew!

Before we left, we phoned NBC and said it was doubtful we could reach Seattle — they should get some backup announcers — but we weren't going to give up. In Portland, we found that the people diverted there had rented cars. I said, "The hell with it, let's get a cab." I still remember the surprised look on the cabbie's face when he asked where we were headed and we said Seattle. He said, "You got *any* idea how far that is?" I said, "Drive. We'll figure out the fare on the way." With that, the cabbie called in sick, shut the meter off, and we agreed on a price — $250 — if he could get us on time to the game. He starts speeding as Dave and I look out the windows, making sure no police were near, as we try to prepare for the broadcast. We had our spotting boards out, the names and numbers. The kickoff was at 4 o'clock and we arrive at 20 to. By then, the traffic is jammed. We got within a half mile of the Kingdome and then thanked the driver, got our bags, ran right through security. People were yelling at us. We yelled back, "NBC coming through!"

We ran to the elevator. By then it was air time and they'd found two announcers. Neither of them had done the NFL before. They were thrilled at getting their chance at network radio when Dave and I rushed in, took the headsets off their heads, and sat down. The guy supposed to do play-by-play asked if he could spot for me and I said, "OK, fine." It was Denver against Seattle and Dave and I were already uptight when a Seahawk intercepted a pass and started to run it back. My spotter was so excited that he accidentally hit me in the head. Off went my microphone as I was calling the touchdown so the audience didn't hear it — but somehow we got through the game. Then came finding a way to *leave* Seattle! We're still socked in with fog. We called all the airlines next morning and they said no flights were leaving. I thought of driving to San Francisco and catching a flight there, but they were booked and it was too long a drive.

Out of desperation, we got the phone book out and started calling air charter reservations and they said it was unsafe to fly. Finally, we found one service that said they would fly us for $2,000. There were myself, Dave Rowe, the engineers, and our producer. I called an NBC executive and told him if they didn't let us charter a plane we would be stuck in Seattle for maybe a week and they'd have to pay meals and hotel and everything. He said, "OK, go ahead." So we chartered a plane and headed for San Francisco. You got the impression that we shouldn't have been flying, but the guy took off and popped through the fog. We got to San Francisco safely and had to stay there all day to catch a flight out at night. An unbelievable story.

Several months later I was in Seattle again, and had a conversation with the girl who worked for the air charter service. It seems that the pilot who had flown us out had no business doing so. He was on the verge of bankruptcy and just wanted our two grand. Given my problems, maybe I should pull a John Madden and just buy a bus.

— *Mel Proctor*

I USED TO live at a place called Half Moon Bay, on a golf course. My home was on the 15th hole. Quite often, I'd see Dwight Clark and Joe Montana walking up the fairway. If I did, I'd grab my clubs, and we'd play the last four holes. This one day,

I go out, drop the ball, hit it, and pull the shot. In fact, it goes two or three inches past Montana's head. What a way that would have been to end my career — kill Joe Montana with a golf ball. It would have been the first-ever lynching in Half Moon Bay.

— *Lon Simmons*

BY AGE 12 OR 13, I knew that I was not going to grow taller or develop athletic genes. But I loved sports, so I wanted to broadcast. I'd watch a football game, lower the announcer's voice, and do play-by-play. Then came the real opportunity — NBC's announcerless game! No competition. What a godsend — just me and the picture. I clipped the Jets' and Dolphins' rosters from *TV Guide* and *Newsday*. I thought, "This is great, I'm the announcer." I looked forward to it for weeks. The game comes on, and I was terrible. Worse, a horrible thought hit me. If this works — games don't need an announcer — what do I do with the rest of my life?

— *Mike Tirico*

WHEN OUR U.S. Open tennis telecast went 11 hours and 16 minutes [in 1984], I had no access to a bathroom because of where the broadcast booth was situated. Going 11 hours without a bathroom was my proudest athletic achievement. But unlike the NFL, it was pretty unglamorous.

— *Pat Summerall*

MY LAST GAME as a player was Super Bowl XXI with the Broncos. I join ESPN, and my first Super Bowl is the Redskins-Broncos — XXII in San Diego. I'm doing the post-game, and our set was on a roof of a building adjacent to Jack Murphy Stadium about 150 yards away. The only way to our set from the stadium was the highway — but our producers told us that if we stayed to watch the game the road'd be jammed. "Don't take the highway," they said. "Just leave the stadium, go down and then up a hill. Oh, and at the bottom of the hill, you'll find a shallow creek."

I stayed and watched the game, then left for our set. It's dark as I go down the hill — 10 minutes to show-time. I've got my notes, sports coat and tie, a real fashion plate. Can't wait. Man, the Super Bowl — my first post-game show! I find the creek and it's 10 yards wide — and shallow, right? I take my shoes and socks off, roll up my pant legs, and in I step — and in I drop. The creek's five feet deep. The only sound I heard was of a guy — me — going under. I lose my notes, the coat is ruined, my vocabulary is heating up, and show-time's in *eight* minutes.

Finally, I cross the creek, and I've never been so furious. Some scouting party — I look like a guy who dove into a mud bath. Our stage manager sees me coming, says, "Oh, my God," and gets me a brand new jacket. I do the show without pants — a blanket wrapped around me. I'm sweating, it's cold, and so steam is coming from my head — I look like an engine that's overheated. Chris Berman says, "Relax, I'll do the highlights alone till your body temperature normalizes." He does, we go to and come out of break, and Chris says, as only he can, "Well, the Broncos got blown out for the second straight year. Tom, it's the kind of game that makes you feel like jumping into a lake."

He says it with a straight face. I'm remembering how he once told me, "TV's like playing. At some point you play with pain." There's chaos in the control center of the truck. We had three cameras in the locker room, three on the roof, and our producer is saying, "Where's [Roof] Camera 3?" He thought I was in the locker room 'cause in the monitor he saw me in my underwear! All the while I'm thinking, "Man, they're never going to forgive me. My career ends the same day it starts." Don't sing to me about over the river and through the woods.

— *Tom Jackson*

A FEW YEARS back I had a heart attack and then bypass surgery. I look at it like this: I lived for 53 years and they gave me a new shot at it. People keep telling me this heart stuff gives you a whole new perspective. That's bull. I'm doing everything I always did. I don't know how to get scared. We're not here for a long time, we're here for a good time.

— *Paul Maguire*

MY THIRD YEAR with the Chiefs was 1987. I remember it because I got married. Our wedding was Saturday, December 20 — great, except that the next day was a game. My wife's from Tulsa, so we got married there — and our present was the worst ice storm in 50 years. The power's out, so we use candles at the wedding and reception. Then we're off to the airport back to K.C. — except that flights are delayed. At 10 p.m. we're still stranded, so we order pizza — our wedding meal. Finally, we get to Kansas City at 3 a.m., I grab a couple hours sleep, and do the Chiefs' game. Meanwhile, my wife is packing for the honeymoon — knowing that the NFL is like the postman. Neither rain, nor snow, nor chill of night, keeps a broadcaster from his appointed game.

— *Kevin Harlan*

THE BENGALS TRAINED in Wilmington, Ohio, where you're stationed in block rooms. They're small and spartan, and you invent things to keep amused. Kenny Anderson was our quarterback. Danny Ross was a tight end. One night Anderson slips into Danny's room when Ross is in the bathroom. The lights are out as Ken slips beneath the covers. Danny comes out, gets into bed, when all of sudden Ken reaches his hands out and snatches Danny around the neck. This starts Danny plotting a little revenge. Several days later we're at the end of a long practice. It's hot, humid, we're sweating as we come back to the dormitory. Ken opens his room, and out storms this baby pig that Danny had gotten from a Wilmington farmer and stashed in the room. He'd been there all day — the pig, not Danny. You've never smelled such a stink.

— *Anthony Muñoz*

SOMEBODY ONCE asked me if there were any girls in the Golic family. I said no, because they wouldn't have been able to get any dates with three football brothers. I mean, a guy comes over and we'd have grilled him. "Where are you going? Good, we're going there, too. When will she be home?" She'd still be a spinster.

— *Bob Golic*

IT'S THE EARLY '90s on ESPN-TV — Michigan at Purdue, a gray day, little bit of a breeze, the feel of fall. Michigan is driving. Elvis Grbac is the quarterback, and they're inside the Purdue 20. All of a sudden I see a shape dart on the field. It's a rabbit. He comes on, leaves, comes back, goes in the end zone. The players are chasing him, he exits, and play resumes. Michigan gets to the 15, and here again comes the rabbit — the camera shows him at the 50, and the fans come alive. The rabbit's on his hind legs, he goes one way, then another, and the crowd is roaring. I decide to join in, and suddenly I start a radio call. "There he goes, to the 40, the 35, the 30, he cuts to his right, the 25, slants to his left, the 20 and 15, there he is, 10, 5, *touchdown!*" This guy had nothing on the Energizer Bunny.

— *Kevin Harlan*

I PLAYED FOOTBALL in junior high school, high school, college, and the NFL. Even when I was with Cleveland and our training camps were probably 10 minutes from my house, my mom would never come. She said, "It's hard enough to watch you get up beat up on Sundays. I don't want to have to watch you get beat up other days, too."

— *Bob Golic*

WE WERE IN Los Angeles against the Raiders when Boomer Esiason gets hurt. Howie Long is playing for the Raiders at defensive end. Into the game comes our backup quarterback, Erik Wilhelm, like Boomer, blond, flowing hair, looks even younger than he was. We come to the line of scrimmage, get into our stance, and ready to snap the ball. All of a sudden Howie says, serious-like, "Where'd you get this paperboy?" Here we are, battling to the death, and we start laughing. Proportion never hurts.

— *Anthony Muñoz*

IN CLEVELAND I talked all the time to business luncheons. They'd send me a note saying, "We request Bob Golic to come and give a motivational speech to our sales people about this and that." Through talking to people at the dinner, I'd get some things in my head and I'd stand up and start talking and people would start laughing. The people who set the thing up at first are going, "Well, when's he going to talk about motivating salesmen?" How could I? I don't know how to motivate salesmen. I'm a football player. What the hell did they call me for in the first place? But by the end they're kind of giggling a little bit, too.

You had different groups of people. Sometimes they would laugh hysterically. I'd always buy them a lot of drinks before I went up there, which seemed to excite their response. But sometimes there were people that didn't get it, and at that point you go to plan B and give them the old garbage — "Well, in the field of sales, the motivational..." You're making something up, and they start taking notes and stuff. Somewhere there's some poor, sorry son of a gun walking around going, "Well, I'm using the Golic technique of motivation." He's doing a different job, because obviously he's been fired.

— *Bob Golic*

I PLAYED BASKETBALL, not football, at Harvard. The funny thing is that later, doing football at CBS, I was paired with Dan Jiggetts — also a Harvard undergraduate, and also black. This was a historic first — the first regular all-black NFL announcing team. We'd kid people, "Historic, yeah — the first all-Harvard team!" Dan covered me in those early games. I made a lot of goofs. One of our first games was in Tampa against the Falcons. Steve DeBerg was the quarterback and on one play he dropped back. "He's going to pass," I said. "No, he's going to run. He takes off, near midfield, he's at the 45, the 50, the 55, the 60." Dan looks at me, like, "What in the world are you doing!?" I get out of that and we prepare to break. I'd been taught to look at our booth clock, not the stadium clock, to see how much time was left. So what do I do? I look at the stadium clock. I go to break by saying, "We'll be right back after this. There's 8 minutes, 99 seconds left." The clock was wrong. So was I. I was never so happy for a commercial in my life.

— *James Brown*

NETWORKS THROW ex-athletes into the booth and say, "Go out and do it." They don't tell you *what* to do. They don't tell you what to *say*. There's no advice, no coaching. Their philosophy is, "If you're any good, you'll know what to say. If you're not, we'll get somebody else." Early on I was doing a game from Tampa Bay. Ray Seals was a defensive lineman. They sent up his head shot into the booth, and all the germane information — height, weight, college. For college, it said, "None." So I said, "Oh, he went to the College of Nun — must be a Catholic college." During commercial, New York called me right away: "Don't you *ever* say anything like that again." Too bad: I liked the line.

— *Matt Millen*

WHEN YOU GO into broadcasting, it's a tough son of a gun. People at home don't know that — they think you just talk. In reality, you're hooked up by ear plug to a producer in the truck. Half your brain is listening to him jabber — the other half is trying to articulate something intelligent to the viewer. Early in my career — 1988, '89 — I was doing a game for ESPN, and I really had to go to the bathroom. I'm listening to our producer give the countdown to my play-by-play partner before a break. He goes, "5-4-3-2-1," and I think we're off the air. What I didn't know was that there's a delay — when he says "1," we're still on the air for two more seconds. He hits "1" — and I go, "Man, do I have to take a leak really bad!" The producer says into my ear, "Fifteen million people just heard you say you're going to the bathroom." I said, "Shit" — it was really embarrassing. The things a young broadcaster does.

— *Joe Theismann*

CHAPTER

16

CAREFULLY TAUGHT

TOM LANDRY

Art Carney, as TV's Ed Norton, said, "I started out at the bottom of this business, and worked my way right into the sewer." Tom Landry's Dallas Cowboys started out at the bottom and worked their way right to the top.

In 1960, Landry's expansion team went 0-11-1. In time, his Cowboys won five Super Bowls, made the playoffs 24 times, and had 20 straight winning seasons. They became America's Team — parading Landry's four-three defense and offensive razzle-dazzle. Doomsday and multiple formations sprang from a computer-loving, committed Christian — football's Gary Cooper at high noon.

Landry's foil was Vince Lombardi — like Nixon and Kennedy, or the Hatfields and McCoys. Their Gettysburg was the Ice Bowl: December 31, 1967, at Lambeau Field. At game's end, CBS announcer Ray Scott said of the Packers' 21-17, last-minute victory: "You have just witnessed a mind-over-matter masterpiece." Unbowed, Landry set *his* mind on taming the NFL. "We were sometimes outscored," he said, "but we were never stopped."

LANDRY WAS imperturbable — one reason the Cowboys excelled at public relations. The first NFL game I saw was in the Cotton Bowl on October 1, 1967. The Rams beat the Cowboys, 35 to 13. I'd just taken over as sports director of Dallas' ABC affiliate. Tex Schramm was Cowboys' president. The day after the game, his aide, Al Ward, told me, "This is out of the ordinary, but we'd like you to be our guest on our charter to Washington for Sunday's game." On the flight Al asked me to do locker-room interviews for the Cowboys' radio network. The problem was that it was on my station's competitor. I didn't care.

This was *Landry* — the Cowboys — I wanted to do it, and besides, who'd even hear this primitive network? So I took a chance, and lost. I interviewed Lance Rentzel and Dave Edwards after the game, and went home higher than a kite. The next morning shot me down. My boss came up to me and said, "I know I must be mistaken. I swear that I heard you on the locker room show." A couple days earlier the Cowboys' PR director had told me: "We want to take care of you." I didn't know that's what they had in mind.

— *Verne Lundquist*

LANDRY WAS REALLY the first guy in pro football history to play defense with a plan. He was the '50s Giants' defensive coach, and explained it to his guys — and they sold it to the entire team. It was unorthodox, because you occupied people, and that freed other people to make the tackle. With us it was [linebacker] Sam Huff. The two tackles would occupy their guards. The two ends would occupy their tackles. And the only person who could get a shot at Huff was the center — and he was always chasing him from behind. I think people adapted to the personalities we had in the secondary and at linebacker. Fans began to accept the same people on a weekly basis. What was going on wasn't dignified school yard. It was done with an organizational plan in mind — and if we just do what Tom Landry says, nobody beats us. And very few did.

— *Pat Summerall*

TOM LANDRY NEVER dodged a direct question. He also suffered fools gladly. I spent a lot of time with him over the years. I saw him angry, confused, but never saw him belittle anyone in the press. I don't mean that he was easy: His players say he could be brutal in film sessions. Landry just had an essential public dignity that refused to let him ridicule a stupid question. I admired that, and his sense of humor. In 1983, I left Channel 8 in Dallas to join CBS. Unbeknownst to me, the station arranged for a little gathering after the 6 o'clock news on my final day. It was a Monday — the day after the Cowboys lost to the Rams, 24-17, in the first round of the playoffs. I walk into the room, totally surprised, and see Tom and Alicia Landry. They'd taken time on what was a crushing day for them to say good-bye. Joe Bailey, the Cowboys' VP, told me later what Landry said when Joe asked if he'd like to attend. "Gosh, yes, you never know how many friends you're going to need."

— *Verne Lundquist*

I DIDN'T KNOW that Landry would become the coaching icon that he became. I did think that you'd better listen to him — and sometimes he was hard to listen to — because he didn't give you much time. Very matter of fact: "You do this, you do that." You never knew if you did it correctly, or to his satisfaction. You knew that he was a fine Christian man. But you never knew where you stood. So I never thought of him as being a great leader of men when he was our defensive coach.

Landry was also my kicking coach because he'd been a kicker in college and in his early days with the Giants. Once, he told me, "Don't ever kick without someone watching you, because you'll develop bad habits when you get tired — and it won't help you to practice bad habits." When Landry was chosen as first coach of the Cowboys, he called me and said, "I'm going to take the job in Dallas." Then he said the Giants were not going to expose me in the expansion draft, which was true. He said, "Just remember, if you miss to the right, here's what you're doing wrong. And if you miss to the left, you're doing this wrong. These are the two things you ought to correct, and you might beat me some day."

I know him well, and spend a lot of time with him even today. But you never got the feeling that he was an emotional person. It hasn't hurt him much.

— *Pat Summerall*

OVER THE YEARS the Cowboys' cast of characters changed. First, Ralph Neely, Lance Rentzel, and [Don] Meredith. Then Staubach. But it took a few years to mature — and until Roger became Roger, the Cowboys meant Landry, period. It was the image, and the constancy. Presidents came and went, economies waxed and waned, but there he was year after year — the coat, tie, and hat on the sideline. He wasn't an easy guy to put in a box — tough to analyze, but easy to remember. Every time you'd get on the Cowboys' plane he'd be in the second row on the left-hand side, behind [owner] Clint Murchison, with Alicia by the window. Tom'd read a Louie L'Amour novel, have one glass of wine, and make small talk — always gracious. You couldn't tell whether he'd won or lost. A stunning constant in a changing world.

— *Verne Lundquist*

GREAT TEAMS TAKE on the coloration of their coach. [See chapter 19.] You think of Pop Warner, Alonzo Stagg, Lombardi willing teams to win. George Halas, intimidating. Landry was different. He didn't want to out*muscle*, but out*think*, you. He enjoyed the mind games — and he played it extremely well. Not everyone could play for Tom — some players weren't bright enough, or wouldn't adapt to his system. I always felt that

given enough time to put together a game plan, Landry could
beat almost anyone.

— *Ray Scott*

TOM'S LAST FEW years in Dallas weren't pleasant. Gracious,
warm, dignified — but there was the feeling that he'd stayed
too long at the fair. Still, I'll never forget tuning in ESPN in
1989 and seeing the press conference where Jerry Jones bought
the club and announced Tom's firing. You remember the "socks
and jocks" line and "How 'bout them Cowboys!" Jones couldn't
wait a period of mourning before dancing on Landry's grave.
It was tawdry and shabby — what a difference between today's
image and Landry, like Mr. Roberts, defending God and the
American Way. The Cowboys used to be like the Yankees —
you might hate, but secretly admired, them. Nobody admires
this crowd. The image problems begin in ownership and seep
through the organization. The irony is that the way Jones fired
Landry only made Tom seem *more* Olympian — which is how
he's regarded today.

— *Verne Lundquist*

CHAPTER

17

HAPPY TALK

THE VOICES ON ONE ANOTHER

Pro football's great announcers have linked theatre, self-aware-ness, hospitality, and individualism. The stentorian Ted Husing. Jack Buck, barbed and satirical. Ken Coleman, whose voice was the voice of a friend. Each linked a fan to the NFL's green and tended fields. If the broadcaster towered, so did the event.

The Eagles' Byrum Saam spoke with beauty and panache. Bob Kelley of the Rams told a clean, lively story-line. To the Second City, Jack Brickhouse seemed as forever fresh as the wind off Lake Michigan. All showed nuance, a naturalistic delivery, a pleasing if not Mt. Sinai voice, and ability to merge fact and illusion. Each knew that you could not separate the salesman from the product.

Like life, football broadcasting balloons with slant. To fan A, Paul Maguire is chicken liver; fan B, chicken salad. What's vanilla to me may taste like chocolate to you. Yet similarities thrive. "Where's the rest of me?" said one-time announcer Ronald Reagan in the movie *King's Row*. Below are men who, more than less, caused fans to lose parts of themselves.

THE KEY TO sports broadcasting when I was growing up was

the good, exciting voice. That, and good diction and grammar. The knowledge of the game was not nearly as important then as now. An all-time great broadcaster, Bill Stern, was noted for the lateral passes he threw during a game to get the correct ball carrier after he scored the touchdown. He made up plays that happened on the field. But his voice was magnificent.

Stern worked for NBC. At CBS was perhaps the best broadcaster of the 1930s, Ted Husing. They did the college "Game of the Week" — often, the *same* game. The schools wanted exposure — so they threw it open. No rights fees. Anyone could broadcast their game, and many did. Among them was Harry Wismer, who also made things up as he went along. He got away with it because there was no way of checking. I remember sitting in the office of the late Tim Mara, founder of the Giants, and listening to a game done by Wismer. Harry would call out celebrities who were at the game. The problem was, many weren't *at* the game.

Tim was sitting in the office at 11 West 42nd Street, in New York, listening to the game with me and several others. You can imagine our reaction when Harry said, "There's my good friend, Tim Mara, in the stands at the 50-yard line." Harry embroidered things, yet was a regular on ABC. Apparently, they didn't mind.

— *Marty Glickman*

IN THE EARLY 1950S I did games for the Liberty Broadcasting System. And it was there at Army's football home, Michie Stadium, that I got to work with a hero of my youth, Ted Husing. One of Ted's qualities was his absolute arrogance. He did nothing to conceal it. And I was never offended by it. In fact, I came to consider Husing attractively arrogant.

In those days, a ramp ran from the back of the press box, where the radio booths were, to the travel road behind. The ramp was bordered with pipe railings, and early arrivals would perch on them to watch for Husing. When he arrived, I was

among the railbirds. Ted was in a Cadillac, and had the chauffeur drive it practically onto the ramp before he got out. As his
feet touched the ground, his eyes were straight ahead, and he
wore a black French beret at a jaunty angle. He had a cigarette
in a long holder, and as he strode toward the booth, dismissing
all cries for autographs, every fiber of his being seemed to shout,
"Get the damned peasants out of the way and make way for
the king."

There is something to be said for being true to yourself.

— *Lindsey Nelson*

I LEARNED A lot by listening to radio football done by Husing.
Stern had a set of pipes that wouldn't quit. These guys made
our job what we have today; I think some current announcers
probably don't know their names. Pathetic. Then came Red
Barber and Bob Neal and Mel Allen and Lindsey Nelson. When
Mel did the World Series — came on the air, you know, for Gillette
— he made it sound like the biggest thing next to the Second
Coming. I took over the Triple Crown of racing from Mel. Before the first one, I thought, "My God, how am I going to do
this like Mel?" So I called him, and he said, "Don't do it like
me. Do it like Chris Schenkel." Best advice I ever got.

— *Chris Schenkel*

I GOT INTO broadcasting by chance in 1960 by rooming with
Charlie Conerly. We were staying and training at Bear Mountain, New York, and I got contacted by accident. I happened to
answer a phone call from CBS' Jimmy Dolan. Radio was much
bigger then, particularly network. Jimmy asked if I would remind my roommate to come and audition for a job by reading a
five-minute script. I had almost hung up when I heard him say,
"Wait a minute. Why don't you come with him?" I guess they
liked how I read, because I did a CBS Radio show in 1960 and
1961. Then I retired, and CBS asked me to be a football analyst.
I began with Chris Schenkel, who taught me preparation,

presentation. If he hadn't been patient, I'd be back teaching school or raising watermelons because I wasn't very good. Chris taught the social obligations that go with being a broadcaster — meeting people, asking and answering questions. Then he moved to ABC and I worked with Jack Buck — a great voice, but looser than Chris. Not that he didn't prepare. He prepared differently. "Hey, this is not a funeral," he'd say. "We're going to have fun, and we hope people watching have fun, too." I'm glad I was there to take Charlie's call.

— *Pat Summerall*

FOOTBALL, BASEBALL, or basketball, Curt Gowdy had a style that you felt very comfortable with. John Updike once described him as sounding like your Uncle Charlie — nice, reassuring. Not many guys did football better than when Curt teamed with Paul Christman.

— *Ken Coleman*

PAUL CHRISTMAN was the first I ever heard say: "It hit him in a bad spot — right in the hands."

— *Charlie Jones*

IN 1964, WABC hired me for the Jets' games. Before then, the team had played in the Polo Grounds. Starting that year they moved over to Shea Stadium. The World's Fair was next door, and there was great anticipation about how many people the Jets would draw as they moved into a big-time park.

My partner, Otto Graham, lived at the Coast Guard Academy in New London, Connecticut, and commuted to New York when the Jets played at home. [Owner] Sonny Werblin owned the team and said, "We'll draw 25,000." People laughed — the Jets had averaged 5,000 at the Polo Grounds. The game was at 8 and at 7:45 there are already 25,000 people. No Otto. They delay the game to let people in. I do the pre-game show. No Otto. Kickoff's at 8:15 before 43,000. No Otto. The first quarter comes and goes. At halftime Otto shows. "Where you been?" He said, "Listening to you. I've been sitting out there on the Grand Central Parkway for the whole first half." From then on he took a taxi.

— Merle Harmon

I ALWAYS ENJOY working with partners who are on the entertaining side — Paul Maguire, Cris Collinsworth, Bill Parcells. It's important that you can kid each other. I believe in having a little bit of an edge to the telecast. You need humor from time to time — maybe a cutting-edge line that sets the tone. For instance, Maguire is a former linebacker-punter from the old AFL days with San Diego and Buffalo. A guy who probably should not be walking the streets of this country, but who is just great to be with on games. At meetings the day before when we get together with coaches and players, I don't think he's ever taken a note. But he remembers everything. Paul is always correct in figuring out what the penalty call is, or whether it's first down or not in a play that is inches away. But a very sick man.

— Marv Albert

THE RITZ-CARLTON in Chicago. WGN-TV's fall premier, a fancy bash sponsored by the sales department. The emcee is Tom Dreesen, comedian. He introduces the sports dignitaries, then says, "Ladies and gentlemen, here's Jack Brickhouse." The usual applause. Then Dreesen adds: "Do you realize that tens of thousands of people grew up not knowing anything about football because they listened to Jack Brickhouse and Irv Kupcinet on the Bears' broadcasts? Right, Kup? That's right, Jack."

Everyone laughed, including me — and they can laugh all they want. The bottom line is that [Chicago Sun-Times columnist] Kup and I broadcast the Bears for 24 straight seasons. How many comedians have shows that run that long? Kup was an ideal partner. He had played the game in college and briefly as a pro. He had officiated in the NFL. And he gave the broadcasts a certain celebrity status because of the guests he attracted at halftime. I'll never forget the day when Harry Truman, Bob Hope, and newly-crowned middleweight champ Carmen Basilio walked into the booth looking for Kup. They found him, like most fans.

— *Jack Brickhouse*

MENTION RAY SCOTT'S name to a lot of fans and they'll respond by saying, "Starr. Dowler. Fifteen yards." That's the way he talked, and it showed the difference between radio and television. On radio, you have to say, "Starr fades back to pass. He throws — picked off by Dowler on the 15-yard line. He goes in for the touchdown." TV's like a Broadway play — just identify the players. Scotty did. He didn't get loud to create excitement. With that voice, he didn't need to.

— *Merle Harmon*

RAY SCOTT WAS never in a hurry to identify whoever made a touchdown or tackle. People tell me that my play-by-play reminds them of Ray, and I guess his brevity is something I've learned. But that's the way I am. If we went to a party, I'd be watching more than talking. It's not copied. It's just something I've always done. In the six and a half years that I was Ray's analyst on CBS I never heard him make an error in identifying a player. Tough to beat perfection. I knew I was supposed to talk when the team was in the huddle. I learned that just because you see a picture, it doesn't mean you have to speak right now.

I know people who come to a game with a list of notes and no matter what the situation, they use them all. I don't think that's necessary. On TV you can see what's going on. You probably don't see as much as I do, because I've been trained at it. There are no flowers, no colorful cliches, and that's just the way

I am. I'm glad people think I sound like Ray Scott. To me, he was the best play-by-play man ever to do pro football.
— *Pat Summerall*

SCOTT IS ONE of the first football announcers I heard. Powerful voice. Very spartan. It was strictly, "Ameche. First down." His style would work today. Curt Gowdy was exciting to listen to. You knew that if it was a big event, he'd be there. I got a kick out of how when I first started doing the NFL on NBC, Curt was winding down. I remember NBC's get-together of announcers at the start of the year. I look around — here's Gowdy, Dick Enberg. I hadn't met them until then. I couldn't believe I was in the same room. All the guys I had grown up watching were here. Whatever Dick does, he brings a degree of class. I like to tell him that as a kid I watched him on "Sports Challenge," one of my favorite shows. He does not accept that readily.
— *Marv Albert*

I ADMIRE FOOTBALL announcers for the same reason I respect broadcasters in other sports — they make the game sing, without becoming a side show, which brings me to Enberg. Here's a guy well-prepared, a wonderful touch, a voice that reflects the excitement level — doesn't go berserk on every play, but calls the big play as well as anyone. A lot of people say football is an analyst's medium, which renders the play-by-play guy invisible. Enberg's had a lot of analysts — not all good — but he makes them look good and doesn't disappear in the process. He makes it seem easy — which, trust me, it's not.
— *Sean McDonough*

I WORKED WITH Dick a long time [1978-88]. A broadcast team is like any personal relationship. It requires several things. First, you need a compatibility. We enjoyed each other on a personal basis — going out to dinner, traveling, our senses of humor. Second, our styles complemented each other. Dick brought

certain things to the table that I didn't. We also both believed in
heavy preparation. Third, and this is a must, both have to be
unselfish. That's an area where we were fortunate. Our egos
were large, but never got in the way of the partnership. So
many other broadcast teams were openly antagonistic. It made
me realize how special it was what Dick and I had.

— *Merlin Olsen*

I DON'T THINK Merlin and I started with flags flying. The
NBC executives watching our first game together, Chet Simmons
and Scotty Connal, looked at each other at some point and one
said to the other, "Do you think we made a mistake?" But people
became comfortable with us. They knew what they'd get —
solid reporting that helps the viewer enjoy the game. We were
kind of colorless. If I'm vanilla, he's strawberry ripple. But we
felt in our blood that the game is the thing.

— *Dick Enberg*

AL MICHAELS IS pure and simple the best play-by-play guy
in the business. He works harder than perhaps anyone in the
business. It's his total focus in life. He has a wonderful wife,
Linda. I introduced them the other night.

— *Frank Gifford*

IN 1976, CBS brought all of its announcers to Miami for Super
Bowl X. They paired me with Alex Hawkins. They were doing
live remotes from different locations, and we were in a place
called the Bowl Bar [near the Orange Bowl]. It was part of the
pre-game show — we interviewed patrons, we're talking with
Dallas and Pittsburgh fans. Typical Super Bowl pre-game stuff.
We finish our spot and go across the street and watch the game.
We're done for the day. But we get over to the stadium and
we're told, "You were good, they want you to do a post-game
thing from the bar."

We go back there and the bar is jammed — the ultimate

firetrap, wall-to-wall people, and everyone's drunker than a skunk. They go crazy when they see us. They know they're going to be on TV and they're screaming and pushing. It's a mad scene, and I'm praying the place doesn't catch on fire. Then we're told through our earpieces that we're not going to go on. They're bumping our spot. Alex and I look at each other: "How are we going to get *out* of here?" This crowd is so rowdy, there's no way we can tell them they're not going onto national television. I'm figuring, "We're not going to get out of here alive."

Hawkins starts going "Quiet!" to the crowd as if we're coming back on. He decides to give them what they want. How do they know it's not actually on television? They're not going to see it. So Hawkins fakes as if we're on the air. As soon as he starts talking into the mike, people are screaming wildly. I'm standing next to him listening to his report and he's saying, "You know, they put us in this bar with all these drunks ..." and so on and they can't hear him. Then he stops talking and they throw the [TV] lights off and we get out of there. It was a stroke of genius. They would have killed us.

— *Al Michaels*

TOMMY BROOKSHIER was a defensive back. He knew offense, because he had defended against it. He knew defense, because he played it. As players — he was with the Eagles — we hated each other. I hated whoever wore green. Then he and I started to work at NFL Films in Philadelphia. Every Thursday we did a show called "This Week in the NFL." We were the co-hosts, and appeared on camera together. We got to be good friends. At this time I was doing games with Jack Buck. The problem was that Bob Wussler, then CBS Sports head, decided that Jack and I sounded too much alike. I said, "If you're going to make a change, I'd like to take a shot at play-by-play." This was midway in the season. I figured I'd have a chance to tape some games and evaluate myself.

Bob said, "When do you want to start?" I said, "I don't

know." He said, "How about next week?" Then he asked, "Who do you want to work with?" And the person who came to mind was Tom. Over the years as we traveled around, having a good time together — probably too good a time — we became very close. I've heard the way we did the game described as listening to two guys at a bar, or in a den, talk about something they enjoy. Which is a pretty good compliment, I think. You don't often arrive at that chemistry between two broadcasters. I once counted the number of people that I had worked with just on football at 108.

If you can find a chemistry like Brooky and I had, you've got something. We didn't have a regimentation. If he was talking when a play started, that was OK with me — and if I talked during the huddle, that was OK with him. We just sat down like we were at a saloon and talked about a game we like. Plus, if I had a brother — I don't — Tom'd be the closest thing.

— *Pat Summerall*

I DIDN'T KNOW if it would work with Pat — that old Giant-Eagle thing. I'd never have had the chance except for how in 1961, I was in the hospital with a compound fracture on my shinbone. I was still partially under anesthesia when a radio station called asking if I'd consider sports. I started my radio show right there. I'd write five minutes of copy and then talk as fast as I could to get it all in 50 seconds. I listen to those old tapes now and all I can say is, they were patient with me.

— *Tom Brookshier*

PAT SUMMERALL Is one of the nicest guys in the world. People say, "How do you get along with Pat?" I say, "If you can't get along with Pat Summerall, you can't get along with anyone." And I'm not the easiest guy. I'm no day at the beach. I'll admit that. I'm all over the place as a person and as a broadcaster. I think Pat is a perfect fit because he's not. He's been through every level of football. He's been a player, coach, analyst, and play-by-play guy. Anything that comes up, Pat's been there as a professional. He's as knowledgeable as you get. I'll say, "Let's do this." Okay, he says. "Let's do that." He's never cross, he's never mean, he's never upset. He's always there. And that helps me, because, you know, I get a little wordy. I'm going here and I'm going there, and talking about this thing, and the airplane, and the blimp's coming here, and the guy's down there. I can say a hundred sentences, and Pat in two words can say what I was trying to say in a hundred sentences. That helps me. I know that I don't have to put a period on every sentence. Or I don't have to finish a paragraph. Pat's there to do both.

— John Madden

PEOPLE ASK what's it like to work with John Madden? We have been together for a number of years now [17]. A few years back, we were riding somewhere in John's bus — you know he doesn't fly — and he said, "We're celebrating our tenth anniversary." I said, "You've got to be kidding." Sure enough, he was right. It just doesn't *seem* that long. John doesn't like crowds. He's shy, not at all the boisterous kind of person he seems. Not many people get close to John. He doesn't like elevators. Strange business for him to be in. But he and I have worked together to where I'm probably, next to his wife, the one person that gets close.

In many ways, he's like Lombardi. He's a great teacher and has a work ethic. That, and curiosity. When John entered broadcasting, he got interested in the industry — why this camera is there, why we take an end zone shot. He learned television terminology, which an athlete coming into the business is totally unprepared for. They don't know what a two-shot is. They don't know what pull back means. Nobody's taken time to tell them. They just say, "You played the game. Now go talk about it." I think the networks make a big mistake. If they hadn't endured a lot with me at the start, I would never have made it. I'm just glad I stuck around to work with John.

— Pat Summerall

WHEN I STARTED Giants' radio, I worked with Sam Huff and Sam was a friend of Madden's. We visited John when the Giants played the Raiders. I told Sam, "Boy, if this guy went into television, he'd be terrific." It's too bad that I didn't advise an agent friend of mine because he would have done extremely well. When John went into TV, someone told me that he was offered at NBC first, and apparently they were not interested. Even at CBS, there were raw moments at the start. At first he wasn't the top game. He did a lesser game for a while before it was said, "Hey, this guy presents football in a special manner." As it turns out, *he* is something special. John has the x and o mentality, and also that entertainment factor — and the result is the most effective color commentator that our business has ever seen.

— *Marv Albert*

MADDEN WAS a lovable bear on the sidelines when he was coaching. It didn't matter if there was a time out, he was full blast. Maybe that's what finally got to him. He said, "I don't need this. I need something a little milder." But he's all-out doing football or an ad for his hardware store chain. I heard him on a commercial the other day, and I thought "Is that John Madden?" He was at a low level. I doubt it's habit-forming.

— *Merle Harmon*

THE ONE COMPLAINT I hear about John and me is that there's too much talk, and I don't think they're talking about me. My style has always remained the same. John has often said, "I can go rambling and drawing pictures and Pat can take it and make it all make sense." I hope that's true. But I haven't changed — haven't had to, because of John. He is the best analyst I've heard in any sport. John knows more about what he's talking about, and sounds like he knows it, than anyone I've been around.

John doesn't mind me adding something to his comments, or make sense out of his comments, as he loves to say, and I don't mind him adding to what I say. It's funny. John gets involved, but has a detachment. He's like Ray Scott. Not many people know that though Ray did the Packer games for many years, he never traveled with the team. He was afraid that personal friendships with players would affect his descripton of the event.

Another similarity: Ray, John, and I think the event that we're doing is bigger than us. We have a reverence about the NFL. Those 22 people down there at a particular time are pretty talented — and it's them that people want to hear about, not us.

— *Pat Summerall*

IN 1988, NBC was getting ready for the Olympics. Michael Weisman was their NFL executive director and since many of his regular analysts were tied up with the Olympics, he decided to bring back broadcast legends like Ray Scott and Chuck Thompson. The first I worked with was Al DeRogatis, maybe the first broadcaster to break down football's complex language so the average guy could understand it. We got together for practice the day before a game between the Browns and Jets. Al watched the Browns for five minutes and said, "I know what they're going to do offensively — prepare for [defensive end] Mark Gastineau, they're keying on him." He's away from the game for years but in five minutes at practice knows the game plan of the Cleveland Browns!

— *Mel Proctor*

I STARTED DOING NFL games in 1989 for CBS Radio after a lot of years doing college ball. That first year I did a Christmas night game with Hank Stram. Hank was the coach of the Chiefs who with that 64 toss power trap became the second AFL team to win a Super Bowl [Kansas City 23, Minnesota 7]. As a broadcaster, Hank had a great sense for anticipating the next play. Hank always kept the monitor into the headphones high. He had it up all the way to 10 that Christmas night in '89. The game got exciting, and the Minnesota crowd in the dome got very hot. Hank took his headphones off, causing feedback over the air, and this fed back into my ears an extremely high-pitched whistle. I said, "Hank, I think you just alerted 250,000 dogs to our broadcast."

— *Howard David*

BY SUNDAY NIGHT, the day's games are over. TNT [Turner Network Television] can look at the big picture, doesn't have to obsess about updating scores, and just turn things over to Verne Lundquist — solid, stable, like a referee who's so great he goes unnoticed. I was told to do the PGA tourney in '95. I'd never done golf, and here I'm at a major. I was supposed to spell Verne Saturday and Sunday — so I asked him for advice. He sat me down, said, "You're a caption writer" — don't overwhelm the picture — and I'm thinking, "Some good guy." Not every broadcaster is that kind of mentor. A couple years back Verne saved [analyst] Pat Haden's life. We're doing a Thursday night game, and on Wednesday Pat started choking on broccoli. Verne does the Heimlich maneuver, and Pat is able to keep his Rhodes degree. We kidded him for just a while.

— *Ernie Johnson, Jr.*

I GREW UP listening to my father. Most of what I know in broadcasting I learned from him. Other than that, I sit down and listen to Al Michaels Monday night — and I'm enjoying what I'm hearing. Another is Summerall, who broadcasts like my father. Pat does what he needs to do — tell you who did it, why they did it, gets in, gets out, works with Madden, puts you at ease. The amazing thing is that in all the games they've done, they almost never step on each other's feet. Go to any dance floor. Most married couples can't say that.

— *Joe Buck*

A LOT OF GAMES today, you can't tell one broadcaster from

another — their voices are so similar. What helped Jack [Buck] and me on CBS [Radio] was the great contrast in our voices. You tuned in, and boom, you knew immediately who was talking. Jack knew when to tell stories, and knew the rules. A lot of broadcasters talk about rules, and don't know offsides from shuffleboard. Jack had been an official at one point in his life. *I* knew *he* knew he had the rules down cold. We were well-prepared, and had a lot of confidence in the other. Plus, Jack has a great vocabulary. The morning after our first game, Dick Brescia, a CBS Radio executive, called and said, "You two have never done a game together. I can't believe your chemistry." Broadcast chemistry is funny. You don't invent it in a lab.

— Hank Stram

A COMMON FAULT of new announcers is to find a favorite word and get so locked into it that you don't realize how much you're using it. I remember one time Jack Buck told me during a break, "Dan, you've used 'fabulous' four times in the last three minutes. Think you can come up with another word?" Needless to say, I did.

— Dan Dierdorf

EVEN DOUBLE-TAKES don't do some stories justice. I served in World War II. So did Jack Buck. My theatre was Europe. So was Jack Buck's. My branch of the armed forces was the Army. So was Jack Buck's. I was wounded in a battle toward the end of the war. So was Jack Buck. My wound was in the shoulder. So was Jack Buck's. Jack and I were both wounded in the same part of the body and in the same battle of the greatest conflict of all time — and we didn't know it until we got to talking one day more than twenty years after the war.

— Lindsey Nelson

AS A KID, I listened to Marty Glickman and Al DeRogatis. Al was somehow able to tell you what plays were coming up and

I always wondered if he was getting signals, or being told the plays. Later, I spotted for and then broadcast with Marty and saw that DeRo was getting signals from time to time — and putting them to good use. Their broadcasts were so popular that they contributed to the success of the whole Giant picture. Marty's style grabbed you — the way he enunciated certain words and names. You'd be driving, and if you put the window down on the car you'd hear the broadcast all over — which was also the case at Yankee Stadium. If he got paid by the radio, Marty would have owned The Bronx.

— *Marv Albert*

I GREW UP six minutes from Shea Stadium. My uncle Frank had season tickets, and so did some buddies — and we'd go see the Jets and bring a radio. By 12 or 13, I knew the game from Glickman. He showed how prepared you had to be. Once he asked my class at Syracuse, "How large is the plate that holds a basketball backboard?" No one knew. He said, "That's part of the game. You have to know." From that conversation, I still carry a rule book with me in the studio and to the game. Marty disliked announcers becoming personalities rather than chroniclers of the game. Each year, the Jets opened on the road while the Mets used Shea. I'd look forward to Marty telling us about the infield — "the dirt baseball skin, meeting the grass where the outfield begins." It all came alive — with Marty, the weather was getting cloudy, the uniforms were getting dirty — marvelous imagery. In television, we don't have much of it left.

— *Mike Tirico*

IN THE 1980S NBC hired me as the first full-time announcing coach. They did it largely because ex-players are thrown in the announcing booth and expected to perform — sink or swim. That's one problem in the business. Another is the fact that almost everyone an ex-player knows is patting him on the back. These are your friends, and they want to appease you, so it's rare when you get an objective opinion. Few people who are qualified as critics appraise your work. It's not easy for a guy to tell someone what kind of job he's doing. So, a lot of these guys think, "Hey, I'm doing well." Then they're gone.

— *Marty Glickman*

I WENT FROM writing to broadcasting. My idol was Jack Whitaker, who has profound respect for the language. I try to make each appearance gramatically perfect and use the precisely appropriate words. There are elements of writing that translate to TV. There's knowledge, and knowledge is comfort. If you quickly need an analogy you can call upon it. You know the right questions to ask, what the viewer needs to know. But in some ways, the transition isn't natural. On TV you're performing — not just disseminating information. That's a learned skill, which is why I looked like I had rigor mortis my first six months on the air. You have to make viewers comfortable with you so they can concentrate on the words and pictures, but it's hard when you're looking into a little lens and talking to 10 million people. As you grow in confidence you risk more. I remember trying my first joke on the air. The Bucs were off to an awful start [in 1990], and I said, "Gee, if they lose another one Ray Perkins is going to have a Tampa tantrum." To tease me, Terry Bradshaw and Greg Gumbel refused to laugh. They just said, "Probably."

— *Lesley Visser*

THE YEAR I left the Giants [1994] and went into TV, I called a few coaches to get some thoughts on football. They all asked about my shoulder. For some reason, every coach I talked to said, "How's your shoulder?" It's like I was crippled. Everybody thought I was not capable of playing, which I said 100 times was not true. I was almost 100 percent when the Giants released me. But once stuff [about his shoulder condition] goes in the paper it becomes fact. So everybody had this preconceived notion that I couldn't do anything. [Including, it seemed, then-ESPN-TV colleague Joe Theismann. In September 1994, Phil Simms and Theismann dueled in the "GameDay" studio. Theismann began, "Speaking of shoulders, how's your shoulder, Phil?" Simms replied, "Fine, Joe. How's your alimony payments?" At that moment, a critic said, he became ESPN's Rookie of the Year.]

— *Phil Simms*

I GUESS YOU can call Monday my day off, because I might as well be brain dead. My secret is there are more than one of me [at ESPN]. It may seem like I am everywhere, but I'm really not. I only do football and baseball and an occasional "SportsCenter." I don't want to be an octopus. [Howard] Cosell was everywhere. I'm not.

— *Chris Berman*

WHEN I WAS first with the network [CBS], everybody was saying I talked too much, so I thought about it, looked at some tapes, and agreed. So you talk less. Then when you say something it means so much more. I think when you first get started, you want to get noticed. You're not as willing to let the analyst in. Now that I'm older, I'm more established. When I hear myself in the old tapes, I think, "Why don't you shut up a bit?"

— *Brent Musburger*

CHAPTER

18 THERE GOES THAT SONG AGAIN

HOWARD COSELL

His monikers included The Mouth, Humble Howard, The Man Who Never Met An Opinion He Didn't Like — especially, his own. He was brilliant and militant, obnoxious and egomaniacal, capable of abrasion and sentiment — critic, gadfly, and in the end, self-caricature — also, the largest broadcaster of our time.

Born in Brooklyn, schooled at New York University, Howard Cosell served in the Army, became a lawyer, and crashed through into broadcasting. He did "Wide World of Sports," became a boxing pop celebrity, and befriended Muhammad Ali. Then, on September 21, 1970, he kicked off "Monday Night Football" — Browns 31, Jets 21, in Cleveland. The noise was insupportable, but pygmy *v.* the furor over Cosell.

Viewers fling rhetoric at most announcers. Cosell's face on television provoked bricks, rocks, and expletives undeleted. From peers he evoked ridicule, respect, exasperation, and not a little envy. Cosell broke old rules, and made "Monday Night" frenzied and still-running. God broke the mold *before* He made the man who professed to tell it like it was.

I THINK THE most successful broadcaster-telecaster-sportscaster

215

in the history of our profession is Howard Cosell. I admire what he started out to do and did and the capabilities he had. To me, he was number one. Yet I think Bob Costas — I still think of him as a kid — has succeeded Howard. It's not just his NFL and NBA studio work, it's his baseball and Olympics and interviewing. I think that Costas has surpassed them all in this business — and at his age, brother. I have neckties older than he is.

— *Jack Buck*

I LIKED HOWARD personally. Before he hit it big, he had a Saturday radio show and would come around the Biltmore Hotel in New York, where most teams were staying. He had his tape recorder, and got players to do his show. Several told me that Howard asked them to "write a letter to the general manager and tell them how much you enjoyed doing this interview with me" — that kind of thing. People said Howard became "Monday Night Football." Yet if you like football, you're going to watch "Monday Night" no matter who is doing it. It's the only game in town. What I don't like is that when you put three men in a network booth, they're making heavy money and almost obligated to talk. [Browns' 1960s analyst] Warren Lahr might see ten plays without saying anything. The people at CBS got on him, but not the fans. I don't think you have to keep bombarding people. Howard never knew that it never hurts to be quiet.

— *Ken Coleman*

YOU EITHER LOVED him or hated him. I loved him, because I did a radio show that he produced, long before he ever got on the air. I knew him better than anybody. Always wished I had his I.Q. I hated to see him get bitter at the end. He was so honest. He called me before one of his books came out and said, "Chris, you're not in my book." I thought, gee, that's strange. He said, "Well, it's a book that knocks a lot of people. I can't knock you. You're my friend." What more can I say?

— *Chris Schenkel*

HOWARD COSELL IS said to have invented the term "jockocracy" to describe too many ex-players in the booth. You have to consider the source. Howard was always bitter that he didn't get as much attention as he felt he deserved. Who's to say that his training as a lawyer trained *him* to be a broadcaster? I always got a kick out of Howard, but I didn't put a lot of stock in what he said.

— *Merlin Olsen*

IN ANY CITY where there was a "Monday Night" broadcast, I will bet that sometime at the height of the traffic in the lobby of the hotel where the broadcasters were staying that Howard Cosell would be somewhere so that people could stop him and gape at him and ask for his autograph. He craved attention. In my years in this business, I don't know of any other broadcaster — with the endorsement of his employers, ABC Sports — who deliberately set out to be obnoxious and succeeded so fantastically.

— *Ray Scott*

HE TAUGHT US all how to be journalistic — how to report a game in a different manner. Before Howard, you always followed the company line. Take the side of the officials in the sport. Don't question the coaches, the ownership, the fans. He taught us we could open a door and go into a new room, and question anything and provide a whole new approach to reporting a game.

— *Dick Enberg*

HOWARD AND I would get on each other's nerves, but it wasn't as malicious as some people thought. I had a lot of respect for the man — even though sometimes I'd have to say, "Man, you're really weird, Howard."

— *Don Meredith*

HOWARD WAS THE sports director of ABC Radio when they

acquired the rights to the Jets. Howard called me in a St. Louis hotel and in typical Cosell fashion said, "Merle, Cosell. ABC Radio has just bought the Jets' rights, and you're the announcer." He did the pre- and post-game shows all those years that I did the games for WABC, ABC's flagship in New York. Never socialized much. I was up at his home once, up in Pound Ridge [NY]. We had some great talks in his office. Never a cross word.

My wife asked me, "Why do you and Howard get along so well?" I said, "I really don't know. Maybe we don't do the same things." He did commentary and his show, "Speaking of Sports." Never could read a script — but, boy, that memory. Just tell him the Bears beat the Packers, 20 to 17 today, and that's all he'd need. Howard brought an objectivity to reporting that wasn't there before. Somebody at ABC once said, "Cosell will not dominate 'Monday Night Football.'" Right. Why'd people throw bricks at him and break television sets? — *literally*. Nobody was neutral about him then. Nobody's neutral now.

— *Merle Harmon*

HE WAS SMART. Never would I knock Cosell's intelligence. But he perfected an act. He was a joke among anybody who knows anything about football. Oh, for heaven's sake, he didn't understand anything about the game.

— *Ray Scott*

HOWARD COSELL IS always asked in terms of what you think of him. I tell you bluntly, although he passed away a relatively short time ago, I didn't like him. He was the key offender in being more important than the game itself. What he had to say took precedence over anything else that took place. So I didn't like him for that. I also didn't like his broadcast demeanor in which he spoke down to the people he worked with, and to the people who were listening. I know it all, and I'm telling you that this is so. I'm not a Howard Cosell fan. I think he was enormously successful. He was very hard working and very, very bright. I didn't like him.

— *Marty Glickman*

THAT FIRST YEAR in 1970, Cosell asked me to come over and have a drink with him at the [New York] Warwick Hotel. We were in there, and he was complaining: "These guys don't know what they're doing, Cowboy." [ABC Sports President Roone] Arledge came in. I waved him over, and he sat down. I said, "Your guy's unhappy here." Roone said, "Wait a minute. *He's* unhappy? All I do is defend you all day with the affiliates. They all want to get rid of you. But I haven't." And he didn't.

— *Curt Gowdy*

HOWARD AND I had a long-running relationship. I wish it could have been warmer. That wasn't my fault, because I think I fit into an arena that Howard put me in — the jock-turned-announcer. In actuality, I put more time into it, in a learning period, than he did. I felt sad when in the later years of his life he should have been the elder statesman of his business, and instead alienated people. Whether you liked him or not, he was a presence that could not be denied. When he opened his mouth and looked into the camera, there was something that happened — and that's what this business is all about: making something happen between you and it. That, and getting their attention — even if you get it by making them uncomfortable. Howard made a lot of people uncomfortable. He also made them think.

— *Frank Gifford*

THE LOVE-HATE relationship that this country had with Howard Cosell had nothing to do with football. We tuned in to watch a football game and people became very much involved with enjoying or disliking immensely a man who happened to be in a broadcast booth with a couple of other blokes, and they were interesting as well. You talk about chemistry. Howard's booth had a graduate degree.

— *Dick Enberg*

THE BEST AND the worst in sportscasting. Remember that marvelous moment when the U.S. won the Olympic hockey championship in 1980? When the game was over you never heard Al Michaels. He knew the picture told the story. He didn't have to say a word. Now think of the World Series game [Six, 1977] when Reggie Jackson hit three home runs. It was at Yankee Stadium, which meant the fans were in an uproar. After the first one, he couldn't hit a second one. Then he hit a second one. Well, he couldn't hit a third one. Then he hit a third one. All in one game. Again, the picture totally told the story. As he rounded the bases, Billy Martin, with whom he had feuded earlier that year, was there to greet him. Thurman Munson, with whom he had feuded, was there to greet him. And above it all was the hysterical babble of Howard Cosell, who was totally unwilling to give up center stage.

— *Ray Scott*

I JOINED ABC in 1974. Cosell left "Monday Night" in 1984. Amazingly, a week before the football season I got a call: "We want you to host halftime — not specifically replace Cosell, but still do highlights." I knew I had trouble. First, I had all of seven days to figure what I was going to do. Second, as I told Roone Arledge, Howard was a societal institution with gargantuan impact. There was terrible danger to me, an apprentice, on the way up. I wouldn't be cut much slack. Maybe they were hoping Howard would change his mind and come back. All I know is that they didn't know what to do with halftime — and here we are, more than a decade later, and they *still* don't. I did my one year — the best I could — and it was a disaster. What ABC doesn't get is that especially with cable, "Monday"

highlights are an anachronism unless you've got Howard's bur-
lesque quality. And where on this planet do you find another
Cosell?

— *Jim Lampley*

ONE NIGHT, after a baseball game in Kansas City, Howard got
out of our stretch limo in a dicey part of town to break up a
street fight. It's amazing what eight vodkas will do for one's
courage, and that was a slow night, too.

— *Al Michaels*

HE WAS THE first out front to take strong stands; he attracted
all the flak and made it easier for us to be more honest. I give
Howard credit for the most courageous stand a sportscaster
has ever taken, and that was over Muhammad Ali and the draft
situation. I'm not sure any of the rest of us, including me, would
ever have had the guts to stand in there and face the enormous
pressure he must have. His impact was tremendous. And his
instinct for a story was unusual in a business where too often
people follow, not lead.

— *Brent Musburger*

TO ME, THE greatest "Monday Night Football" game we ever
did was in 1978 — Houston 35, Miami 30. [See page 141.] I
went back and watched the game a few years ago to see if it
was that good. It was. But what's interesting is that there were
only two of us involved. Don Meredith wasn't there for a personal reason. Howard and I did it alone. As the game progressed even Howard realized that it was almost as important
as he felt he was — terrific, technically, and from the story-line.
What I remember most is turning around and seeing Howard's
beloved wife, Emmy, who traveled with him and was maybe
his only confidante. She was calmly doing her needlepoint —
didn't look up once. It moved me. After she passed away,
Howard was never really the same.

— *Frank Gifford*

I HAVE GREAT respect for what Howard Cosell accomplished, particularly in his early days — his heyday. I think later on, he became a caricature of himself. But that's not how we remember him. We remember him for making "Monday Night Football." It was his perfect stage. I know he liked to make it appear as if he were the show. Looking back, perhaps he was.

— *Marv Albert*

CHAPTER

19 MR. WIZARD

COACHES

"I am willing to admit that I may not be always right, but I am never wrong." Don Shula, or Chuck Noll? Samuel Goldwyn — but the tissue connects. Like teams, coaches embrace the good, bad, and ugly. Some seek a niche as General Patton of the gridiron. Others mime sport's Mick Jagger — bad-boy poster children of their time. All affirm the fact of little boys within the men — never allowing the boy or man to wander far away.

Often, coaches fashion teams in their image — Bill Walsh, and the galvanic 49ers; Bud Grant, the defense-hardened Vikings; Paul Brown, to whom repetition was dearer than Godliness — and secrecy dearer than both. Most lacked, shall we say, a harvest of proportion. "Losing the Super Bowl is worse than death," said the Redskins' George Allen. "You have to get up the next morning."

As long as *pro* precedes football, how likely is "play-to-win" to change? Reply blares another Goldwynism: "In two words, im-possible." Ask any NFL announcer. A-for-effort attends another school.

GEORGE HALAS coached hundreds of great players. One was

223

George (Moose) Connor, who weighed two pounds at birth, then grew up to become a football immortal at Notre Dame and with the Bears. Vice-President Gerald Ford was in the audience the night Moose laid it on me at a Frank Leahy memorial dinner in Illinois.

"I was a rookie with the Bears in '48," Connor said, "and Coach Halas needed a kicker. I had handled the kickoffs at Notre Dame and now Halas wanted me to go in and try my first field goal. I figured this was my chance to become another Lou Groza. Bulldog Turner, our center, snapped the ball, J.R. Boone put it down, and I moved toward it with my size 15 shoe. I swung my leg mightily — took out a big divot — and kicked a low line drive which hit Bulldog Turner right in the hind end. And up in the broadcast booth I am told that Jack Brickhouse hollered, 'Watch it now — the Bears got a trick play, Hey-hey ...'"

"Hey-hey" is my trademark phrase. I don't remember using that, but Moose got a big laugh and I can't knock success! Moose and I both laughed at a story Henry Jordan of the Packers told about another football coach, at another banquet, about the Packers' Super Bowl I game against Kansas City. As Jordan told it, Chiefs' owner Lamar Hunt entered his team's dressing room before the game and said: "If you men beat the Packers, I'll double the jackpot."' When word of that offer got to Green Bay's coach, Vince Lombardi, he told the Packers, "If you win, you can call me by my first name!"

You all remember who won. Green Bay, 35 to 10.

— *Jack Brickhouse*

I WENT DOWN to see George Halas at the hotel in Chicago. This was in the early '50s. Happy to see me, anything he could do for me. I said, "What I need are your rosters. Who did you bring with you, and what are their numbers?" He took me through the whole team — number, position. Just great. So I sit down the next day and made up little charts to try to work from, and I found that seven names Halas gave me didn't even make the trip. In those days, that's how coaches were.

— *Chuck Thompson*

MY TIME IN sports was when players and broadcasters and writers were one family, along with the coaches. We traveled to cities by train. We'd go to the ballpark together during practice sessions, and walk out on the field. Often we were admitted to the chalk talk sessions that the ballclub had. There was not today's adversarial situation between coaches and the media.

The change occurred because the money became so important. Some individuals, especially management, did not want to give anything away. I remember Paul Brown, then Browns' coach and general manager. I would go to him before every Browns-Giants' game and show him my spotting board with the Browns' starting lineup. I asked, "Is this going to be your lineup?" He'd make one or two changes and say, "This is it." Not once did he give me the correct lineup. He was concerned I'd go back to whoever was coaching the Giants and say, "These fellows are starting."

I understand that Brown was never popular with the media anyhow, at Cleveland or when he later coached at Cincinnati. But the feeling went beyond Brown. I was the enemy, and that attitude was further developed by the money that later came. Sadly, a little different than when we traveled by train.

— *Marty Glickman*

EACH YEAR PAUL Brown had a first-week training meeting that lasted over two hours. He had all the players and assistant coaches there and television and radio announcers and print media covering the team. He introduced everybody and told the players that when it came to the media, "These men have a job to do. I want you to cooperate with them. Be courteous. Help them. But don't you ever say anything that'll hurt our football team." Fuball — fuball team is the way Paul would say it.

Brown had each player write down everybody else's plays — *all* the assignments, not just yours. He said, "Keep notebooks, and write the plays down in long hand. I want them in long hand, because that way you retain them better." Then he gave them pencils, and said where the sharpeners were — the first floor there at Hiram College. That's how detailed he was. Brown invented the two-minute drill. In the 1955 championship game, he used it and ran up a big score [Browns 38, Rams 14]. Afterward, you could tell that he was thinking, "Now that I've invented it, how am I going to stop other teams from using it against *me*?"

Brown invented the draw play when Marion Motley and Otto Graham got mixed up in an exchange of the ball. The line was set up for pass blocking. They're retreating when Otto goes back and fumbles. Marion gets the ball and he's going downfield. That's how the draw play began — by accident! Paul was the first to have a full-time coaching staff. He took the films home, broke down every play, and worked all winter. But his greatest ability was spotting talent. During the war, Paul got people like Motley, Lou Groza, Dante Lavelli, and Horace Gillom — players that folks didn't know about. He's never received enough credit for being, in my view, the greatest coach of all time.

— *Ken Coleman*

TO A LOT OF people Paul Brown seemed cold. He wasn't. It's just that he had such a passion for the game that it obscured everything else. Things we take for granted today were Brown inventions — full-time coaching staffs, calling plays by messengers, exact pass routes. But what really impressed me was that he got livid if any of his players intentionally hurt the opposition. Today, you see a lot of players doing dirty — gouge, cheap shots. Coaching has changed. So, sadly, have the times.

— *Jimmy Dudley*

IN 1952, TWO fellows came knocking at my door — representatives of Lang, Fisher, and Stashower Advertising in Cleveland who represented Carling's Black Label Beer and Ale. Carling's sponsored Browns' games on WTAM, managed by Hamilton Shea, which was an NBC-owned-and-operated station in Cleveland. I was then doing events for NBC, and hoped to join them full-time. Bob Neal had been the Browns' broadcaster, but a rift had happened and the job was open. They wanted to know if I would come there for a personal interview with Paul Brown.

I flew to Cleveland, and Shea met me at the airport. We went to Brown's home on Saturday morning for the most thorough exam on football that I have ever undergone. I had done a game between the Browns and Giants, and Brown wanted to know what I remembered about it. Among other things, I remembered that the Browns had stopped fullback Eddie Price on the one-yard line. Great coaches always tell you about their defense. Monday, I was back in New York at [NBC sports head] Tom Gallery's office to report on my trip to Cleveland. I explained that I had promised to quickly let Cleveland know my decision. Tuesday, Gallery said nothing to me as he picked up the phone and called Shea. "We've decided," Tom told them, "that Lindsey will stay here." Then Tom turned and stuck out his hand. "Welcome aboard," he said.

Years later, when Gallery was asked why he had hired me, he said, "Well, among other things, Paul Brown in Cleveland was about to hire him, and Brown is no dummy." Soon Ken Coleman was on his way to Cleveland from Boston to begin a long and distinguished career as Voice of the Browns. Still, I wonder. Otto Graham and Jim Brown and Bobby Mitchell. Paul Brown and I — we'd have had some fun.

— *Lindsey Nelson*

I DIDN'T PLAY for Paul Brown, but I saw a lot of him with the Bengals. He was their founder, and he was the boss. You never called him "Mr. Brown" or "Paul Brown" — he was the "Coach."

It was my third or fourth year with the Bengals, and we were in camp in Wilmington, Ohio. One day this rookie tight end from Pittsburgh was crossing the quadrangle when he ran into Coach. They start conversing. The rookie tells him how things are going. He's about ready to leave when he asks Brown, "By the way, why do they call you Coach?" The Coach about fell over. Here you've got a guy — a legend, like Papa Bear Halas — and this kid is totally ignorant about his background. We ought to teach a lot more history than we do.

— *Anthony Muñoz*

YOU PICK UP great stuff the day before a game — tip-offs on what to look for in situations. Sometimes this runs counter to what you've picked up at a film session. Sometimes it doesn't. Sometimes you're in the position of knowing both sides to a story and knowing it's not what it seems to be, and you can't utter a thing. Often, stuff comes from the two opposing coaches — or from a coach and another player. Like the time I talked to Paul Brown and Joe Namath before a Bengals-Jets' game in 1969.

I asked Paul how he planned to defense the Jets, since the Bengals were primarily a zone team and Namath was great at destroying zone defenses. Paul said he planned to switch to a man-for-man because Namath was murder on zones. "It's Broadway Joe's meat," I remember Paul telling me. Then I asked Joe how he planned to attack the Bengals. He said that since the Bengals played zone, he intended to use plays that would force them into a man-for-man which they weren't used to using.

There I was with both points of view — each of which turned out to be right. Talk about frustration. I was in the worst world for any broadcaster: I couldn't say a word.

— *Charlie Jones*

IT DIDN'T TAKE me long to learn what a violent game pro football is. Just after World War II, I was working at WIBG in Philadelphia when Greasy Neale, then coach of the Eagles, asked if I would like to visit the sidelines during an exhibition game. I said sure. Keep in mind that these were the days before facemasks. After 10 minutes, I kid you not: I had heard enough grunting, screaming, and other horrid noises out of *Animal House* to last a lifetime. I went over, tapped Greasy on the arm, and said, "Thanks a lot."

"Giving up, kid?" he asked.

"Yeah," I said. With that, I left before Greasy had a chance to shame me out of my decision. Believe me, since that day I have great respect for what the men between the sidelines do.

— *Chuck Thompson*

AROUND 1960, I was working in Kansas City. Ben Martin, head coach at the Air Force Academy, was on a recruiting trip and had stopped off to attend a sports luncheon. Afterward, we got to talking about the academic requirements at the Academy. It was fairly new then and talk said that the academics surpassed even the Army and Navy — the toughest in the country.

Ben had developed a good football team and had a fine quarterback named Rich Mayo — all this in a couple years. I asked how hard it was to coach in such a place with good academics and did it interfere with the time his kids had to practice football. I'll never forget his answer. "Well, do you mean after they come on the field to practice?" I said, "I guess." He said, "Once they're suited up and come out I have them for 45 minutes. Of course, some of the kids don't practice each day, because they have lab sessions which interfere with football practice and they have to go to lab."

I said, "How can you coach a winning football program if you only have your players 45 minutes a day?" His response was, "My guys can remember the plays." It's tough to beat brains.

— *Merle Harmon*

WHEN THE DALLAS Texans of the AFL moved to Kansas City in 1963, they became the Chiefs. The Texans' first coach was

Hank Stram. We remember him for leading the Chiefs to victory in Super Bowl IV against Minnesota. Hank was one of those guys who was always thinking. You could be at lunch, dinner, riding in the car. You'd look closer and see that faraway look in his eye. You knew that he was thinking.

That first year in Kansas City, Hank and his wife Phyllis and my wife Janet and I became very good friends and we went to a movie together one night — *Around the World In 80 Days*. It was hilarious, but long, and had an intermission. In the first part I never saw Hank laugh so hard at some of the movie's crazy parts — yet every once in a while he'd nudge me and say, "I've got something to tell you during the intermission." He'd pull out a piece of paper and make a note and then go back to the movie.

At the intermission, we were saying how much we were enjoying the movie when Hank pulls out that paper and he had some x's and o's on it. He tells me, "Here's a play that would really work." Talk about a guy who never lets go.

— *Merle Harmon*

A COACH NEVER leaves coaching — even when he starts broadcasting. I once worked on the dock in a General Mills flour mill, and I've been on the assembly line at a Chevrolet transmission plant. You're not on the 50-yard line of publicity. You're working, and not enjoying what you do. Coaching's different. Never did I feel like I went to work. It was my life, not job. The real heroes are the ones who don't get the glory. Not every man can be an NFL coach. The reason is because it takes a special wife and kids to help. They have to sacrifice time because you're not home. Tom Landry can tell you that — a John Madden, Bill Walsh. Forget Tuesday, Wednesday, or Thursday during the football season. Hell, forget other days. You're invisible. That's the bad part, but the good is the greatest thing going. Talk about something that sticks in your blood.

— *Jerry Glanville*

WEEB EWBANK WON [1958-59] titles at Baltimore with Johnny Unitas and then came to the New York Jets and won Super Bowl III. Weeb was a grandfather-type. Everyone loved him. Today, coaches have 10, 11 assistants. Weeb went to the Super Bowl with five. He was definitely in charge. Once he said, "Come on the field an hour before the game and I'll tell you our plays, give you an injury rundown." The Jets were playing in San Diego and the center was Mike Hudock — 6-foot-2, 240 pounds. Hudock hurt an ankle or something in a practice before the game. The Jets were without a center. So from the taxi squad in New York flew out John Schmitt. They gave him number 52. Hudock had been 53.

I go down before the game and I didn't know Hudock had been hurt. I'm watching the center snap for the punter — keep in mind that Schmitt's about the same size as Hudock — and I see that he's 52. I said, "Coach, did Hudock change numbers?" He said, "Shh." I said, "What do you mean?" He said, "Hudock's not here. We had to fly John Schmitt in from the taxi squad. If the Chargers know they'll come after him" — John hadn't played much — "so we're trying to hide the fact." Weeb knew the Chargers would catch on. He just wanted to prolong the inevitable so that the Chargers wouldn't put Ernie Ladd on Schmitt's nose.

The game starts. The Jets ran two plays, the Chargers called time out, and when they came back they put Ladd, 6-foot-9 and 330, on Schmitt. The first snap John makes, Ladd leveled him and John saw the Hollywood stars. The nice thing is that he later had a terrific career as an all-star center. The memorable thing is how Weeb was from the old school — don't ask, don't tell.

— *Merle Harmon*

BUD GRANT. What image comes to mind? Dour, taciturn. You'd expect him to brutalize his players. Think again. Before Ahmad Rashad joined NBC, he was the Vikings' all-pro receiver. He tells stories about Bud's practices — short, sweet, few pads, little hitting: He saved his players. Look it up: The Vikings had very few injuries over the years — and kept their stamina late in the year while other teams were worn out from pre-seasons. What irony. Known for their brutality, the Vikings were taught to avoid brutality — one reason Ahmad, Carl Eller, Jim Marshall all had long careers. Bud'd tell receivers to dance out of bounds rather than get hit. Ahmad says he never got his uniform dirty in all the years he played! My friend is a very funny guy. Thanks to Bud Grant, he's also a very *healthy* guy.

— *Jim Lampley*

NINETEEN SIXTY-EIGHT. Weeb Ewbank of the Jets and Al Davis of the Raiders — two coaches who'd do anything to win. That year, they played the AFL championship in Shea Stadium, which can be brutally cold in December with all the water that surrounds the park. It was just bone-chilling cold as I arrived on Sunday morning at the usual time about 10 o'clock. I looked down on the field and on the visitor side below our WABC broadcast booth I saw this crazy construction. It was a long sort of dugout like they have at baseball parks in Seattle and Montreal. Actually, it was Al Davis looking for an edge. He'd put a bunch of 2-by-4s together and a polyethylene cover over it. He had heaters. Al hadn't missed a trick. Weeb came out and hit the ceiling. "Take it down!" he said, and of course it came down before the game. "Winning is the only thing" didn't start with Vince Lombardi.

— *Merle Harmon*

MY FIRST YEAR of working with CBS Radio was 1989 — RFK Stadium, the Redskins versus Cowboys. Maybe you remember the Cowboys that year. Jimmy Johnson has tried to forget. It was his first year as coach, and they lost their first eight games. So what happens? They come into RFK on a Sunday night — November 5 — and beat the Redskins, 13-3, for their only win of the year. The 'Boys finished 1 and 15 — dreadful. The next year, 7-9, then 11-5, then a Super Bowl in Johnson's fourth year, beating the Bills — and it all turned around that Sunday night. Nobody remembers that game now — at the time, it meant nothing in the standings. But I'll never forget what their performance told me about where Johnson might take them. *Might?* He did.

— *Howard David*

I'LL NEVER FORGET the Super Bowl [XXIII] in my last year with NFL Films as a writer and producer. It's the game where the Bengals were ahead, but the 49ers went 92 yards in the last three minutes. We had Bengals' Coach Sam Wyche miked, and I went down on the field with NFL President Steve Sabol before that final drive. Just listening to what Sam was saying, he knew they'd given Joe Montana too much time. He kept picking the Bengals' defense apart — five yards here, 11 there. Every play, Montana got the 49ers closer and Wyche is dying — he knew that Joe was going to pull it out. Arguably, it was the best Super Bowl ever. [With 34 seconds left, the 49ers scored to win, 20-16.] You often *see* a person's anguish. With Wyche, we *heard* it, too.

— *Andrea Kremer*

AFTER SUPER BOWL XXIII, Wyche and Bill Walsh broke down in their locker rooms — Walsh because it was his last game as 49ers' coach, Wyche 'cause the Bengals lost in the final seconds. I liked it because they humanized a sport that can be pretty buttoned-up: You felt what these two guys were going through. It also shows what happens when you win, or lose. There's the buildup of two weeks before the Super Bowl. Everything in you gets invested in the game. One team wins, and goes to Disney World. The other — a week later, people don't remember they played. The losing team can't wait to get out of the locker room. The winner stays forever. No sport has more of a gulf between winning and losing than the NFL.

— *Jim Hunter*

REPORTERS WALK a fine line with coaches. You have to be close enough to obtain information, but distant enough to criticize when you think they're wrong. In 1990, the Miami Hurricances spent a whole year trying to improve their reputation, and they were doing OK until the Cotton Bowl. The good news: Miami beat Texas, 46-3. The bad: They got 16 penalties. I was working the sidelines and reported that the Miami players were vowing to physically hurt Texas, then doing so. I said, "So much for 'Miami Nice.'" Some people didn't like it, including [Miami Coach] Dennis Erickson. I'd tell him what I would any coach: "I'll be glad to talk with you any time. I'll give you my reasoning and explain why I think what I said was an honest comment. If I think I made a mistake, I'll tell you that, too. But talk to me. Don't carry a grudge." Most coaches are great guys, but we have different responsibilties and constituencies. The last time I looked, no coach signed my paycheck.

— *John Dockery*

I'VE HEARD, BUT didn't see, this story — yet knowing the principals I'm sure it happened. It's the Senior Bowl, and Ray Perkins was the coach of one of the teams. Derek James was graduating, and knew he'd be a high draft choice. It was tough for anybody to keep him in line. On the day the players are supposed to report Mr. James wasn't there. Mr. Perkins picked up the telephone and said, "Derek James, aren't you supposed to be here today?" Derek said, "Yes, sir." Perkins said, "Well, your ass is supposed to be here." Derek doesn't say much. Perkins says, "Get a car or bus or plane, and get your ass up here today" — and he did. Who says coaches aren't authority figures?

— *Eric Clemons*

MY FIRST GAME at Fox involved Carolina, and I've never been as impressed by a person at first glance as [Coach] Dom Capers. You could tell that day that it wasn't going to be long before they were something else. Most teams like to train in cool areas. That's why so many go up to Wisconsin for pre-season. Not Capers and [general manager] Bill Polian. They train in Carolina — in July! My partner, Anthony Muñoz, was down to watch the Panthers work out and asked, "Are you worried about wearing down in the heat?" Capers pointed to tents they had around the practice field, as many teams do. Not only did he make the players come out from beneath the tents — condition yourselves, get ready for the heat — he made the fans come out, too! Get 'em ready for the long haul. Cowboy fans'll wear down before Carolina does.

Capers keeps a journal. It's like a diary that you or I would have, and he'd catalogue everything — what kind of day it was when we worked out, what time of day, how hot, how cloudy, the wind — all to see who performed how, when, and under what conditions. Then he'd log it over several weeks to judge his players. Long before the Panthers were a hit, you knew that if there were a formula for success, this guy had it written.

— *Thom Brennaman*

YOU LEARN A lot if you play long enough. Our first Bengal team to make the Super Bowl [XVI] had Forrest Gregg as coach — a Vince Lombardi-type, military training, and eternal drills. Our quarterback was Ken Anderson, a great player but not verbal — didn't ooze arrogance, like some say a quarterback has to. All he did was complete 70 percent of his passes. The next Super Bowl coach was Sam Wyche — no disciplinarian, did magic tricks, the media loved him, had us in T-shirts, not pads. What a difference between he and Gregg — and between Anderson and Sam's quarterback, Boomer Esiason. Six-foot-four, blond, the type of guy who in his first pre-season game comes into the huddle and you'd swear he'd been your quarterback for five or six years.

People say you need a Ditka or Jimmy Johnson kind of coach to put fear into young players. Sam Wyche didn't. Mike Holmgren isn't a martinet, and he just won a Super Bowl.

Football's played on the field, not a computer printout. What I learned is that all types can win, as long as they gain your trust.

— *Anthony Muñoz*

A LOT OF COACHES have gone into broadcasting, and they'll sympathize with this story. After I left Kansas City, I did my first announcing in a Dolphins' pre-season game. Today, they give new broadcasters trials, critique them. Not then — they just put me in a booth and said, "Talk." I had no idea what was going on in the production truck — the director and producer — didn't know they'd be talking in my ear, or that I wasn't supposed to talk back. After a while, I learned to take what they told me — "Focus," say, "on Dick Butkus" — and translate it to the audience. Not that night. After the game my wife said, "Who were you *talking* to?" I spent half my time on the air talking to the truck: Viewers must have thought I was talking to myself. Poor Hank, it's a good thing he's no longer coaching. The pressure finally made him crack.

— *Hank Stram*

CHAPTER

20

THE NEW KIDS IN TOWN

FOX AND CABLE TV

Until 1987, network television had pro football to itself. The sport then proceeded to build a new window on the land. First, cable's ESPN and TNT joined football's family. In December 1993, the family changed: Football's Godfather — CBS — lost NFC rights to Fox. The NFL without CBS seemed as strange as the British Empire *sans* India. Yet it thrived as Big-Game America — the welcome beckoner of a thousand afternoons.

In 1933, Art Rooney bought a pro football franchise for $2,500. In 1993, teams were awarded to Carolina and Jacksonville. The price tag: $140 million each, or 280,000 *times* what the Mara family paid for the '25 Giants. Imagine two men stranded on a South Sea isle from, say, Bangor and San Diego. The strangers differ in age, religion, income, and career. Their common denominator is a game played on mud and sloth and inside domes.

Fox et al is the NFL's latest stop on a road from DuMont via Cosell to Madden, Summerall, and the VCR. The comedian Fred Allen once called TV "a collection of passport photos." Looking back, it propelled pro football to big-time from oblivion. Said Jack Whitaker: "Our weekends are different because of it — and so, in a sense, are we."

IN 1993, I WAS invited to a 25th anniversary party for "60 Minutes" — a program I had promoted for years. Having broadcast the NFL for 30 odd-years with CBS, I was sitting next to a CBS executive. Negotiations for the TV contract were coming up, and I asked him about the future. He said, "As long as there is pro football on Sunday afternoon, CBS will be a part of it." A comforting thought. I had grown up in broadcasting with CBS, and I thought, "This is going to continue until I get ready to retire."

A while later, I was sitting on a flight from Minneapolis to Dallas with the owner of the Cowboys, Jerry Jones. Jerry and I went to Arkansas, and were talking about the old school. Then he said, "How long is your contract with CBS?" I said, "I frankly don't know." He said, "Can you get out of it?" I said, "Why would I do that?" He said, "I think Fox is going to be a major player in these negotiations." Jerry was telling me that something might happen. I didn't worry about it. Then, one weekend I arrived in Detroit for a game between the 49ers and Lions, and one of our broadcast assistants was on the elevator at the same time I was. He said, "Did you hear the news?"

The rumor had been that ABC might lose its rights, or maybe NBC lose the AFC. Its ratings were not good. I said, "What news?" The assistant said, "We lost football." I said, "What?" He said, "We lost football to Fox." I said, "You've got to be kidding." He said, "No, it's true." I met John [Madden] and the producer and director that night. We had dinner at the hotel, and it was a wake. Everybody was in shock. What am I going to do now for a living? I'm no longer connected with the NFL. Another CBS executive came to John and me and asked if the NFL knew what it was doing — Fox was a nonentity. Maybe, but if money talked, Fox's dollars were played at full blast.

— *Pat Summerall*

WHEN CBS LOST football, it was the biggest shock that any of us had. Maybe people can say now they saw it coming. But none of the people that I know did. CBS had always been there, and thought they always would be. I thought that I was always going to be at CBS. Pat did. Everyone else did. I was on the bus from Chicago to Detroit, and I got a phone call that Fox has the NFC — we don't have it any more — and the first thing you say is, "That's unbelievable. It can't be right." More calls and more talking, and it's happened. It was all over that quickly. Just one thing, boom. There was a little talk, well, maybe we'll get the AFC from NBC. Then, in a couple days, that went away.

It was very difficult. We were football broadcasters for a network that didn't have football any more. We weren't needed until Fox came along. Even though I coached in the AFC, I did CBS football for 13 years — so I kind of became an NFC broadcaster. I always think that the NFL happens on Sunday, and I wanted to be part. So when I knew that Pat was going to Fox and Bob Stenner, our producer, and Sandy Grossman, our director, it was easy to make the move. On the one hand, it's a new situation — Fox. That was scary, because there was no sports there. But on the other hand, we were doing the same things with the same people.

You can't tell me that familiarity breeds contempt.

— *John Madden*

THE STORY OF how John and I went to Fox has rarely been told. The weekend that CBS lost football we did a game at Giants Stadium, and a CBS executive told me, "We don't think the NFL was loyal to us. We're going to form another league. We'd like you and John to be our lead team on the broadcast. Have you been approached by anybody else?" John and I had been approached by Fox, but neither of us had signed anything. So I said, "OK. How long do you want me to wait?" He said, "I'll get back to you." I said, "Where do you stand on the formation of this new league?" He said, "On a scale of one to ten, about a three." So we didn't sign anything. We waited eight or nine days. Meantime, I had an offer from Fox. But John and I kept waiting. Then CBS called back and said, "Would you wait a little longer?" I said, "Where are you on the scale of one to ten?" He said, "About a six."

We started the playoffs, and John told me that he was having dinner with Fox head Rupert Murdoch. I said, "I can't imagine at this stage of my career broadcasting with anyone else." John said, "I feel the same way." So to make a long story short, or shorter, we both signed with Fox at different times. No collusion. They told us, "We think you two guys are the best. You give us credibility. Keep doing what you're doing." I heard from one Fox executive in all the first year [1994], and that was to tell a joke. Otherwise, they just left us alone. And we did what we've been doing.

— *Pat Summerall*

FOX STARTED WITH nothing. You'd go there, and they said Fox Sports. But all they had was football. So it wasn't even Fox Sports. It was just Fox Sport. They had one sport, and about five people working. This was in January and you say, "How are they going to put all this together?" Well, by August, we were doing pre-season games. We did the first pre-season game in San Francisco and I said, "I just hope that when we turn on that monitor and it comes up at 6 o'clock, a picture hits the screen." What Murdoch and [Fox Sports head] Dave Hill did is amazing. I mean, pushing, saying we want the NFL, then getting it — and because of that, getting more affiliates. They didn't go in the side door, didn't say, "Well, I'll do ice skating events, a couple fights a year." Murdoch said, "I want football." How they did it, I don't know, and I'm not going to tell you that I knew it would be successful. There were times when I had no idea if we'd even get on the air. Of course, we did. Now Fox has hockey and baseball. Finally, they can put the s on Sport.

— *John Madden*

I'LL NEVER FORGET how I heard the news [of CBS' loss]. A

radio report called me and said, "Fox just got the NFC." I told him he was nuts and hung up. Then I started calling people. I couldn't get through to anyone. I went down to the lobby and started wandering around. Then I just went to the bar. Later, Greg Gumbel came over in a state of shock. When I saw him I started to cry. I'd been at CBS for 10 years. The people there were family.

— *Terry Bradshaw*

I WAS WORKING on St. Louis' KMOX one night on "Sports Open Line" when at about 7 I went to the wire ticker, tore off the stories, and took them back on the air. The seventh or eighth sports story was that CBS had lost the NFC to Fox. My first thought was of my father — all the days I spent at the stadium seeing him do games. I couldn't imagine the NFL without CBS. Jimmy the Greek, Brent Musburger, the "NFL Today" — I mean, this *was* the NFL. What a shame. I just felt sorrow. Never once did I wonder, "Who'll Fox use?" Nobody'd ever heard then about the Fox Box, putting the score on the screen, or natural sound. Nor did it cross my mind that I might be among the used.

— *Joe Buck*

NO ONE AT CBS ever thought we would lose this thing. We talked about it, but would always say, "Nah, it could never happen." I've always said this is a cruel business, so maybe I should've expected it. In the back of my mind I always thought I was a lucky guy who could get a job tomorrow. This taught me in this business, there are no tomorrows.

— *Terry Bradshaw*

IN DECEMBER 1993, I learned that Fox had gotten the rights. Before you knew it I'm headed to Hollywood. As fate would have it, I auditioned with James Lofton, the great wide receiver who wound up being hired by CNN. We sat in a studio and broadcast a quarter and a half of a Green Bay-New Orleans game off a big screen — my indoctrination into the NFL. Fox decided to hire three veteran crews and three groups of "newcomers," and I was hired with Joe Buck and Thom Brennaman and some color analysts. That first season, people had all sorts of skepticism. Would Bart or Homer Simpson be in the booth? Would Fox keep the same quality as CBS had in the 38 years they did the NFL? In June, Fox had all the broadcasters for a couple of days to meet everybody and take photos — basically, a PR session — and amazing was the group dynamics. You had one group of John Madden, Pat Summerall, Howie Long, Jerry Glanville who'd been around football for 30 and 40 years — many with CBS. You had newcomers like myself and Joe and Thom and Tim Green and Kevin Harlan who sat off to the side and listened to their stories. The camaraderie of the veterans was incredible to see.

What stands out is a dinner. The younger guys are keeping to themselves and listening to the stories when a waiter comes around. All of a sudden you hear that great voice of Pat Summerall's as he orders an appetizer: "I'll have the the kick-ass chili." You're so used to hearing Pat say on CBS, "Coming up next, 'Murder She Wrote.'" "Kiss-ass chili" wasn't quite out of Cabot Cove. The whole table broke up. Right then, we didn't need ratings to tell us that Fox football would work.

— *Kenny Albert*

I WAS IN '94 spring training with the Cubs, and got a call from my agent. He said, "Fox wants to talk to you about football." I said, "Who is Fox?" I knew they were a network, but they didn't do sports. He said, "They're doing football big-time." I said, "Don't bullshit me. Did you tell 'em I was a football announcer?" As of that moment, I had never done a football game in my life — pee-wee, high school, college, pro.

My agent said, "They saw you broadcast a basketball game, and its pace is like football — they think you can handle it." I said, "OK, when's the audition?" He said, "Next week." I gulped and called my friend, Cris Collinsworth in Cincinnati. I said, "Big problems. I've never done a game, and here I'm auditioning." He said, "Relax," and then, "Who do you like?" He meant which broadcaster was my favorite. I said Dick Enberg. So Cris sent me four tapes — three of Enberg, and a fourth of another guy so I wouldn't try to mimic everything Dick said.

I got the job, and we've all grown — the announcers, and Fox. In the CBS days, the technical people stayed at a different hotel from the announcing and production people. Not Fox. They're not afraid to try anything. They turn off some people. Not me. My favorite part of the year is the Fox seminar. I go there to learn — just shut up for four days. That alone should tell you how I love this job.

— *Thom Brennaman*

IN STUDIO, I miss the thrill of being at the game. Still, we have our fun. One colleague, a Hall of Famer [Terry Bradshaw] — the other two who'll be there [Howie Long and Ronnie Lott]. People say, "How do you fill an hour show?" We've got so many games to talk about that an hour's not enough. Ray Nitschke was once in the studio. He came up and said, "I know you played basketball, but you're OK." My rites of initiation. Ray and Terry went to our simulated football field. Terry said, "Let's be honest, you couldn't play football today. You're not fast enough." Big mistake. Ray took his coat off, threw his glasses away. Terry sees the fire in his eyes and says, "Ah, I'm sorry. We don't have time to complete this segment." Bright guy.

Another time, we're coming out of break and learn that we've got two minutes left to talk about the games — *our* games — on Fox. Fine — except that Terry isn't listening. We come back, and Howie talks about Fox games — Washington and New York. Ronnie talks about Fox games — Green Bay and Chicago. Terry starts talking about an *AFC* game on *NBC*. The funny thing is that he was so good I didn't have the heart to stop him. The things you remember have nothing to do with first and ten.

— *James Brown*

244 of M pages

PEOPLE ASK IF Fox has changed the way we broadcast football. Not one iota. We've got maybe better, maybe newer, equipment than we had at CBS. But we've got the same director and producer that we had at CBS. There were 17 people who joined us in the move from CBS to Fox — so I'm hearing the same voices in my ears that I heard for all those years. Maybe John and I are a little better now. The pre-game show is different. The halftime show is different. The post-game show is different. The shows that we promote are different, and aimed at a different demographic area. Other than that, I can't see any difference in how they broadcast football. What I can see is a difference at CBS. In their sports department, it's not like when we were the Tiffany network. Then, everybody's desire was to be at CBS and have your show. I've seen a decline since the NFC went to Fox. Because of pro football, more people are aware of Fox and its sports department. I'm told that the dollars are countless that Murdoch and Fox have gained from the NFL association. More than ever, people ask me, "Where you going to be this Sunday?" Somewhere, that's for sure.

— *Pat Summerall*

AT CBS, DURING the fall when football would start, we would still have golf. We had U.S. Open tennis. And we would have baseball going on. So we were one of four things. Plus, they had the Winter Olympics. When we started at Fox, all Fox Sports had was NFL football. We weren't spread out, and I kinda' liked that. Everything just pointed towards the NFL. Now Fox has hockey and baseball, and baseball's going on during football. Maybe we should go back to Fox Sport.

— *John Madden*

AT THE END OF TNT's first year, we played a little Walter Mitty. Our last game was in Atlanta — home base — and so the remote and the studio crews were both in town. The day after our final game, stop the presses — man, we had a touch football game to end 'em all. Pat Haden quarterbacked the remote crew. Snake Stabler quarterbacked the studio. What a thrill — we're in the huddle and Stabler's saying, "You all just get open, and I'll find ya' somewhere." We did, he did, and the game ended, 21-all. The camera crew shot it — and now this documentary for the ages sits in the bowels of the Turner archives. We could show it on TNT — except that it has enough comedy series as it is.

— Ernie Johnson, Jr.

LOTS OF CHANGES since TNT got football. My role has changed from doing highlights to game hosting live. We go to the city Friday, interview Saturday, do pieces for Sunday and then the post-game. But what's really changed, sad to say, are the fans — so classless in many cases. I'll get home Monday and talk to my wife and shake my head. So many times a couple great teams try to knock each other off. When one loses, their players show the guts to come on our post-game show. It isn't easy — they'd rather be in the locker room — but they come out and how are they rewarded? They hear, "You stink," or "You guys suck," or worse — all by idiots who don't have a brain or a life.

Once, at RFK in Washington, the Redskins won a game and afterward a couple visiting players come on. We're waiting for the studio in Atlanta to switch to us, and all we hear are expletives undeleted. I go over to these fans and say, "Your team *won*. Show some class" — and for that I got more expletives. It's extraordinarily depressing. What's worse is what it says today not just about football — but life.

— Ernie Johnson, Jr.

ESPN'S DONE FOOTBALL for a decade. Game thoughts: They're not afraid to review their product and make it better. ESPN started out with three men in the booth, it didn't work, so they dropped it. Most networks have extraneous field reporters. For example, who needs a sideline reporter for medical reports? If a guy's hurt, the news goes from the team to the booth and then down to the field: The sideline reporter is the *last* to know! We use our guy — Mark Malone — as an extra pair of eyes of analysis.

Halftime and post-game thoughts: Once, you had to wait till halftime of "Monday Night" to see Sunday highlights. Not now. We give them Sunday night — not 20 or 30 seconds a game, but two or three minutes; not just the long bombs, but the crucial third and ones. If it's pivotal, we've got it. All this, in turn, forced "Monday Night" to change the way *it* does the halftime.

Pre-game: Chris Berman is right about the glut of programming. "At this rate, in a couple years our pre-game show will start the night before." Ours balances information, journalism, entertainment. Sure, we did a story on Steve Young's [1996] concussion. Everybody did. But for the Super Bowl, we looked at incentive proposals: Literally, teams *pay* for hits. Everybody's *heard* about Jerry Rice's workout program. We went to his home and *showed* how hard it is to take his hill. The Marines would have envied it. That's us — we keep charging up the hill.

— *Andrea Kremer*

FOR MY GENERATION — the generation right after Generation X — ESPN's "NFL PrimeTime" is a habit. I also know, from the inside, that it's constantly on the verge of disaster. I say that because of what we're up against — most games ending at almost the identical time, and only a few minutes to get all the highlights on. For that, we turn to Chris Berman. It's like he's fourth and long on every play, and always hits the bomb. ESPN has never missed a game highlight in "PrimeTime"'s history. That almost ended in 1996. I'm at home watching two TVs. On one is NBC's Bills and Patriots on my dish. Chris is on the other. The game goes into overtime. We can't show a thing till it's over — our show goes off at 8 — and it looks like the game won't end by then. At 7:59:30 I see Steve Christie kick a field goal to win for the Bills. On my other TV there's Chris, and the highlight comes on at 7:59:40. The streak lives! — showing each week's insanity and our desire to get it right.

— Mike Tirico

IN 1987, WE started doing the NFL — courtesy, in part, of the America's Cup. That year, we purchased the Cup rights. Now, a boat race is as exciting as flies crawling up a drape, but the pictures were nice and it was a rare instance in which the United States was an underdog and that got everyone's interest. The fact that we could make something like this interesting I think amazed the NFL. They looked and said, "We might not think we're ready for cable, but we're ready for ESPN."

— Chris Berman

GOING FROM NFL Films to ESPN was like leaving a propaganda machine for sports journalism. Each treats football in a different way. The great thing about both isn't the great games, or the Super Bowls, but the people I've come in contact with. Good stories come from access to athletes as human beings, and none was better than Anthony Muñoz and his wife, DeDe. DeDe suffers from agoraphobia, a fear of public places. She had never talked to anybody about it. I spoke to her about an interview, and she talked to her therapist, who advised against it. Months later, I revisited the issue — and this time DeDe talked with Anthony and her therapist and said yes.

I spent four or five days with the Muñozes, and it was unforgettable. DeDe goes to games, but can't drive — the anticipation is too much. She also had two kids who didn't know about her condition. We shot her going to the game, sitting there, then we went out to eat. Then back to their house for the interview. Anthony put the kids to bed and then said, "Can we come into the kitchen for a moment? I'd like to say a prayer." We stood around the table, holding hands — Anthony, DeDe, myself, our crew — and Anthony says, "Thank you, God. Bless this interview. Thank you for these people coming into our lives, and the chance to help other people with this condition by letting them know they're not alone."

I was in tears, and had to compose myself before the interview. ESPN, Fox, or TNT: After moments like this, touchdown passes seem pretty tame.

— Andrea Kremer

21 LOOK WHAT YOU'VE DONE

OWNERS

In 1919, Earl (Curly) Lambeau talked his employers at the Indian Packing Company into spending $500 for uniforms and equipment. In 1925, Tim Mara and Billy Gibson opened their checkbook and bought the New York Giants for $500. For years, as the NFL seemed a Magi of empty seats, franchise shifts, and anonymity, both parties feared they overpaid.

There was something akin to Coronado about the founders of the NFL. In Illinois, George Halas, athletic director and player-coach of the Staley Starch Company, forged the Decatur Staleys. They netted $1,800, after expenses, for 22 players to share. "The players voted me, as coach and player, two full shares," Halas said. "We practiced every afternoon, six days a week, on a very well-kept baseball field owned by the Staley Company."

Many early teams rose, and folded, the same year. A few lived via owners' life-support — to wit, Halas, Mara, Art Rooney, Charles Bidwell, and George Preston Marshall. Today, the more robust-than-ill patient is ministered to by owners — improbably, their *heirs* — like Al Davis, Jerry Jones, and Art Modell. Some use this to disprove the theory of evolution.

I WAS THE FIRST announcer who did two games in one day.
In the 1950s, the owner of the Browns [David Jones] said, "You're
the one we want to do an exhibition game between Detroit and
Cleveland" — a Saturday night game — "because you've done
the championship game between those teams before [1953-54]."
I said, "Well, I can't because I have a game Saturday afternoon
at Cornell between the Redskins and the Giants." So they asked
if they sent a private plane to Ithaca, New York, could I catch it,
fly to Cleveland, and do the game. I said yes and did both of
them on TV — the first time anyone had done two pro games in
one day. It's not something I recommend.

— Chris Schenkel

IN 1956, CBS made its first contract with numerous NFL teams
— not a big deal, and not much money. The Giants, for instance, got $50,000. The important contract came in the early
'60s. This meant a lot of money then [$333,000 a year per club],
but more vital was the genesis of the concept now being fought
by owners like Dallas' Jerry Jones — revenue sharing.

Back then, the Maras met with Pete Rozelle and decided
that with all this money now coming from television — and
foreseeing the great amount that might be over the horizon —
the only way to keep the playing field balanced for teams like
Green Bay and St. Louis in the lesser markets was to share the
revenue equally. Unlike baseball, football is unattractive if one
team is killing the other. Without revenue sharing, the Giants
would have had far more money than Green Bay to lure players. They'd have bought all the best talent — but if they kept
beating up a little nobody, the attraction would disappear.

So it was farsighted by the Maras and Rooneys and the
great families who founded this league and went through the
tough times. They sacrificed for the good of the whole — which
is the difference between them and the new owners who've
come into the league. I understand why they need to maximize
the profit — luxury boxes, and the rest. But the truth still ap-

plies: We need a level field. It may be difficult for some to see, like the Jerry Joneses. But it happens to be true.

— *Frank Gifford*

BEARS' OWNER and founder George Halas sat in an automobile showroom in Canton, Ohio, and helped draw up the plan for the NFL. He was the toughest person I've known from a physical, emotional, and business sense. The agony and pain he experienced before and after hip surgery was staggering. He lost his wife and his son. His response was to keep going. Halas' other side is that nobody privately gave to more charities. There were many players and associates whom he helped and who then turned around and bit him on the hand. He wasn't always wealthy. It wasn't until 1959 that George didn't have to go to the bank to open the season. The first year the Bears played their home games at Wrigley Field, Halas had to wait for the first $20 so he could take it and go across the street to buy tape for his players.

His respect for the buck is legendary. We were playing golf one day after he signed Dick Butkus to a $200,000 contract. I said, "George, knowing you that is $1,000 a year for 200 years." He and Butkus had their problems. Yet when Dick was inducted into the Pro Football Hall of Fame, he asked Halas to present him with the award. There was a time when I received an award at a function and I, too, asked Halas to present it to me. Never again. The good news is that there were three standing ovations. The bad is that Halas got every one.

— *Jack Brickhouse*

A LOT HAS changed in football, but not the owners. Many play flamboyant roles in their organizations. In his imperial manner, George Preston Marshall *was* the Washington Redskins. GPM was called Mr. Marshall by his office staff, his uniformed chauffeur, his coaches, and the telephone company that installed a direct line from his seat in Griffith Stadium to his team's sideline bench. "Ever get any wrong numbers?" I asked in jest one day. Fixing me with a cold stare, he snapped, "Just wrong plays." That was my sole delicate attempt at light conversation.

Mr. Marshall did not shy away from publicity. One year prior to the Redskins' invasion of New York to play the Giants, he led about 10,000 fans and the Redskins' band playing "Hail to the Redskins" in a big pre-game parade down Broadway letting everybody know that they were in town. George liked the color green, but for a long time enshrined the color white. For years, Shirley Povich, the Hall of Fame columnist of *The Washington Post*, prodded Marshall to let blacks play on the Redskins. When they started to advertise color TV, Povich wrote, "Now that TV is entering all the natural hues, it is high time that Marshall makes sure his team shows its best athletes in living color."

"Living color" was a slogan of the time selling color TV. When Marshall saw the light and integrated the Redskins, it helped sell his team as well.

— *Bob Wolff*

IN THE EARLY '60S I was in Washington when a guy who liked to talk baseball when the Yankees were in town came over to discuss another sport. Marshall said, "How would you like to do the Redskins' games?" Being the owner, he was in a good position to make that happen — 'cept that Harry Wismer was already doing them. Marshall explained that Wismer had bought the New York Titans of something called the American Football League. It wasn't public, but Marshall said he'd have to replace Wismer in a hurry with *somebody*. Later, I realized, hell, that wasn't much of a compliment. "I appreciate the offer," I told him, "but until Harry says he's leaving there's no job open." Soon Harry discloses he's going to New York. Marshall calls — now, it's open. Final problem — I do college football Saturday, and don't know if I can get wherever the Redskins are playing the next day.

Marshall says, "We'll take the chance" — so for two years I

call his games. One time I did USC-UCLA and with the difference in time get to Washington at 3 A.M., wake up at 9, and the
city's socked by snow. The park has snow on top of a tarpaulin
on top of grass. They delayed the game — by itself, unusual —
for 45 minutes hoping for a miracle. Finally, they give up and
put up wooden stubs for markers 10 yards apart. You only knew
the goal lines because they were a different color. Add the fact
that these Redskins weren't the greatest of all time. But I loved
players running in deep snow — a football *Babes in Toyland*. That
day they were the Boys of Winter.

— *Mel Allen*

I ONCE HAD a disagreement with Bert Bell of the NFL. I broadcast a game in which George Blanda fumbled twice, and late in
the game there was a fight. Later that week, Bert called and said
he would appreciate it if the NFL broadcasters did not deal in
negatives. He said, "Instead of saying the man fumbled the ball
say it escaped him." And he said the league wasn't selling fights
— it was selling football. I asked him, "What was I supposed to
say about the fight? That they were dancing around the May-
pole?" The phone conversation became a little heated. But I
stuck to my guns. Then, again, I was talking to the NFL Commissioner. The next day I went in to see George Halas and asked
him if Bert Bell could cost me my job in broadcasting. Halas
looked at me with a funny expression on his face and said he
probably could. But then he added, "But I'd never let him."

— *Jack Brickhouse*

IN 1963, THE Pro Football Hall of Fame opened. I was the MC
at the opening, and I got a kick out of being able to salute Tim
Mara, late president of the Giants, one of the original induct-
ees. I was at CBS, and they had me do a 15-minute show on its
opening. It was scripted, but I memorized the whole thing word
for word. Twenty-five years later, all the good folks in Canton
had a dinner party and after dinner they showed that film which

amazed a lot of people. I'm sure Tim would have been delighted to learn that broadcasters can think as well as read.

— *Chris Schenkel*

FOR YEARS, NBC broadcast the games of the Colts and Steelers. Then came 1961. The Justice Department decided that it would be all right for the league to negotiate an exclusive TV series. The NFL meeting was held at the Warwick Hotel in New York. We at NBC Sports often had lunch across Sixth Avenue from the RCA building. Austin Gunsel was a former FBI agent, now on the NFL staff, who had been interim commissioner of the league after Bert Bell died and before Pete Rozelle was named. This day Austin came into our restaurant from the NFL meeting to say that they were having a hell of a time getting everybody together. That wasn't news. The NFL frequently had that problem.

In this case, though, CBS had offered $9.3 million for the package — an awful lot of money. They had voted several times, but it had to be unanimous — and every time they came to the Steelers, their owner, Art Rooney, clutching a cigar between his fingers, rose and said he could not vote for the deal because he still had a handshake agreement with my boss, [sports director] Tom Gallery of NBC. So the NFL and CBS were being kept from this deal by Rooney's inherent sense of honesty.

I raced across the street to Gallery's office to tell him what was happening. He hadn't expected that. "I called Carroll," he said, meaning Baltimore's owner Rosenbloom, "and told him he was released [from his NBC contract]. I assumed that Art would know that we couldn't do anything with one team." But to Rooney, a deal was a deal until it wasn't anymore. Gallery got him on the phone to tell him that he was released and that NBC would not contest the package. When the next vote was called, Rooney voted with the rest — and CBS had $9.3 million worth of football, including the Pittsburgh Steelers.

— *Lindsey Nelson*

EVERYBODY LOVED Art Rooney. But he'd never won anything. Then they started to draft Terry Bradshaw and Joe Greene
and got better. It's December 1972, and they're playing the
Raiders in the playoffs. The Steelers are behind [7-6], time's
running out, it's fourth down and 10 yards to go and Rooney
said, "I better go down in the locker room and congratulate my
boys in a losing but courageous cause" and this and that. Walking
out, he threw a cigar to me on my table, said good-bye, and got
on the elevator.

Seconds later, Bradshaw faded back, ran around scrambling,
and heaved a ball down the field. Oakland's Jack Tatum tipped
the ball to Franco Harris, who was lumbering down going nowhere, just looking around — and suddenly here's the ball! He
grabbed it above the knees and runs like hell for the goal line
and scores the winning touchdown. They called it "The Immaculate Reception" — and it did come out of the heavens.

Mr. Rooney got off the elevator, ran out, and the place was
going crazy. He says what's this — is there a riot? They said,
No, you've won the game — congratulations. He couldn't believe it. Thankfully, he got the chance to *watch* a few more titles.
— *Curt Gowdy*

THEY DON'T MAKE them like that anymore — "they" referring to Whoever made Mr. Rooney. Maybe the greatest thing
about my time in Pittsburgh was the chance to play for the
Steelers' owner and patriarch. Today you've got your conglom-
erates owning NFL teams — they make their bucks in oil, or
real estate. Mr. Rooney was a bettor, former boxer and baseball
player, a guy who loved horses and didn't have big bucks: He
made his *living from* the Steelers. Their breed doesn't exist today — the sportsman, football man, the Halases and Maras.
What a wonderful guy. What a terrible loss.
— *Mark Malone*

WHEN YOU RETIRE as a player and go with a network, you're

forced by default to deal with people that you haven't have a great relationship with. In early 1987, I retired from the Broncos. That fall, I'm with ESPN and assigned to a feature on the Oakland Raiders' camp. I arrange it, fly out to the Coast, and the night before my interview get a call from Al LoCasale, the Raiders' PR guy. He said, "Sorry, Tom, you can't come out here and do your story." I said, "What's the problem?" He said, "It's Al Davis," the Raiders' owner. "He's just not comfortable with people who've been with a team" — in my case, the Broncos — "and the next year come to our practice." In other words, Davis thought I'd steal secrets and give them to Denver.

I was livid. "Look, I've been sent out by my company to do a job. I'm going to show up. If you keep me away from the players, you'll have to do it on camera." We get there — me, my cameraman, and producer — and see two of the biggest guards I've ever seen, 6-foot-6, 290 pounds. They say, "You're not allowed into the practice facility." So we sit on the curb. I figure I'll wait until practice ends, then interview players on the way home. After a while, who shows up but the guy keeping me out? It's Al Davis, saying in the friendliest way, "Hey, Tom, how you doing?" How'm I *doing*? I say, "Not so good." He says, "Come on over," puts his arm around me, and takes me to the entrance gate.

I tell him, "Al, I'm really upset. I'm working for ESPN, not the Broncos. If I took what I saw here and told the Broncos, it's espionage — the end of my career." He whispers to me, "Tom, if you played for the Raiders and then went to ESPN, I'd *expect* you to report back to me and tell me everything you saw." I started laughing. How you going to argue with ethics like that? With the Broncos, coach Dan Reeves once saw a couple guys on a roof two blocks away and stopped practice till we got rid of them. Paranoia is part of the football business.

— *Tom Jackson*

MY TOUGHEST INTERVIEW was my first — Al Davis in Oakland. My partner that day left the booth and I had no one to rescue me when Al got going. He said he could spare only two minutes, but talked for three minutes and ignored the guy signaling a break for a commercial. Finally, the guy tore up the signal cards and threw his hands in the air. Who says Al's a blabbermouth? He talked through two commercial breaks.

— *Paul Maguire*

SOME COACHES HAVE owners who constantly interfere. I never had that problem with [Redskins' owner] Jack Kent Cooke. When I got my first contract, I knew he would leave me alone. He came in with a bunch of accounting books and said, "I have the damndest problem. I have to pay $16 million in taxes unless I can find a way around it." I thought, "Good, he's preoccupied."

— *Joe Gibbs*

CHAPTER

22

WAY OVER YONDER

ON AND OFF THE FIELD

Recall Hal Smith as Otis Campbell — *The Andy Griffith Show*'s town drunk. "The funny thing is," he said, "I don't think I've ever been drunk in my life." By contrast, pro football can drive a broadcaster to a distillery and/or monastery. Memorize the numbers, and huddle with the analyst. View film which accents the dancing patterns on the field. Learn the shorthand of pro ball's "Technologyland," as Norman Mailer calls America — tendency charts, scouting reports, and computer-fed information.

Like IBM, NFL Voices digest, inhale, and spew an Everest of fact. Moreover, their life extends beyond the screen — cab rides, late planes, lost keys, missed reservations, meals cold, drab, and skewered. "You don't get a chance to think during the pell-mell of a game," said Lindsey Nelson. "You make up for it waiting three hours on the tarmac at O'Hare."

Say hello to clamor, pressure, deadline, and scrutiny — vocation, not romance — what announcers confront behind and beyond the mike. Below, mikemen explain why they brook it, conjure memory, and tell how they view their craft.

I DID FOOTBALL radio for fun and television for money. On

radio, you're the contact. On the other hand, NBC proved something with its '80s announcerless football game in Miami. They just used the P.A. system in the background, and people actually followed it. Do that with radio, and you have three hours of dead air.

I love Jack Buck. He says radio beats your brains out — but if you lose a play on TV just look in your monitor and see some guy running and say, "Look at him go!" TV's bad side is that it's hard to focus on language with that IFB — Interrupted Feedback — in your headset connecting to the production truck. The IFB's in one ear, your partner in the other, the crowd roaring — and you have to hear the cues coming toward commercial while you're reading the introduction to commercial! Tough? I'd leave a TV game and say, "What in the world happened?"

Try this some time. Get the cues right; get the game on and off the air; include your partner — all at once. You have number 67 holding. So you ask, "What do you think of this, Billy?" And Billy'll talk about something he's seen on the replay monitor before it hits the screen. All these things add interest. You used to have one or two replay machines. You might have seven. You might have 13. Might have 20 on a Super Bowl. The announcer has to balance it all. On radio, people can't see your mistakes. They sure can on television.

— *Merle Harmon*

I WORKED WITH Vin Scully and Pat Summerall and Al Michaels — but I remember Jack Buck on CBS Radio — a Monday nighter in Chicago — when the fog came off Lake Michigan. It was like we were in an ocean, like the Titanic sank. Jack and I couldn't see a thing. But that didn't stop him from doing play-by-play. He invented guys blocking and tackling, feinting and jabbing: To Jack, it must have seemed like broadcasting in an aquarium. Like old guys doing re-creations, Jack's job was to keep things moving. My favorite play was Jack handing the ball off and then lateraling — when actually it was a forward pass. That's my definition of a pro. If you were listening, you heard me laughing. Thank God we were doing radio, not television.

— *Hank Stram*

YOU CAN'T DO football unless you spend the whole week preparing to do the game. In baseball, you're immersed in it day in and out. In football, you think way ahead about names and numbers and putting your spotting boards together and looking at movies. My football radio delivery was much more up than baseball because it's a different game and there's 22 people in motion at the same time. Yet I didn't want to overtalk. When I started in 1952 with the Browns, I was told by a gentleman with the ad agency that hired me that they'd rather get mail from listeners saying that our announcers don't talk enough than that they talk too much. I feel the same. The announcer is there to put captions on the picture and not insult the audience by giving you play-by-play. Ray Scott once said to me, "You know, I picked up your style, because I like it on television better than anybody." Ray knew what I did. Don't tell the audience what it already sees.

— *Ken Coleman*

I'VE OFTEN SAID that they probably should have collected money from me to do the games — but paid me 10 times as much getting ready to do them. Because it's preparation.

— *Ray Scott*

I'M NOT BRAGGING, but I had a good memory. A lot comes from Elocution lessons my mom made me take when I was ten years old. I had to memorize the poetry and give it to the teacher. If I didn't memorize it word for word, boy, she'd be all over me. Especially in sports that I love, I remember plays from 20 years before — and I'd use 'em in a game. A good memory helps in football, where you have to put the number with a player. They're in a mass down there, you're way up, and you can't identify them by the uniform. It's that number you go by, and I'd woodshed them. Saturday night before a pro game I never left the room. I went over the numbers till I had them down cold. Sometimes guys will write a lot of notes and can't find them when they're broadcasting. The more work you did, the more you had in your head. Notes were superfluous. Preparation is 60 percent of the battle — especially if you train your memory.

— Curt Gowdy

IT'S THE TRAVEL that kills you. You walk up to a hotel desk and the person just looks into a computer screen for 90 seconds, hands you a plastic key, and walks away. If you get a second-floor room and you say you don't want a second-floor room, they say, "That's where you've been assigned."

— Keith Jackson

MONEY IS ONE change between now and when I started. Another is that sportscasters probe more. Diplomacy played a vital part in the early days of TV because each club had such a large stake in deciding which sportscasters would be employed. Telecasting the Browns many years ago I used to hear about Paul Brown's celibacy rule. The players told me that Brown wanted his men to abstain from sexual relations on Friday, Saturday, and Sunday morning preceding the game. His theory apparently was this would increase their strength or perhaps their irritability. This wasn't mentioned on the air. They weren't topics of the 1950s.

Today, such mild subjects would seem too tame for most TV talk shows. Perhaps a reporter might do a feature on whether abstinence medically had an effect on the players' games. This might make a funny sketch on "Saturday Night Live." There are no secrets these days that have not been unearthed, or come out in book form, with big money in advance. Crude and lewd sell more than compassion and understanding. Negative attracts more headlines than positive. Most broadcasters today are more independent in voicing their views. Imparting the truth is mandatory if one wants to be known as a true sports journalist.

The computer age has brought other changes. TV news rooms are as quiet now as public libraries. No longer a clatter of typewriters. All reporters have beepers and cell phones. They carry their office with them. Better, or worse? Just different.

— *Bob Wolff*

IT DOESN'T MATTER if you're a player, coach, or broadcaster. You're not an individual. You're preparing with your team. The only difference in broadcasting is that you don't have the highs that you get as a player or coach of winning. Nor do you have the lows of losing. There's nothing better than winning, and nothing tougher than losing. In broadcasting you don't have either one. But I had them before I got into TV, so I don't feel like I'm missing much.

— *John Madden*

EX-ATHLETES ARE like the man who writes a travelogue. Unless he's been to the place, he can't write a story that would be nearly as warmly felt or as seen with the insight that taking the trip would provide. The ex-athlete has more insight into the game than the man who hasn't played it.

— *Don Meredith*

COVERAGE OF SPORTS has changed so drastically in the past few years you'd barely recognize the way it was done in 1972 — which seems like 1822 when you watch tapes of telecasts from 25 years ago. But the funny thing is that for an announcer the fundamentals are the same. It's still the principles of jour-nalism — who, what, when, where, why, and now. You have to remember that you're reporting. You're also entertaining, and it's great to have a sense of humor, be casual about it, and be the viewer's friend. The technology has changed — the way it's

covered has changed — the anticipation that people have for the quality of a telecast has changed. But the basics haven't.
— *Al Michaels*

MY MOST UNUSUAL day in broadcasting was 1962. I did the Red Sox then, and they were at Comiskey Park in Chicago. They moved the night game to day so it wouldn't oppose the football game between the College All-Stars and the NFL champs — that year, the Packers — and I was assigned to the football game, too. As the baseball game went along, Bill Monbouqette of the Sox hadn't allowed a hit. Eighth inning, no hits. Last of the ninth, boom, the final out. A no-hitter. I close my briefcase, hand it to somebody, and say, "Keep this for me." Then I pick up my *football* briefcase, get a cab, and go to Soldier Field. The All-Stars had some future AFL guys, but the Packers clobbered them [42-20]. A no-hitter by day, the mighty Pack at night. I always thought a sports announcer should slide from football into baseball into basketball. The seasons overlap now. You can't do it as much. But a fellow should do all the sports he can.
— *Curt Gowdy*

IN SOME CASES today announcers think that what he has to say is more important than the game. I don't like that. The announcer should always talk about what is taking place on the field — not his personal approach to what's taking place, but what he knows about the game. Too many announcers are more concerned with how they are represented to the audience than with the game. To me, as Shakespeare said, the play's the thing. Let announcers analyze, but don't let them get self-absorbed. Don't impose themselves upon the listeners and viewers. After all, without the game, we wouldn't have much to broadcast.
— *Marty Glickman*

TWENTY-FIVE YEARS after winning Super Bowl III, the Jets'

owner, Leon Hess, invited everybody that participated in that championship season to come back to New York for a Saturday night dinner. The players were honored the next day at Giants Stadium in East Rutherford. I was invited as the Jets' announcer, having done them for nine years. I'd seen a few players from time to time like Don Maynard and Joe Namath. There were some that I hadn't seen since I stopped broadcasting the Jets.

The dinner was at what used to be the Summit Hotel, and it was interesting to see the guys and meet their families. When had they gotten old? When had I? I recognized everyone except a fellow who came up and shook my hand. He was about 6-5 and 240. He had a little gray interspersed with black hair. "Merle," he said, "how are you?" The look in my eye said I didn't know him. Finally, he said, "You don't recognize me, do you?"

I said, "I am embarrassed. I just can't identify you." He said, "I'm Verlon Biggs." I said, "Oh, my, Verlon, I'm sorry, my goodness, you've taken off so much weight." I couldn't get over it — the last time I saw him he was almost 400 pounds. I said, "You look like a basketball player." He took it as a compliment. The evening ended and we had a good time. A little while later, Verlon died of cancer. I felt so terrible that I said he'd lost weight — now, I knew why. He never commented on *my* comment. Such a fine individual. I'm glad to have seen him once more.

— *Merle Harmon*

IN THE 1960s and '70s, everyone arrived on Saturday in a given city — the crew, producer/director, the analyst and play-by-playman. You'd go to the stadium and see the home team go through their paces. Next came a five- or 10-minute visit with the coach to see who was hurt and to say hello. We had our production meeting. Then came the *real* business: Where were we going to have dinner and have a nice social evening? That evening often went to 3 in the morning. The endurance was if you could stay out and have a few drinks, socialize, and be in decent condition to do the next day's game. Today, our production crew and analyst, Matt Millen, get to the stadium on Friday. We see a couple of hours of film, then meet players and members of the coaching staff. The next day, more film. Then, the visiting team arrives and we go to their hotel for the same paces. Finally, our production meeting. We look at the graphics our people have put together. What are the story-lines — the guys to look at? A little different than, "Where's my next drink?"

— *Dick Stockton*

I'LL BE SITTING somewhere, and thinking about my past career. It's interesting how the bond with your teammates severs when a player becomes an ex-player. It's like one of those old Marlin Perkins nature films where the lion chases the zebras. One zebra's a little slow and the lion gets him, but you notice that the other zebras don't slow up or look back. Once you quit, you're like that slow zebra. Oh, you're still one of the guys, yet you're really not. They know you can appreciate what they're going through, but you've got a different job — you're the media. Ask them a question they'd rather not answer and you see a wariness. You're the media — the lion.

— *Randy Cross*

THE FIRST play-by-play that I did was 1968's first pre-season game — the Steelers and Cardinals. The Cardinals' Cid Edwards carried on the first play, was tackled, and a strange thing happened. The clocks and sticks were moving and I thought to myself, "This is the fastest game I have ever seen. I wish they would slow it up." I wanted them to let me catch up because things were zooming by. The more pro football you do, the slower things seem. Today, when there's a play being run, I see everything in slow-motion. I see a blitz develop and receivers going out. I see the patterns, the quarterback going, the whole peripheral scene. At the start of '96, I talked to [Fox's] Ronnie Lott about being a sports broadcaster. I said, "When I started out I was going a mile a minute and now it's a crawl." People say experience is the great teacher. They're right.

— *Dick Stockton*

PEOPLE ASK ME to describe a typical NFL broadcast week. First, the preparation is much greater in football in terms of getting ready. I've worked hockey and filled in on television for the NBA and major league baseball and there's no comparison. You're working for a network — so there's more at stake than with a home-town team or small cable network. With only one game a week and 16 games per year, you may hit a game where you've never seen the two teams before. Add the wide audience watching — don't forget those satellite dishes — and you have to know everything about their team because if you screw something up, they'll know. So on Monday, we get back into town and unpack. Monday's sort of most people's Sunday. We rest for what's to come.

— *Kenny Albert*

I DON'T THINK I've ever done anything that I'm satisfied with. I've never watched a tape of a game that I've done or listened to a tape — because I can't watch myself and I can't listen to myself. I often thought that I probably won't like it — and if I don't like it, what am I going to do? I know there are a lot of people that study tapes of themselves, and at Fox they send us tapes of our games. CBS sent us tapes. I've been doing this 17 years now, and I've never watched a tape — and I won't.

I mean, have you ever seen a picture of yourself you like? I don't like to look at pictures of myself. You never think you look like that. I don't like to listen to my voice on a radio because I don't think I sound like that. And I don't want to hear myself on television, because I think I'd cringe. So if that's the truth and you see something you don't like — but it's you! —

what are you going to do?! That's the hand you're dealt. If you can't change it, why antagonize yourself? Why look at it?

The other thing is, you're always told to be natural — just be yourself. Well, if you try to change, you're no longer *being* natural and just yourself. So why look at it? If you don't like it, you're not going to change what you are naturally. You know what I'm saying? I'm going to be myself, you know, good or bad. Or average. Just me.

— *John Madden*

FOR A NUMBER of years I was NBC's in-studio pro football host — every Sunday, often from noon till after dark. It may have the highest visibility of any TV job in sports — given the number of people who watch, and number of hours you're on. I enjoyed it to a point, but never found it as fulfilling, say, as when we took our show on the road for the playoffs. You were out-doors, it was snowing, there was a real sense of reporting from the scene. What I did mattered to the show — the highlights, acting as traffic cop, getting off a good line here and there, ana-lyzing a down-and-out to Vance Johnson. I don't mean to deni-grate it; the role takes a not inconsiderable skill. But after a while, the physical and mental constrictions take over. Each week, it was like doing the same dance steps. Now, I do one piece a week for NBC football — an interview, or essay or com-mentary. They're only four to five minutes, but I put more of a personal stamp on them than all the host work combined. Dif-ferent job, different satisfaction.

— *Bob Costas*

TUESDAY, THE studying starts. First comes two Federal Ex-press packages from the two teams you're doing Sunday with a huge pile of clippings and statistics from the last couple weeks. Then, another Fed Ex with two videotapes: one, our game of two days earlier so we can review our work; the other, the previous game of the teams you'll see that week. Say you have an Arizona-Washington game coming up. You get a package from both teams, and a tape of my game and a tape of the Arizona and Washington games. Another Fed Express package gives you notes and stats that come out every Tuesday from the NFL. You take a breath and start with the videotapes. This lets you see the game in terms of numbers and stats. Haven't seen a team yet? Now you do, and get an idea of what the announcers were saying — what stories they told, what not to duplicate, what to stress. It takes forever to do it right — especially the reading. I read it all because I don't want to miss that one great note in some article. Then turn off the lights. The real homework is still ahead.

— *Kenny Albert*

PEOPLE WONDER WHERE commentaries come from. In football, spending an afternoon watching Jim Brown or seeing Johnny Unitas win a game in the final minute seemed to leave a part of me unfulfilled. I thought there was more to be said than just describing the play. Those are special things and I felt they deserved some special treatment. I wanted to tell the audience what they *really* meant. I still do.

— *Jack Whitaker*

WHEN I DID football for ESPN, I didn't spend a lot of time talking about the four-three defense. "Boy, the nose guard really cracked down on that play" — that wasn't interesting to me. What were people trying to say about Tony Dorsett? Would he be traded? Did he get along with Herschel Walker on the Cowboys? That was interesting. That's what people wanted to know. Opinions and commentary. Not Bill Murray or Walter Cronkite, but a mixture of both.

— *Roy Firestone*

WEDNESDAY AND Thursday, you're watching tapes and reading and memorizing and inhaling the NFL. Keep the coffee ready. Preparation is where Sunday is make or break.

— *Kenny Albert*

FOLKS TELL ME, "Gee, I like how you do football. Why don't you call baseball the same way?" Or, "Love your baseball. Wish you'd broadcast football just as well." They don't realize you can't *do* both sports the same on radio. Baseball's conversational, and daily. You can't wear yourself out — or the guy listening. Football, you're on once a week. You detail everything — how the team is leaving the huddle, what the quarterback is checking off — and in a heck of a hurry. Sometimes, I'll do a football game Sunday, come back to baseball Monday, and find myself calling baseball in my football way! I've said everything there is to say about a batter, and the ball's still in the pitcher's hand. Believe me, I change back pronto. Apples and oranges. You confuse the two sports, and you'll be in a new profession quick.

— *Bob Starr*

FOOTBALL IS THE easiest sport to broadcast — there's a natural rhythm with your partner. The play starts, and the play-by-play person speaks. When it's over, the analyst steps in. You don't have the gray area like in baseball between pitches — sort of awkward, where you and the color man sometimes step on each other's lines. In football, "I talk, you talk, I talk, you talk." The hard part is that football is by far the toughest sport to prepare for — all the numbers to memorize, the minutiae to learn. It's even worse in college than the pros because the players aren't as familiar. If you don't do your homework, don't bother showing up. Most of your work is done long before the game.

— *Sean McDonough*

FRIDAY, WE FLY into the city of the home team and go into their practice area. Let's say it's the Cardinals, and the public relations director has set up the meeting. Four of us from Fox are there — me, Tim Green the color analyst, and our producer and director. Add four or five players and maybe the defensive and offensive coordinators. This takes anywhere between five minutes and half-an-hour depending on if they're productive. The analyst is looking for strategy game-type situations. I'm more interested in the story aspect. Maybe a quarterback was coached in college by a coach from the other team. Maybe Ty Detmer's brother is playing in a bowl game the next week. Anything that says human interest is what I want. I'll watch the home team's film — they shoot from up-top as opposed to network tape: You see formations and plays developing. You look for certain trends. Finally comes our production dinner at a restaurant. Good food. What you're really tasting is a good game.

— *Kenny Albert*

MY TWO YEARS at Oxford had a profound change on my life. When I went to England in September 1975, it was the first chance I had to *breathe* — to *not* play football — since the sixth grade. I loved the competition — sports and academics in high school and USC — but never had the chance to examine things. The pace of American life is incredible. Oxford brought me to a halt. The pace was slower, emphasizing the quality of life, enduring things. We had three-hour dinners, social evenings at which I heard some of the great minds of our time discuss social and philosophical issues. I put football in perspective. Like most players, I'd been consumed by it since I was 12. Once I had a chance to step back, I found the win-at-all-costs attitude destructive. On a universal scale, a single game is cosmically insignificant. We lost sight that this is a *game* that allows us to express and improve ourselves. A *game*, not a *war*.

— *Pat Haden*

NINETY PERCENT OF viewers don't have a great grasp of strategy and context. It's intricate stuff — only megafans have it.

Most watch to enjoy the physical contest. So you relate the strat-egy — each side's strengths and weaknesses, and whether that strategy will work. Then comes the important focus: the people who play the game — their background, personality, the game within the game. Say a lineman is battling Reggie White. I talk with him about what in his experience prepares him to face Reggie. Maybe the Packers' Robert Brooks knows for months that he has to beat the Bears' cornerback. Does he train in the off-season on weights so that he can break that guy's tackle on the down-and-out? It's funny. When I was playing, you're part of a whole — the team. But I was also writing my first two novels — so I stepped back to capture the poignancy of playing in the NFL. Now I'm broadcasting and I try to do both. Remove yourself, analyze the game — but also relate what it's like to play pro football. Do one, and you cheat the viewer. Do each, and you get some sense of what a great game it is.

— *Tim Green*

SATURDAY MORNING. More talk. More film. More hoping for a close game. We get together and watch the previous week's tape. Saturday afternoon, we go to the visiting team hotel when they arrive and go through the same drill. Saturday night, we have our production meeting where we talk about our open — what we want to do at the start of the game on "Fox Watch" — stories for the pre-game — graphics we need. By now, it's too late to learn much new. You've got it, or you don't. Lights out.

— *Kenny Albert*

A PET PEEVE of mine is what too many play-by-play guys do. They wait until the play develops, then call it in present tense — but by the time they call it, it's *past*. They're protecting them-selves by giving themselves more time. A basketball analogy. Michael Jordan tries a jump shot. Some guys wait until he shoots, then say, "Jordan — swish." The problem is he's scored *before* they speak: They should put it in past tense. That, or call it earlier, just as it happens: "Jordan tries a jump shot." Be honest. Don't cheat by waiting till the play's occurred.

— Tom Hammond

I WENT TO THE University of Kansas to get into radio/TV. Between my junior and senior years in 1981, I got an internship in Avon, Connecticut, at the now defunct Enterprise Radio Network — the forebear of ESPN. My roommate was Sean McDonough. A lot of the producers and directors at this place had worked at the networks — CBS, Mutual. They'd retired, or been let go, but they loved the business and they worked here for nothing. I don't know if *they* know this, but these veterans changed my life. They were radio people, and exposed me to old games and sportscast history. I'd listen to the archival tapes and fall in love with how the old guys did it. Pioneers used *language*: "The shadows are creeping across the outfield," a guy "adjusted his cotton shirt," "wiped sweat from his brow," "there's a long drive to left-center field. The left-fielder turns, takes three steps, moves to his right" — great detail. Nobody does that now. Even on radio, guys bring a TV approach — don't say much, skip the verbal expression — and I say, *Why*? You're cheating listeners if you skip the word-pictures. I wish that network were still alive.

— Kevin Harlan

SUNDAY IS GAME time, but your time started months before. Each summer, Fox holds seminars for the producers and directors. [See page 242.] One day we'll talk about TV-related experience. We see tapes of last year's games. Jerry Seaman, head of officiating, explains new rules. The Commissioner comes by. On the third day, they have satellite hookups with coaches getting ready for training camp — a question/answer session headed by the Howie Longs and Jerry Glanvilles and John Maddens. People think a guy making $8 million a year might not be as interested in this as everyone else. With Madden, they'd be wrong.

Madden just sits in the hotel lobby talking about football or TV or anything else that comes to mind. Once he gets off on a tangent he can circle a paper towel or napkin blowing on the field and get a story. I remember a seminar when Madden asked why Barry Sanders is often taken out of the game in goal line situations for the Lions — and someone says, "Because they have Ty Hallock," who was their backup running back. Someone else says, "Who needs Barry Sanders when you have Ty Hallock?" — and all of a sudden he became a running joke the rest of the seminar. Every time something came up, Hallock's name would be mentioned. Just hearing it come out of Madden's mouth broke you up.

By Sunday, you've consumed the production meetings. I learned in one about George Seifert's wife, who'd just gone on safari and climbed Mount Kilimanjaro. We talked about it on the air. Human interest — a coach's wife's going around the world. Sometimes players talk other sports. One day, Boomer Esiason says, "Hey, the Rangers are 7-0-1 in their last eight games." In the middle of his season, he's still a hockey nut. Anthony Muñoz is a huge pro basketball fan. We'd go to Houston and find time to squeeze in an NBA game. We use our access to players to learn things that reporters or local broadcasters probably don't know.

Jeff Brady is a Vikings' linebacker: We joked that we brought him in before the coach because they're on such rigid schedules that when they arrive everything stops. Put him *after* the coach, and Jeff's still talking. Sam Wyche'd sit for hours and talk about his private plane. Every player we talk to gets a Fox hat — Madden said they're like currency. Warren Moon wanted one for his son. In '94, we talked with the Rams and our hats hadn't come yet from the office. They come looking for them later: John's right — the hats are gold. Our typical week. It happens every Sunday — but really evolves from the whole year.

— *Kenny Albert*

I'M SITTING HERE, looking out at the lake [Skaneatelas, in Upstate New York], working on my fifth novel. It takes a lot of work, but it's pleasurable, like broadcasting. Say I'm going to a Jets' game. I get to talk with Bill Parcells and ask how he's going to attack the Bears' defensive line. That's the business that you must attend to. Next comes the stuff I love. "Where did you go on your vacation?" "What's your favorite artist?" "When you'd last go to a museum?" The personal things that take characters beyond cardboard cutouts and let the viewer identify. A couple years back I was talking with Lions' quarterback Scott Mitchell. I said, "You've got three great receivers who all want the ball. Do they try to lobby you?" He laughed. "This guy whines," he said, "this one threatens, this guy pouts." I said, "Has anyone bribed you?" He said, "Yeah, Herman Moore offered me fishing gear." So I put a graphic together of Scott and fishing — and all of a sudden, fishermen regard Scott as a kindred soul. Even if you don't fish, here's a guy making millions of dollars, and he's like me — he likes free gear. The key to broadcasting isn't complex — it's making the actors live.

— *Tim Green*

SOME CITIES HAVE real jerks as fans — rude, crude, and stupid. Then there's Arizona — you get heat, and that's about it. On the other hand, take Denver — great place, terrific ambiance, you stand on the sidelines, look up at the three tiers, the parkas, the crowd, and say, "Man, this is football like it ought to be." Or Kansas City — my favorite place. You go there in the morning, and fans can't wait to get into Arrowhead. You get a sense of it on TV, but even more in person. I did the pre-season game there when Joe Montana made his [1993] Chiefs' debut. As soon as he stuck his head out of the tunnel, the stadium started rocking. Kevin Kiley said, "That's a bumper" — goosebumps. It's a feeling which Montana once or twice has caused.

— *Ernie Johnson, Jr.*

PEOPLE ASK about being a woman reporter in the NFL's man's world. I relate the first year — 1982 — of my first job as sports editor of the *Main Line Chronicle* outside Philadelphia. Back then, women weren't let in the locker room except on game days. Yet the day after the regular season ended — obviously, a non-game — I got in and talked with the Eagles' Mike Quick, who was going to the Pro Browl. He was sitting in one stall, I'm in the next, and suddenly he looked at me. "Wow," he said, "you really know what you're talking about." I started laughing and said, "What do you think I'm doing here?" Maybe it hit him then that in journalism, gender doesn't count. I've done funny, poignant, and x's and o's stories. I remember a story on how people defend the 49ers' Jerry Rice. He showed me how he used his feet, how he bumped, did a "rat-a-tat" move with his feet at the line, almost like a dancer. Then I went to Carolina, met two of his former roommates, watched some tape, and talked about how you stop him. The consensus: not easily, or often. Two things I'm proud of: I haven't been pigeonholed, and I've proven that a woman can cover football as adeptly as a man.

— *Andrea Kremer*

THERE ISN'T A subject in the world I'm more adamant about than franchises moving. Because the whole thing depends upon the emotion of those people in that city. I mean, that's what you're existing on, that's what you're trading on. To make it a floating crap game — moving on to the next town with the biggest television base or a new arena — is just ridiculous. Maybe we ought to remember who pays the bills for these teams — you and me.

— *Brent Musburger*

IN MY ONLY nonfiction book, *The Darkside Of the Game*, I have a chapter, "The Second Death." Every player faces it — the day you're finished as a player, it's like dying before you die.

You can't replicate the experience of being an NFL player
— the angst and the thrill. But as a broadcaster you come close
— go down on the field, talk with guys from both teams, feel
the energy and intensity. Each time I do I feel an ache to play
again. Then I go to the booth, and there's anxiety, too. People
ask me what it's like for a former player to now announce. I
compare it to methadone for a heroin addict. You're still ad-
dicted to the thrill — you don't get a drug — instead, you get
your fix. That's how you survive The Second Death.

— *Tim Green*

SINCE COLLEGE, I have accepted Jesus as the major part of
my life. It's interesting that more players now seem to be following — a growing spirituality, a turning to God, whatever
you call it, there's more exposure. When Reggie White was in
Philadelphia and he'd talk about religion, the media would go
to other players like they didn't want to hear him. Now the
media is more respectful. It's like they recognize the country's
yearning for something bigger than ourselves. Being a Christian isn't saying, "I'm perfect": it's the opposite, that we're not
perfect and need God's grace. And it doesn't make you soft or
less intense. My experience is that it makes you strive harder,
be more self-disciplined. Are more players awaking to the spirit,
or just more of a spotlight? Either way, it's good.

— *Anthony Muñoz*

I SPENT SIX years [1984-89] with NFL Films as a producer, director, and on-air reporter. It's grown exponentially since then,
but still exists to humanize the game. Every fan wants to be
vicarious, become part of the NFL. So NFL Films uses the hits
and wiring to take you *inside* — into the locker room, the sidelines, into players' lives. They did it before other sports — and
what amazes me — think about it — is how they achieve the
miracle of taking these oversized, faceless beings who wear helmets — almost gladiators — and making them *poetic*! Each show

employs writing, music, and film to capture the two elements of football — the beauty and brutality, athleticism and savagery — all melded together. Everything has a dramatic flair, with a flow, all told in a storytelling vein. Every game is elevated beyond a contest. Plus the silver lining. If a team goes 1 and 15, you'd never know it from the video yearbook produced by NFL Films. If the video lasts 30 minutes, the one win will get 25!

— Andrea Kremer

I'VE HAD AN uphill battle all my life as a broadcaster because I talk. People said I talked too much when I was a player. They said it because I gave interviews — what a crime! I liked to talk to the press! And I'll admit that as a broadcaster I've had to learn discipline — say things in a more succinct fashion, don't go off in a thousand different ways. So I've worked hard to do my job, but I'm saddled with this reputation as a guy who babbles on. It's frustrating, and I think people who hear me — who *listen* to what I say — know it's a bum rap.

— Joe Theismann

MY FAVORITE MEMORY is my first assignment on joining ESPN in 1989. I got to interview Deion Sanders at his house the day he signed his huge bonus. He was typically understated — had expensive sunglasses, the glowing jewelry — and prompted the first words I ever uttered for ESPN: "Gee, Deion, it looks like you're wearing your signing bonus." What a difference from NFL Films! There, no controversy — here, Deion's girl-friend, Carolyn, now his estranged wife, got into a heated fight with his mother. She goes outside, runs down the street, and everybody follows her. Total chaos. It was like "Peyton Place" — in other words, with Deion, a portent of things to come.

— Andrea Kremer

FROM 1990 through '94, WGR-Buffalo aired Bills' games on radio. I was the sports director, and discovered how a program director can make life hard for you as you're working with an NFL team.

Chuck Phinney wanted to put billboards up in Dallas before the Bills met the Cowboys in their 1993 Super Bowl — this to benefit an FM station that the company owned in Buffalo. So up goes a billboard, "Bend over Cowboys, grab your spurs, here come the Bills." It had the logo of the FM station in Buffalo, which was strange. No Buffalo FM station has ever been *heard* in Dallas. Bill Polian, Bills' general manager, was livid. He called WGR to say he didn't want any more so-called locker room bulletin board material appearing in the enemy's home lair.

You won't believe this, but I've had confirmed by a couple of sources that this was to be only the first in a *series* of billboards. The next one was to say, "If Dallas couldn't protect JFK, how can it protect Troy Aikman?" Thankfully, that one was intercepted and never put up. It just shows how sometimes a team's biggest problems aren't on the field.

— *Pete Weber*

I HATE THIS business. It's cruel. That's why I'm looking at movies and sitcoms. That's why I'm still in the horse and cattle business and that's why I'm real conservative with my money. You get a new boss every three or four years who has a different way of pickin' talent. You get comfortable with one guy, and he's fired. It's tough to make friends because you sense how these people are trying hard to make it. It's such a talk business. There's so much bleep going on behind people's backs. Most of these guys don't know what it is to depend on somebody else for their livelihood. I'm talking about the meaning of teamwork. The analysts know about it, but the play-by-play guys, the pretty boys with great voices — well, that's another story.

— *Terry Bradshaw*

I WAS WORKING on a local station, doing SEC basketball, when I got to know some NBC people as they came through Kentucky.

It's through them that I was hired to call NBC's first Breeders' Cup. I had done a lot of horse racing. Afterward, their director, Michael Weisman, told me, "We didn't know we had a broadcaster here. Would you like to do other stuff like the NFL next year?" *Would* I? So they had me do a practice pre-season game.

Dick and Merlin Olsen did the game over NBC. Sam Rutigliano and I did it into a tape machine. Later, NBC executives reviewed it. Other teams were vying for our spot, and they had us all to a dinner where the number one producer, Larry Cirillo, starts holding court. He starts talking about the people competing for this position. "I don't know how I get these guys," he says. "Last year, they foisted an auto racing announcer on me for football. This year, it's worse — a horse racing guy."

He's speaking, and I'm sitting right there. Or should I say slinking, because that's what I start doing. I think Dick Enberg was the only one who realized my embarrassment. Anyway, I got the job, so it's all forgotten. Sort of.

— Tom Hammond

I DIDN'T HAVE any formal courses in broadcasting. I don't know of any book that tells you how to inject your personality into a game. My whole *modus operandi* is to be a teacher. I want people to grow. I want them to turn to a friend — the guy sitting at home, or a bar — and say, "You know, I learned something from Joe Theismann that I didn't know." My critics will not believe it — but that's the legacy I'd like to leave.

— Joe Theismann

YOU'VE GOT TO know players as people so that they take you into your confidence. A few years back Derrick Mayes of Notre Dame was on the brink of breaking the touchdown record. I said to him, "If you could orchestrate the record-breaker, what would you do?" He said, "I'd hit the end zone, find my parents in the stands, jump up, and take them the ball." I said, "Nice thought, but what happens to the game? Lou Holtz might have a little problem with you taking a sabbatical." That week, Derrick scores the touchdown. I'm in the end zone covering the game for NBC, and here comes Derrick to score. He finds me, gives me the ball, and says, "Hey, would you take this to my family?" I was honored, but I couldn't believe it. So I trip over some people, show my vaunted speed — just kidding — and find his parents. I was his emissary, and it came from preparation. Anything that adds humanity, *do*. Football players aren't just athletes. They're people, too.

— *John Dockery*

PLAYERS DON'T like to be criticized by the media, especially during a game. What's different from when I played is that they don't need us [broadcasters] anymore. With the Redskins, I *needed* announcers, was always glad to talk with them. They could help my reputation and career. Same for my teammates. Now, they make so much money they don't give a damn. Joe Theismann? What he can do for *me*? So it's hard to make contact with them — that, and there are so many announcers — that, and before they talk with me they have to talk with maybe five people at ESPN, and if not with ESPN at one of the other networks. It's just too crowded — and because of that hard to develop relationships. I liked it better when it was a kinder, gentler NFL.

— *Joe Theismann*

IN THE EARLY '90S, Dolphins' defensive back Liffort Hobley had a baby daughter who fell into a swimming pool, drowned, and died. He used football to get through it — focused on the game, tried to block out everything. I contacted the Dolphins about talking to Liffort, and they put me in contact with his wife. She hadn't talked about this publicly, so we spent a long time on the telephone, getting to know one another. In the meantime, they had had a son. Referring to the daughter, I said, "What do you tell him about her?" The wife said, "We tell him she's playing with the angels." I went over and we did the interview — a special day. As we're sitting there the mother pulled out the program that they had at the memorial church service. It reads, "She's playing with the angels." We all burst into tears.

— *Andrea Kremer*

CHAPTER

23 FINALE

FOOTBALL NATION

A Dublin ballad said, "Being Irish means laughing at life knowing that in the end life will break your heart." Being Irish was a lark *v.* the NFL's lot in pre-TV America. Bill Stern was lucky to have a warm booth and carbon microphone. Al Michaels uses technology by way of *Star Wars* straight out of "Captain Video." Early Voices broadcast a game with less passion than asterisk. Today's play-by-playmen vend sport's Tiarah of our time.

Television made pro ball addictive; *sans* screen, the game might still brook anonymity. Instead, it blankets the USA as a community peregrination — brutal, complex, and self-awardly human. Diversion and/or obsession — to millions, pro football 'r' us.

Why do more people behold the NFL than any institution? When was it, exactly, that even football widows conceded — or converted? Few remember the Akron Pros, Muncie Flyers, or Buffalo All-Americans. From their backwash 1920s, fake a down and out, deke your defender, and go deep to the '90s. Read why the medium *is* the message — and the message is gold.

IT'S VIOLENCE that makes pro football. You may not want to

say that, but to many it's one of the most attractive things. Plus, if you sat down and wrote something for a television show and said, "Here's the way I want you to do it," football would be the result. The fellow would say, "I want you to huddle. I want all eleven guys to get together on each side of the ball. I want them to talk to each other for just a second. I want them both to decide what they're going to do, and then go do it. Then they'll come back after it works or doesn't work, and they'll talk it over again. It gives you a chance with the quarters and half-times and commercial timeouts to analyze as a fan. It gives you a chance to get up and get something to drink." It's as if football were perfectly scripted for television.

— *Pat Summerall*

NOTHING WAS MADE for television like football. Most sports, like soccer, are non-stop. Say you're doing the World Cup. How do you pay for it? You've got to go to a commercial — and while you're away maybe the best play happens of a 2 to 1 game. You can replay it, but you missed it. We don't miss much in the NFL.

— *Frank Gifford*

TODAY, SUNDAY afternoons revolve around the NFL. It wasn't always so. Bert Bell hoped that families would embrace NFL football. He also realized on Sunday that people should go to church. The Maras, especially, were very devout Catholics. They wanted to balance religion and football, so they didn't start the games until church was long over. People could have lunch before our telecast started. This was appreciated by the fans, and it was planned that way by the Maras. You didn't have to miss church for football, or the other way around. Today, you have all these teases on what's coming up. Not us. We came on with the billboard and kickoff. Hook fans when they tune in. No extraneous stuff. Get to the game. *Bull Durham* talked about the Church of Baseball. The Maras helped preserve football's.

— *Chris Schenkel*

I'VE BROADCAST football at every level — high school, college, and professional. It's the best game that a young man can play. It's the best teacher of civics that I know of — playing according to the rules. Listening to your coaches. Working together with your teammates. And respecting your opponent. It's learning the ability to get hit and hurt, and come back and continue to play. It's the greatest instructor of young people I know. I enjoy football more than any other sport. One, because it teaches. Two, every time the ball is snapped, so many things can happen. Every play, it's something new. Basketball is exciting, but it repeats itself. Hockey the same way — up and back, up and back. Football, not so. Perhaps that explains why I've loved playing, then broadcasting, then watching the game.

— *Marty Glickman*

PRO FOOTBALL in the east at 1:00 on Sunday afternoon is more than a habit. It's a tradition now — something that you expect to do when the weather starts to get cold. Once Labor Day is over, you go back to the city, whatever the city, and look forward to watching pro football on Sunday. It's just part of America's life. People come up to me in the airport and say, "I grew up with you" or "My father introduced me to you." And I've never met your father or met you. But people feel like they know you. A lot of people object to that notoriety. I don't at all. It's a warm feeling to feel that, hey, you have grown up with part of this country and presented it in such a way that people enjoy. You don't last as long as a lot of us have in this business if people don't get a sense that you like what you do. That's why I keep doing it. That, and the tradition.

— *Pat Summerall*

FOOTBALL ON RADIO means having to talk more and fill in gaps. When I was doing CBS-TV, the network let me freelance. I'd do a radio game on Saturday for NBC. God, it was difficult. I'd get to Penn State or somewhere, and I'd have to shift gears.

But by halftime, you'd say, "Boy, isn't this fun." I had to describe what I saw, and make people visualize it. I enjoyed it — but not as much as football enjoys TV. Television captures the enclosure around the field. It's chilly, it may be snowing, a fan builds a fire in the seats to keep warm — whatever it is, TV catches it. In golf or baseball, certain things elude you. Not in the perfectly defined area for the perfect TV sport.

— Chris Schenkel

SOMETIMES I THINK the NFL talent is spread thin. I don't think there's enough good players. On the other hand, there could be more teams, because there's more cities. Baltimore should have a team, because they supported the Colts — and they've got a team now. But the team they took was Cleveland's, so Cleveland should have a team. There's no team in the Los Angeles market. That's ludicrous. There's going to be more teams because there has to be a team in Los Angeles. There has to be a team in Cleveland. I can see the day that there's going to be teams in Canada and Mexico. Some day there'll be a team in England. So I can see expansion within this country and outside. That's one part of my brain. The other part says the talent is spread too thin.

— John Madden

PETE ROZELLE WAS very bright. I first met him when he was the Rams' public relations director. Even then, he was aware of the importance of media and of Madison Avenue and advertising. It was he who helped keep together the various rugged individuals who owned teams in the National Football League. It was he who put together the concept of oneness of NFL play. He was terribly important in the development of the NFL as perhaps the leading sports organization in America today. When you watch the NFL on television, you're really watching his child.

— Marty Glickman

I FIRST MET Pete when he was with the Rams. I found him affable, and very pleasant. What I didn't see was his potential to become the commissioner of the league. In 1963, football and television were still in an early relationship. I remember visiting with Pete before the 1963 title game between the Bears and Giants. Instead of being at Wrigley Field for the entire game, Rozelle watched at least a part of the game on closed circuit television, looking ahead. [See page 65.] Some people have common sense. Some people have vision. Pete had both.

— *Jack Brickhouse*

THE NFL HAS never been healthier, nor more precarious. It's the biggest sports thing in America, and it's skating on thin ice. NFL owners laugh at baseball's debacle — the strike of 1994, their inability to market. They also marvel at the NBA and how David Stern has promoted the league. The question is which road will the NFL take. The owners don't like the last labor agreement they signed — so they're stockpiling strike insurance. The players don't like it. They thought they'd hit the free agency jackpot. To them, the system was to reward veterans and take money from the young kids. It's turned out just the opposite. Football has survived franchise shifts and strikes — but it's not indestructible. That's what they called baseball — and look what happened there. The enemy of the NFL isn't pro basketball or computers. It's the awful illness called greed.

— *Randy Cross*

I HATE THE NFL's rule against end zone celebrations. We'd better be careful or we'll legislate ourselves to boredom. Next thing you know, they'll make the fans wear suits.

— *Terry Bradshaw*

THE NFL'S IMPACT hit me in the late '60s, where you realized most of the male population on Sunday was occupied with watching whatever game was coming to that particular area.

By then, football had begun to seize the American public. Add "Monday Night" — which meant entertainment. It made football more than a game, which points out the foresight of people like Rozelle. Even now, I don't think that Rozelle has gotten enough credit for the perception he brought to the NFL. He knew it had the advantage of being a once-a-week sport, so you could build to that particular game. With nationwide exposure, you had people all over America keying into games in other locations. People in San Diego are interested in what happens between Kansas City and the Jets. This doesn't happen, say, in baseball. Today, the NFL's on five networks [ABC, NBC, Fox, ESPN, and TNT]. You would not have envisioned that. In the past the feeling was, "We'll lock it up on one network and have an exclusive." But today the feeling is to get on as many networks as you can.

There's the NFL, and there's everybody else.

— *Marv Albert*

WHAT MAKES football for TV, and keeps it exciting, is you only do it once a week. There'll be a Monday night game, but basically you do it Sunday. So there's no games on Tuesday, Wednesday, Thursday, Friday, Saturday. That's its advantage over the other sports — the build-up time to the next game. I mean, there's a pro basketball game on every night. Same thing, baseball. Same thing, hockey. But after Monday night, you can't watch a pro football game until the next Sunday. You have the game, and then you talk about the game for a day or two. Then you start talking about the game that's coming up for a day or two, and then play. Like anything, whether it's a championship game, a heavyweight fight, the anticipation is a big part of the event.

— *John Madden*

WE JUST HAD so much more fun playing when I did. We were all making about the same amount of money, so we were all pretty close. We partied together every Tuesday night, and everyone showed up. Now, these guys make so much money, they hardly know each other. It's a shame. They're missing a great part of pro football folklore.

— *Paul Maguire*

THE MARK OF a good general is to surround himself with quality people. Paul Tagliabue does. An example is [broadcast director] Val Pinchbeck, who's responsible for putting out the schedule. That means the networks constantly pound him over the head. "We want this or that game and you gotta' give us the best schedule on Monday night and Fox and NBC each want the best schedule on Sunday afternoon." It's a good thing that Val's so engaging. No matter how mad you get at the schedule, you can't get mad at him. Having said that, probably in the next couple of years Val is going to say, "Enough, already! I'm going to go hit the links and forget this aggravation!" [Retiring in 1998, he will.]

— *Howard David*

WHEN I LEFT coaching, I wasn't going to go into announcing. I just coached ten years, and I said, "That's enough. I'm going to do something else." Then CBS wanted me to do four or five games, and I said no. I never saw myself as that. Finally, I got bored, and I didn't have anything else to do. So I said, "Yeah, I'll try it," and the first game I did was New Orleans at San Francisco. I loved it. I said, "This is it." What I love is that I'm still part of the game. See, what happens to a retired player or coach is that you've been in this all your life. And you've always had a season — August until January. That's your season — then, off-season. Your whole life is that way. Then you retire, and soon there's no difference between November and May. You need your season. So I went from playing to coaching, and when I got out of coaching I went into broadcasting. Had

I not had television, I would have gone back into coaching. You need your season. That's what I learned when I got out of coaching.

— *John Madden*

I KNOW A GUY from Orville, Ohio. Fellow's name is Bobby Knight. Bobby told me one time that on Sunday afternoons, he and his father would not only close the door to his house — they would lock it, just sit there, and watch the Browns play football. Each Sunday was the same. I knew a priest down in Washington Courthouse, Ohio, who came to most Browns' games. He'd get somebody else to handle his Sunday masses for him during the football season. When he couldn't get somebody, he'd do it and afterward close himself in a room: just he and the Browns. The habit of watching NFL football Sunday afternoon was very special. Was, and is.

— *Ken Coleman*

I AM NOW retired for years from broadcasting pro football. Yet I set aside every Sunday each fall to watch the game in person at the ballpark or watch it on TV. I must say mostly on TV now, because it's more convenient. It's a habit — Sunday afternoon or "Monday Night Football" — which combines excitement, the attractiveness of the game, and weekends renewing themselves. In a sense, it recalls how at Yankee Stadium in the '60s I had tickets for the games — same seats. From the end of one season until the start of the next, my family would not see the individuals in the adjacent seats. But at the start of the next season, it was like one big family gathering together again.

They would ask about each other's children, what occurred during the last year. You were interested in them, and they in you. It became a ritual — to be in the stands or watching at home on TV. Has it changed? Yes, it's grown.

— *Marty Glickman*

FOOTBALL CAN BE cruel. In 1968, I was a Bengals' rookie — one of 266 guys trying out for the team at Wilmington College. I came in late the first night and a guy in bed stuck out his hand and said, "I'm Wally Scott, a defensive back from Arizona State." I said, "I'm Bob Trumpy from Utah. I played against you. We'll talk in the morning." I saw him briefly at breakfast but we never got to talk. By the time I got back to the room he was gone.

— *Bob Trumpy*

THE REASON PEOPLE watch is to see what's happening during the game — now, not them. Some of these guys talk about when they played. Who cares? Who cares what Paul Maguire did 30 years ago? It's a game for 12-year-olds played by 25-year-olds for millions of dollars. It's never been work, I swear to God. The hardest part of the whole deal is making it through the traffic when it's over to catch the flight home.

— *Paul Maguire*

THE GAME IS the thing. We're doing, you know, San Francisco at Dallas, people are going to tune in, and they want to watch the 49ers play the Cowboys. I'm a firm believer that it all goes on between those lines. The camera should never be taken off the field. So it doesn't matter who you're doing it for — CBS, say, or Fox — you don't do it differently. You can't say, "Well, I want more passing" — and have a director say, "Okay, pass more." It doesn't work that way. Whatever happens, the director covers.

Same thing in the booth. Whatever the play, the play-by-play guy calls. Whatever the play, I talk about it. When you forget that and say, "Yeah, I'm going to do this or that," you're full of baloney — because you can't format a live event. You don't know what's going to happen. You can't say, "At 1:35, we'll do this." If, at 1:35, Steve Young throws a pass to Jerry Rice, you'd better be watching Steve Young throw the pass to Jerry Rice. You know what I'm saying? You have to react to

what they're doing. And you'd better be prepared. You don't
know what's going to happen on the field. So you have to be
ready for anything that can happen with anyone doing it. You
know what I mean?

— John Madden

I'VE COVERED football in the West, the South, and out of New
York. It may be the best sport. It's certainly our most popular
sport. Doubt me? Visit any bar Sunday afternoon.

—Dan Hicks

THERE'S AN OUTER circle and an inner circle on every team,
and the inner circle consists of the starters. If you're hurt and
can't start, suddenly you're on the outside looking in. At meetings the coaches are talking to only 11 guys, and you're not one
of them. It's a feeling of loneliness, of being cast aside. I retired
in February [1978]. I went back in August for an exhibition game.
I walked into the locker room with a suit and tie on, and everyone made fun of me. I was a civilian, and was no longer in the
inner circle. I knew I never would be again. The funny thing is,
you miss the adrenaline euphoria of the games. Having never
taken drugs, I've found no substitute whatsoever — nothing close.

— Bob Trumpy

HERE'S HOW MUCH I love the NFL. As a youngster growing
up in D.C., Sammy Baugh was my favorite. He made the trans-
formation from the single wing to the T-formation and was the
greatest pure passer that I ever saw — also, a remarkable punter
who holds a ton of league records. I'm just glad to have broadcast Super Bowl V — the Jim O'Brien field goal for Baltimore
here in Miami [January 17, 1971, with five seconds left, beating
Dallas, 16-13]. Jim Simpson had been sent away to Europe to
do some skiing and they asked me to do that game. I could talk
for hours. The NBA has it all wrong. "I love *this* game."

— Jay Randolph

INDEX

C

Caesar, Sid 42

California 78, 172

Campbell, Earl 141

Campbell, Otis 258

Canada 40, 285

Canadeo, Tony 113

Canton, Ohio ix, xi, 7, 51, 114, 251, 253

Canyon City, Colorado 33

Capers, Dom 96, 234, 235

Cappelletti, Gino 106

Capra, Frank 120

Cardinals (St Louis) 7

Carney, Art 192

Carolina (Panthers) 95, 96, 99, 129, 234, 235, 237, 275

Caroline, J.C. 58

Carson, Johnny 149

Central Michigan University 8

Champiagn, Illinois 30

Chandler, Don 20

Chapel Hill, North Carolina 3

Chesley, C.D. 166

Chester, Pennsylvania 159

Cheyenne, Wyoming 37

Chicago, Illinois 5, 12, 20, 30, 40, 42, 45, 47, 51, 57, 58, 65, 72, 76, 113, 129, 155, 175, 176, 178, 183, 201, 224, 239, 243, 259, 263

Chirkinian, Frank 49

Christie, Steve 136, 246

Christman, Paul 58, 85, 86, 105, 200

Christy, Earl 156

Cifers, Ed 33

Cincinnati, Ohio 3, 6, 26, 86, 96, 127, 134, 138, 160, 225, 243

Cirillo, Larry 279

City Park Stadium 66

Clark, Dwight 184

Clemons, Eric 5, 161, 234

Cleveland, Ohio 6, 8, 14, 42, 43, 46, 47, 48, 54, 55, 61, 62, 65, 81, 82, 88, 94, 102, 113, 130, 131, 133, 137, 138, 151, 155, 156, 171, 188, 189, 225, 227, 250, 285

Coca, Imogene 42

Coleman, Jimmy 32

Coleman, Ken xi, 3, 43, 47, 55, 65, 69, 85, 150, 151, 153, 154, 166, 197, 200, 215, 226, 260, 289

Collins, Gary 69, 154

Collinsworth, Chris 6, 92, 93, 94, 128, 138, 159, 160, 161, 162, 201, 243

Colorado (University of) 4, 11, 15, 22, 37, 38

Columbia, Tennessee 29

Columbia University 8, 14, 18, 24, 29

Columbus, Ohio 55, 172

Comiskey Park 40, 58, 263

Concourse Plaza, New York 53

Conerly, Charlie 52, 53, 55, 59, 60, 61, 74, 166, 199

Connal, Scotty 203

Connally, John 17

Connecticut 3, 55

Connor, George 75, 78, 224

M

ABOUT THE AUTHOR

Curt Smith is an author, radio and television commentator and documentarian, and former presidential speechwriter. *Of Mikes and Men* is his seventh book. Prior books include *America's Dizzy Dean, Long Time Gone, Voices of The Game, A Fine Sense of the Ridiculous, The Storytellers*, and *Windows on the White House*.

Smith does award-winning essays for Rochester, New York's National Public Radio and NBC-Television affiliates WXXI and WHEC, respectively. He also appears on the Empire Sports TV network, writes for *Reader's Digest*, and teaches Public Speaking at his alma mater, SUNY at Geneseo, and the University of Rochester. Recent documentaries include three 90-minute prime-time ESPN-TV "Voices of The Game" specials Smith wrote and co-produced based upon his book. One special originated at the Pro Football Hall of Fame in Canton, Ohio.

Formerly a Gannett reporter, *The Saturday Evening Post* senior editor, and chief speechwriter for President Ronald Reagan's cabinet, Smith wrote more 1989-93 speeches than anyone else for President George Bush. Among them were the "Just War" Persian Gulf address; dedication speeches for the Nixon and Reagan libraries; and the speech aboard the battleship *USS Missouri* on the 50th anniversary of Pearl Harbor.

After leaving the White House, he hosted a smash series at the Smithsonian Institution, based on *Voices of The Game*, before turning to radio and TV. Smith lives with his wife Sarah in his hometown of Rochester, and jokes that the Stairway to Heaven favors fans of Broadway musicals, "The Andy Griffith Show," and the Boston Red Sox.